The Overthinking Cure

The Overthinking Cure

How to Free Your Mind and Focus on What Really Matters

Dr Jessamy Hibberd

monoray

First published in Great Britain in 2026 by Monoray,
an imprint of Octopus Publishing Group Ltd
Carmelite House
50 Victoria Embankment
London EC4Y 0DZ
www.octopusbooks.co.uk

An Hachette UK Company
www.hachette.co.uk

The authorized representative in the EEA is Hachette Ireland,
8 Castlecourt Centre, Dublin 15, D15 XTP3, Ireland (email: info@hbgi.ie)

Distributed in the US by Hachette Book Group, 1290 Avenue of the Americas,
4th and 5th Floors, New York, NY 10104

Distributed in Canada by Canadian Manda Group, 664 Annette St, Toronto,
Ontario, Canada M6S 2C8

ISBN: 978-1-80096-316-0
eISBN: 978-1-80096-318-4

A CIP catalogue record for this book is available from the British Library.

Typeset in 8.5/17pt Libre Baskerville by Six Red Marbles UK, Thetford, Norfolk.

Printed and bound in Great Britain.

1 3 5 7 9 10 8 6 4 2

This FSC® label means that materials used for the product have been responsibly sourced.

Publisher's note
All reasonable care has been taken in the preparation of this book but the information it
contains is not intended to take the place of treatment by a qualified medical practitioner.

Before making any changes in your health regime, always consult a doctor.
While all the therapies detailed in this book are completely safe if done correctly,
you must seek professional advice if you are in any doubt about any medical condition.
Any application of the ideas and information contained in this book is at the
reader's sole discretion and risk.

This monoray book was crafted by Jessica Minocha, Leanne
Bryan, Mel Four, Emily Campbell, Clare Sivell, Claudia Martin,
Sarah Parry, Erin Brown and Rosa Patel.

For Max, Edie and Bibi – I really hit the jackpot
when it came to you three

Contents

INTRODUCTION

The overthinking cure

Do you get caught up in anxious thoughts? Do you play over your mistakes and failures in your mind? Do you ruminate over things you've said? Or do you get stuck trying to work out where you've gone wrong in life, and how to change it? Maybe you can't shake the thought that you're no good, or that you're not measuring up? Perhaps you worry about these endless thought patterns and fear that you'll never be able to stop them?

If so, you're suffering from overthinking.

Overthinking is when we put too much time into thinking about something or analysing it in a way that is unhelpful. When we feel unhappy, anxious or stressed, it's natural to try to think about why, but as we deliberate the issue, we make it more complicated in our minds.

Overthinking can stem from a need to understand things or to resolve something difficult. You want to work out what's going on and find a solution. It begins with a good intention: perhaps it starts off as a way to try to improve and be on top of problems so you don't get caught off-guard. It feels like a helpful way to manage anxiety, to improve your mood or to gain a sense of control over the situation you face in life. But, instead of finding clarity, you become trapped in a loop of replaying the same thoughts, and analysing every possible outcome in your mind.

I worked with Olive, who often suffered from overthinking. Her overthinking normally focused on her work life or home life. When she felt overwhelmed by her emotions, she would try to take control by thinking over everything in detail. This would lead her to question herself and the things that she felt she'd got wrong, and her thoughts would play on repeat in an attempt to make her feel less anxious and more in control. Her overthinking was particularly bad when she really cared about the outcome. Olive described to me a job interview she had recently been to: 'I really wanted the job and I thought the interview had gone well, but I know if I think I've done well I won't get it. I feel like lots of things I've wanted in my life haven't happened, so I don't want to get my hopes up.' Olive hated not knowing the outcome of the interview, and she didn't dare hope it had gone well in case it made it more likely that it wouldn't work out as she wished. Ultimately, her overthinking left her feeling far more overwhelmed.

A health warning

If you consider yourself to be an overthinker, you are not alone. It's something we can all relate to. I see it in myself, and in my friends and family, and I come across it often in my work as a therapist.

Overthinking has always been an area that fascinates me. It's the problem that disguises itself as the solution. Unlike issues such as panic attacks or depression, people often feel ambivalent about letting go of these thinking patterns. Although they recognize the difficulties that overthinking causes, it is also seen as a useful coping strategy, a way of trying to solve problems, with the hope of feeling better or finding certainty. We tell ourselves that, if we just think about something for long enough, we'll uncover the answer, or we assure ourselves that thinking deeply about things offers the truest meanings and a clearer view of the realities of life. It can feel wrong to put the thinking to one side. You might feel justified in your angry thoughts, you might feel you deserve to have some time feeling sad, but there's a difference between thinking things through and becoming stuck.

In my clinic, I frequently see overthinking as a precursor to mental health problems and also an offshoot of them, which is why it's so important to take action and manage the problem before it becomes a bigger issue.

Dr Susan Nolen-Hoeksema,[1] a Yale professor who spent her career studying overthinking, called it the 'secret to unhappiness'. Decades of research corroborate the causal link established by Nolen-Hoeksema and prove that overthinking has multiple negative consequences: it exacerbates problems, magnifies and prolongs negative mood, impairs problem-solving and makes us more pessimistic about the future.

One of the biggest problems for overthinkers is the idea that they should always feel good or happy. The American Psychological Association[2] examined two different aspects of pursuing happiness: aspiring to be happy and being concerned about our level of happiness. Over 1,800 participants answered questions about their beliefs about happiness, as well as their psychological wellbeing and depressive symptoms. The study found that the pursuit of happiness, or viewing happiness as an important goal, didn't have a detrimental impact on wellbeing. However, judging how happy you are and having concerns about personal happiness levels were associated with lower overall life satisfaction and psychological wellbeing, as well as greater depressive symptoms. This related to fears about not measuring up or not being as happy as other people. The research also found that having concerns about our own happiness was associated with greater negativity about positive events. This suggests that having high expectations about how happy we *should* be can be detrimental, as it makes it more difficult to achieve the level of happiness that we are expecting. This is an idea we'll be coming back to throughout the book.

The research is clear: those who overthink are unhappier. It might seem like a discrete issue, but it is in fact the common denominator of a multitude of issues. It presents as not just a symptom of many far more serious problems; it is also a root cause.

Overthinking should come with a health warning:[3]

- It makes life much harder, because it leaves you feeling frequently overwhelmed, angry, sad, anxious, ashamed or guilty.

- It takes up huge amounts of your time that would be much better invested elsewhere.

- It can lead you to live in a constant state of dread.

- It amplifies your problems.

- It saps your energy and motivation, impairs your ability to focus and limits your ability to feel joy.

- It damages self-worth, is linked to low confidence and low self-esteem, and pulls you into problematic comparisons with others.

- It negatively affects your relationships, because it can make you more reactive and can make it difficult to set boundaries.

- It makes you more likely to make unwise decisions and engage in problem behaviours like binge-eating, substance misuse and self-harm.

- It can lead to chronic stress, which in turn can lead to physiological problems such as systemic inflammation, increased cortisol and disrupted sleep.

- It is strongly associated with perfectionism. Studies have suggested that the higher the level of perfectionism,[4] the more psychological disorders you may suffer.

- It contributes to physical health changes, including higher heart rate, blood pressure and sympathetic nervous system activity. Over time, the corrosive effect of this psychological agitation can lead to higher rates of heart disease, cardiac arrest, stomach ulcers, arthritis, back problems, headaches and chronic pain.

- It contributes to the onset, maintenance and recurrence of multiple mental health problems, including depression, eating disorders and anxiety disorders such as post-traumatic stress disorder (PTSD), social anxiety, health anxiety, obsessive-compulsive disorder (OCD) and generalized anxiety disorder (GAD).

It's important to see that there is nothing good about overthinking! Once you see this clearly (and I mean really *know* it, beyond a shadow of a doubt) it makes it much, much easier to take the next steps.

The second arrow

Imagine you are hit by an arrow,[5] then, a few minutes later, a second arrow comes and strikes in the exact same spot. The first arrow really stings and hurts, but after the second arrow, the pain has not only doubled – it feels ten times more intense.

When we suffer misfortune, two arrows fly our way. The first arrow is the difficult event and the impact it is having on us, physically, mentally, emotionally, economically or socially. This is unavoidable, and it's natural to feel pain. The second arrow represents our reaction to the bad event. When we experience pain, whether it is physical or mental, it is important that we recognize it, but we must be careful not to amplify our feelings or add more pain and suffering. While we can't stop the first arrow, it is within our power to control the second.

I love this Buddhist parable, as it sums up overthinking for me. When we don't feel right and question what's wrong with us, that's the second arrow. When we feel depressed and question why these things always happen, or when we get angry and revolt against what's happened, it's the second arrow. When we feel things are unfair or when we worry too much and imagine all the worst-case scenarios – you've guessed it, it's the second arrow.

While I'm not suggesting we deny our reaction to suffering, I want to show you how you can avoid the second arrow – and unnecessary suffering – by following my five steps. You have a choice in how you react to a painful situation, and this book will show you how.

I have seen first-hand how freeing yourself from overthinking can have dramatic results. This is why I want to share these ideas with more people – I've seen the difference they can make. It's like letting go of a heavy weight: you will feel lighter and more confident. Fix overthinking, and it won't just leave you with more capacity, energy and clarity to function and enjoy your day to day – it will radically change your life.

How to use this book: breaking the overthinking habit

The good news is that overthinking can be cured, and I'll show you how to do so in this book. So often we are told that our problems are because of what we have experienced in the past, our genetic make-up or something else impossible to influence or change. The truth is that the way you deal with life's ups and downs can be changed. Research shows that thinking patterns are not fixed but are in fact trainable.[6] In short, if you work at beating overthinking, you can free yourself from it.

In Part One, I'll be explaining how overthinking operates and why it's so difficult to break free from it, alongside why it is so important to learn how to change. I'll help you to develop a greater awareness of your overthinking and give you a better understanding of yourself. The better you become at recognizing overthinking, the more easily you'll be able to catch it in action – and when you catch it, you have a choice. Rather than reacting automatically, you can intentionally choose your response and break free from repetitive negative thinking.

In Part Two, I'll be looking at the *why* of overthinking. This section details my thoughts on why overthinking has become so prevalent. I'll look at what's going on in our brains when we overthink, and why it can be so difficult to stop overthinking once we've started. I'll also be looking at the problems that feed into overthinking, including self-criticism, comparison and our capacity to manage, alongside what we can do to overcome these things.

In the final part of this book, I'll be introducing you to my five-step plan to cure overthinking for good. I'll give you the techniques to future-proof your life against overthinking. At the very end of the book, I've added an appendix where you'll find specific advice for problem areas that overthinking loves: health anxiety, social anxiety, people-pleasing, relationships and intrusive thoughts. You can come back to these and use them as a reference for the future.

Here are the five steps we will be going through:

1. **Notice** the thought.
2. **Choose** what you let into your spotlight of attention.
3. **Challenge** your thinking.
4. **Accept** the reality of how life is.
5. **Face your fears** to overcome them.

To stop overthinking, you first need to increase your awareness of how it operates. When you notice it, you can choose your response and broaden your 'spotlight of attention' (more on this in Chapter Three) to help your brain become unstuck. This will allow you to build new, healthier habits so you can switch overthinking for strategies that actually work. You can then challenge your thinking and move on to acceptance. Finally, I'll be asking you to face your fears so you can stop avoidance and get back to the things you enjoy.

I'll also include brief case studies throughout the book. It can be easier to see how overthinking operates when your own emotions aren't involved, and there can be a relief in seeing that other people think as you do. The better you become at recognizing overthinking in others, the more easily you'll be able to see it in yourself. The case studies are not specific individuals; they are based on the many people I treat/work with in my clinic and are an amalgamation of the common themes and patterns I see.

Get ready to see things differently

In this book, you will learn that:
- Overthinking is the problem, not the solution.
- When you overthink, you are making yourself go through the very experience you are trying to avoid.
- Thoughts and feelings are not facts.
- Avoidance is not the answer.
- Not everything comes back to you.

I will teach you to:
- Zoom out from your feelings.
- Boost your mood to disrupt overthinking.
- Change what you focus on and change how you think and feel for the better.
- Build new neural pathways in your brain to break the overthinking habit.
- Do rather than think, and see that experience is the key to emotional development.

When I talk about overthinking, I'm thinking about worry and rumination. Worry tends to be future-focused, while rumination tends to be past-focused. These thinking types overlap, and so the treatment approach for dealing with worry and rumination is the same.

In this book, I will be referring to 'negative emotions' or a 'bad mood' for ease. I'm thinking of emotions like anger, shame, guilt, sadness, anxiety and low mood. I want to make it clear that, although I'm calling them negative and bad, all emotions are important, and they serve a valuable and useful function in our lives. It's not about trying to get rid of them; it's just about ensuring that we don't get hit by the second arrow.

If you are struggling with overthinking at a level that is causing you significant distress, or you think you may be suffering from an anxiety disorder or depression, it's worth going to see your doctor. They may suggest seeing a therapist, who can help you put these ideas into practice and support you with whatever you are facing.

How to get the most from this book

The fact you have picked up this book is a brilliant start. It means you hope for things to be different. Hope is the key to change, and it's an important first step. Yet, to truly break the overthinking habit, you'll need to do more than just read the book; you'll need to translate the ideas into your own life and try out all the strategies (yes – all of them).

This is a bit like learning to drive: it's all very well passing your driving theory test, but that doesn't teach you how to drive a car. Psychology is the same. The theory is really helpful (and interesting), and a first step towards understanding your mind better, but putting these ideas into practice and carrying out the strategies will really make a difference to how you feel.

I know it's hard to stop and do the exercises, but it's only by trying them that you'll have a chance to see the difference they can make. Try each one for the first time when you are feeling good, as it will be easier to put them into practice. Then, when you really need them, they'll be more familiar.

The strategies in this book are just an introduction. I want you to think about this as an ongoing project: it's really about getting to know yourself and seeing what works for you. In each step, I'll run you through different approaches. There's no 'one size fits all', so you need to work out which ones work best for you.

People are often surprised by the strategies that work best for them and the benefit of trying new things. I am certainly guilty of this. When my husband started cycling, I wasn't sure about it – the Lycra seemed a bit much to me. But, just before my fortieth birthday, and after yet another running injury, I thought I'd see what all the hype was about and give it a try. Now, cycling is something I love and it's not an exaggeration to say it's changed my life. Our natural response is to stick with what we know, but this approach is so limiting. So I want you to try all the strategies in this book, even the ones you think you won't like. The more you try, the better chance you will give yourself of breaking this debilitating habit.

While I'm all for trying new things, I also believe that you should always reserve the right to change your mind. If a strategy is not working for you, don't keep going just because you said you would. Stop and try something different. It's going with what feels right for you at the time that will make the difference.

Make notes

Take time to reflect after reading a chapter or trying a strategy. There are blank pages at the end of this book for note-taking (see page 335 onward). Writing things down lets you keep track of your progress and what's been helpful. If you prefer using your phone, you could write in the Notes app. Taking notes is a great way to keep hold of any ideas that resonate with you and also a way to gain new perspectives. We learn much more from our experiences when we reflect on what we've done.

Make a note of how you feel before you try the strategy, and then make a note of how you feel afterward. This will let you track how you get on and see the difference each strategy makes. You can also look back at your notes the next time you're facing something difficult as a reminder that you can do it. Holding on to this feeling is key to doing it the next time.

Highlight the strategies you like and the ones that work best for you. You may even want to think about which ones work best for specific issues. If you normally overthink when you're angry, which strategy is a good replacement for this? Or, if you overthink when you fear how you're coming across, what can you do instead that works better? The techniques that work best may change depending on the problem or what's going on in your life.

It's also important to talk to others about overthinking to actively open up the conversation. You'll be (pleasantly) surprised by how many people will relate to the way you feel.

Change takes time

When I work with people, I find that they're able to think differently fairly quickly as long as they're ready and motivated to change. However, it can take a bit longer for the new habits to really take hold. Give yourself time; things won't change overnight, but with perseverance you'll see a huge difference in your life.

Together we will plant the seeds of change, but it is up to you to nurture them, take care of them and bring them into bloom. You will feel uncomfortable at first, but don't worry. Growth isn't meant to be comfortable; I'm pushing you out of autopilot and into uncharted territory. You will learn new skills and they will stretch you, but, with regular practice and hard work, you will begin to improve and feel less self-conscious.

Have faith in the process; I promise it will be worth it. Hard as it might be to believe, you're not so far away from the life you want.

Small steps add up

Consistency is key. My motto is that what we do every day makes the biggest difference. It's small steps that lead to the greatest change. How we feel is a natural product of all of our choices, but especially the small choices that each of us makes every day. When put together, all these small changes can have a massive impact.

Small steps might not sound so dramatic, but they add up. You don't set off up a mountain and then suddenly reach the top; it's many steps that take you to the summit. Remind yourself that, if you do what you need to do today, it will get you to tomorrow, and in the longer term it will get you to where you want to go. Keep this idea with you as you work through the book.

Before you continue, take a minute to think about your reasons for change and write them down:

- What do you want to gain from this book?
- What do you hope will be different?
- What impact would this have on your life?

Well done. You're ready to begin!

PART I

UNDERSTANDING THE PROBLEM

Chapter 1
Overthinking is the problem, not the solution!

By the end of this chapter, you will:

- Know what overthinking is and why we do it.
- Understand the difference between abstract and concrete thinking.
- Recognize overthinking is a bad habit and understand why it becomes habitual.
- Appreciate why you can't think your way out of a negative feeling.
- Understand how doom spirals operate.

What is overthinking?

Overthinking is when our minds get stuck on certain thoughts and feelings, usually negative ones, and we can't stop thinking about them. They could be things such as worries, replaying events in our minds, or endlessly questioning why something has happened. It's normal to think things over, to revisit your past, or work through alternative options for a situation, but persistently dwelling on how you're feeling and your thoughts causes problems, particularly when there's no escape at night-time and sleep is disrupted.

I'm going to show you that, rather than helping, overthinking magnifies the problem, increases self-focus and creates a vicious cycle amplifying negative moods and thoughts, so we are constantly going over the same feelings or events again and again and again. This type of thinking becomes habitual and out of control, adding to our troubles rather than relieving them. Overthinking is the problem, not the solution!

Why do we overthink?

Thinking through problems is obviously not all bad. In fact, it's an evolved and adaptive response – the brain is always trying to understand the significance of events and keep us safe from danger. Overthinking is triggered when the brain alerts us to a 'goal discrepancy' in our lives. The brain is constantly monitoring and reacting to discrepancies between where we *feel* we are and where we *think* we should be, or how we're feeling emotionally and how we *want* to feel. This goal discrepancy can be either real or imagined.

The brain sees the gap as a problem to be solved and tries to work out the best way to bridge it. To do this, we focus on the issue, break it down

Goal discrepancy

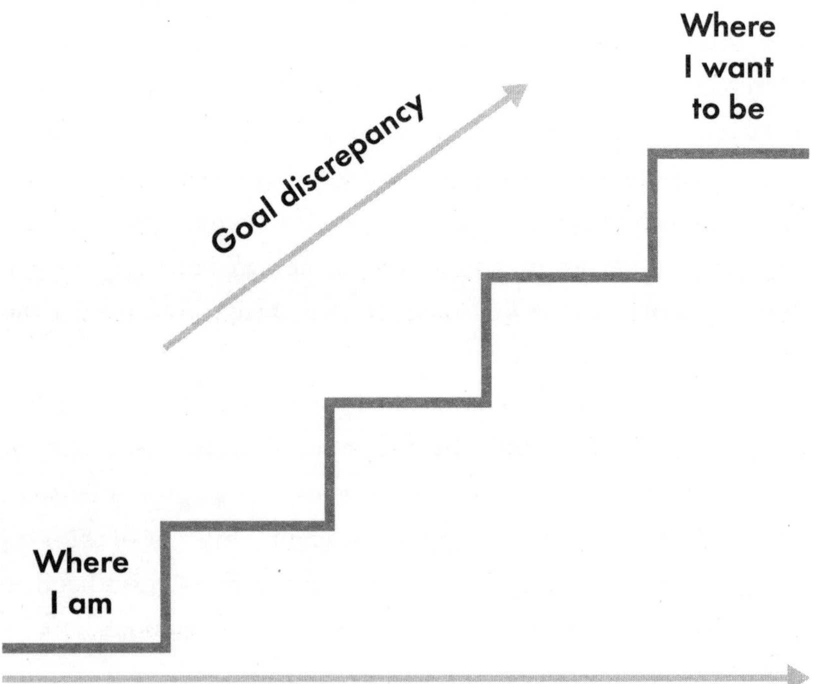

and analyse the best way to narrow the gap. This can happen consciously or outside our awareness.

It's human nature to think things over to make sense of them, and when done in the right way, it can be useful. It's a way to notice something that is off and work through a detailed analysis to solve the problem and close the gap. Or, if we're working towards a goal, it's a way to ensure we are making progress and staying on the right path.

This type of analytical thinking is brilliant when it's concrete, which is when we think about a specific issue and problem-solve solutions with a focus on what's happened and how to take action. It's helped us build cities, treat cancer and travel into space. It's also helpful in our daily lives, whether it helps us with organizing the specifics of our week or taking action on what we need to do. It helps us work on a project, organize childcare, get our cars booked in for a service or train for a marathon. Giving some time and energy to the problem allows you to think of a solution, helping you to move forward.

However, this type of thinking becomes problematic when we shift to abstract thinking, moving from what's actually happened to overgeneralizations, imagined scenarios and unsolvable thoughts. The initial issue might be a mistake you've made, but from there you begin to generalize and think about the fact you always mess up, or that you're no good at all. Before you know it, you're thinking about the fact you're a completely useless person. This is what Frankie often did. Frankie hated making mistakes. She had high expectations for herself and, if she felt she hadn't done everything she could, she'd blame herself.

When I found out I'd failed my mock exam, I sunk into the lowest mood. I was so cross with myself and I felt ashamed. It was like I was stuck to my bed, just sitting there thinking. I found it impossible to move. I couldn't stop thinking about it for two days, completely overwhelmed. I couldn't sleep so I didn't get a break at night. All I was thinking was, how could I have been so stupid? Going over and over where things went wrong, imagining what other people would think. The thoughts swamped my mind and I couldn't rationalize them. I got angry at myself for allowing them to run through my head, but I just couldn't cope.

When we overthink, we focus on the gap between where we *feel* we are and where we *think* we should be, finding ourselves at fault for not matching up to our ambitions. Our beliefs also feed into the problem. If we think we should always have a plan a, b, c and d, or that we should be perfect and never feel bad or out of control of life, then this gap will be regularly triggered when we believe that we're not happy enough or not doing well enough, or that we're failing at being the person we wish we could be. These goal discrepancies can be thought of as an expectation gap. Our minds are trying to help us make sense of what's going on so we feel better, but instead they are doing the opposite.

The problem that pretends to be a solution

When we notice a goal discrepancy (we're not making progress as we'd like to or feeling as good as we believe we should), we believe that the solution is to go over it, so we can understand it, take control, feel better and avoid ever feeling like this again.

Even though overthinking causes lots of problems, many people who overthink don't tend to see it as intrusive or unwanted. As we've already seen, it can arrive in camouflage, pretending to be helpful and coming under the guise of useful thoughts. It promises to lead you to new insights and bring a new understanding to how you're feeling or to the problems you're facing.

This is the first and biggest mistake we make. You can't think your way out of a negative feeling – it's like digging to get out of a hole. Focusing on the gap in these situations is actually one of the worst things you can do.

Overthinking typically starts with 'why' or 'what' questions. Why did this problem happen, why am I feeling like this, what is wrong with me, why do these things always happen to me? But when we worry about the future or go over every possible scenario, we then move on to 'what ifs'. What if I embarrass myself? What if I make the wrong decision and fail?

This type of thinking can trigger a cascade of negative memories and self-critical thoughts, as we dredge up past regrets and imagine future catastrophes. In one sense, our brains are trying to be helpful by looking at the problem from all possible angles. But this highlights all the problems in our lives and leads to us trawling through negative feelings, upsetting memories, bad experiences and potential future problems. We then delve into any potential or perceived problem, making ourselves feel worse. This amplifies the negative feelings we're already experiencing and drives our mood lower as we consider the future. This is how Ely often felt.

It was my birthday, but I just wasn't in a good mood. I was just thinking, What's wrong with me, why am I feeling like this? Why aren't I happy? I looked back over the past year and, although there's some stuff I'm happy with, I feel like I'm not enjoying myself. There isn't much happiness in each day. I shouldn't be feeling like this all the time. It made me really question if I'm getting my life right. Am I making the most of it?

I'm not sure my work is right anymore; I don't know if it's what I should be doing. There are days when it makes me so miserable, and it's hard working alone and having to motivate myself every day. I'm trying to do all the right things, like seeing my friends, doing my running, but it doesn't make up for the days when work's hard and I'm not productive – when I'm sitting at home trying to work and I don't feel good. If I was doing something I enjoyed more, I'd feel better, but I don't know what that is. I just feel depressed by being another year older and not having life worked out yet.

If we place an extreme value on happiness and the importance of not experiencing negative emotional states, we are much more likely to overthink like Ely. Our mood then drops lower as we think not only about the initial problem, but every past, present and future problem, too. It's like being pulled into quicksand.

One psychological study[7] created a way to get people to overthink in a lab by asking them to focus on how they were feeling. They split the participants into two groups: the first were classified as low in mood, and the second group were classified as non-depressed (those that felt good). Participants were randomly assigned to spend 8 minutes focusing on their emotions and how their lives were going (the overthinking group) or on descriptions of geographic locations and objects (the distraction group).

The overthinking group were given the following instructions:

- Think about your level of motivation right now.
- Think about your goals for the future.
- Think about how happy or sad you feel right now.
- Think about your relationship with your family.

The distraction group were asked to:

- Think about a cool breeze blowing on a warm day.
- Think about a plane flying slowly overhead.
- Think about the shape of the Statue of Liberty.
- Think about the layout of the local shopping mall.

The study found that those participants who were already low in mood became sadder after doing the overthinking task for only 8–10 minutes, whereas those who did the distraction task for the same amount of time became significantly less sad and depressed.

Those who weren't sad (the non-depressed group) when the study began, showed no mood changes in response to either the overthinking or distraction task. Therefore, thinking about yourself isn't inherently

Time spent overthinking negatively affects mood

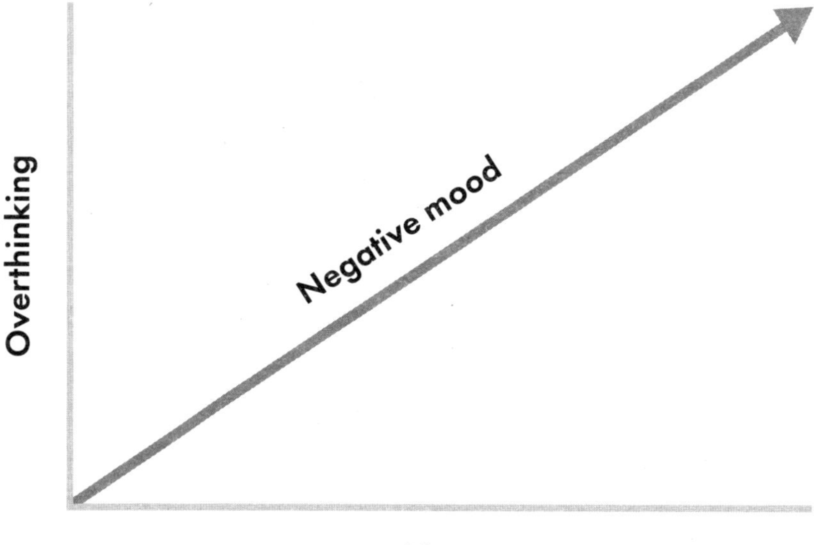

depressing; it only depresses your mood if you are already feeling low. This is a key idea to hold on to as you work through the book.

The overthinking that we thought would help us solve the problem or stop us from feeling so bad is making everything worse. Instead of helping us to move forward, we end up stuck in a negative downward spiral. When we get stuck obsessing about something, it can persist for days, weeks, even months. When it's really bad, it can be incredibly distressing and overwhelming as these thoughts snowball out of control, gathering momentum.

Overthinking is a bad habit

You'd hope that when you were feeling overwhelmed by overthinking, your mind would jump into gear and start supporting you. Sadly, the overthinking only continues, adding to your problems and making them harder to resolve. Overthinking is best thought of as a bad habit, like vaping or overeating. What starts off as a small release soon becomes habitual and addictive.

Once you begin to overthink, it is self-perpetuating, becoming hardwired into your brain over time (you'll find out more about this in Chapter Six). Instead of being triggered by a goal discrepancy, we become so practised at this type of thinking that it becomes an automatic response and is triggered any time something goes wrong or we feel bad (due to factors such as negative mood, anxiety, discomfort or tiredness).

What was once a conscious process that we engaged in as a way to take our problems seriously is now out of control. It's happening all the time, often without us even realizing it. You might also associate certain places with overthinking: just as you might link the refrigerator to thoughts of food, you can link places, like home, to all the jobs that you need to do and haven't done. Or when you spend time with family, it might trigger memories of the ways you have felt let down by your family in the past. Consequently, it's easy to fall into passively engaging in overthinking. Your brain thinks it is being useful by reminding you of these things, and your response (to think intensely) automatically kicks in.

Doom spirals

Overthinking is both triggered by low moods and a cause of them. When we're feeling good, we rarely do a deep-dive analysis into why things are going well. We don't wake up feeling great and run through all the reasons why. Yet we feel the need to go back over and over the things we got wrong – those embarrassing moments, arguments and perceived criticisms. We question ourselves and what we're doing with our lives, or compare ourselves to a previous better version: 'I never used to be this tired, this nervous, or find life this hard.'

When I first met Xiang, she told me how hard things were for her. I could see the pain she was in and how trapped she was by her thinking.

I've always felt insecure, especially in my friendships. I just don't feel like I click with people. I question absolutely everything. 'Is what I'm wearing OK? Am I coming across in the right way?' It makes it impossible to look forward to anything. Socializing can feel like a nightmare. Before I go out, I try to prepare as much as I can as a way to feel safe and in control. I make sure I know what's happening in the news, what other people might be interested in. I try to think of questions and things to talk about. Sometimes I spend so long trying to prepare myself that I make myself really anxious and end up convincing myself not to go.

When I'm there, it's hard to enjoy seeing people. I feel like I have to come across as fine, and that if I show I'm feeling anxious people will judge me. I don't feel I can trust just being myself, so I try and adapt myself to what I think other people want me to be. Sometimes I feel like I don't even know myself anymore. I run through so many scenarios before admitting that I don't even know what I actually think. I convince myself that whoever I'm talking to is finding me boring or stupid. I feel like if people really knew me, they'd see I wasn't someone they'd want to know.

I want to be part of the conversation, but I also hate it when everyone looks at me. I feel like they're all scrutinizing me and what I'm saying, and that they're not thinking anything good. I can't bear the embarrassment of standing on my own. I hide in the loo when I can't face talking to other people and it all gets too much. Or I go on my phone.

Then afterwards, I'm plagued by uncomfortable feelings of how I came across. I replay it in my mind from every angle. I analyse every comment and their body language: 'When I said that, what did they think? Did they want me to leave? Did I appear closed or rude because I felt so anxious?' At one point it got so bad that I started drinking before going out to numb the feelings rather than have this constant noise in my head, but the next day the hangxiety made everything ten times worse.

I often avoid saying yes to plans as I just can't face it. Or I seek reassurance, like 'Do you actually want me to come? If you're not in the mood, don't worry, we don't have to go.' I feel insecure about whether people actually like me or if I'm bothering people, so I'm always apologizing. Even though I often bail last minute, if I'm not invited I feel upset that they're doing things without me. I know people are allowed to have their own friends, but I still feel really lonely and rejected. I can't help but worry I've done something wrong. I end up going on my socials to see what everyone's up to and see pictures of everyone out together, all having fun without me.

Other people seem to find it so much easier to make friends. I compare myself to everyone and try to work out how to be more like them. I literally compare myself on every little thing. I look at other people and ask myself: 'How do they do it?' Other people find it so much easier than I do. I'm struggling to cope, and it's not even over a real problem. I feel so overwhelmed.

Overthinking can destroy your confidence and leave you feeling hopeless. I felt so sad for Xiang as a young woman in her early twenties. Her overthinking was stopping her from seeing what I could see: that she was intelligent, interesting and thoughtful. However, I also felt hopeful, as I knew that I could help her to see this too – and that the first step to doing this was to stop her overthinking.

When we are in these negative mood states (e.g. low, anxious, angry), our brains have a negative bias. We start to think more negatively and we recall negative memories and thoughts. For example, if you overthink when your mood is depressed, your brain links to all the difficult and dark times in your life that have been marked by failure, loss and disappointment. These sad thoughts and memories flood your consciousness, making you even more depressed. This is because our emotions are intrinsically linked to our thoughts, how we feel physically, and our behaviour (I'll explain this further in Chapter Six). As you can see in the mind map below, they are all connected: the brain tells the body what to do, but the body also guides the brain. Feelings can trigger certain thoughts, memories and reactions, just as certain actions and thoughts can trigger feelings. This means that when we are overthinking, it has an impact on how we feel and how we approach life, as well as what we expect.

Overthinking mind map

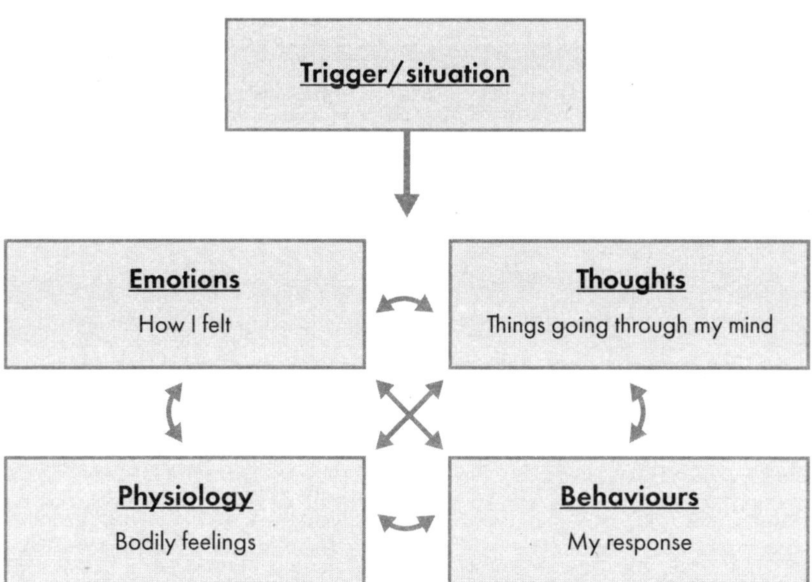

Overthinking mind map (example)

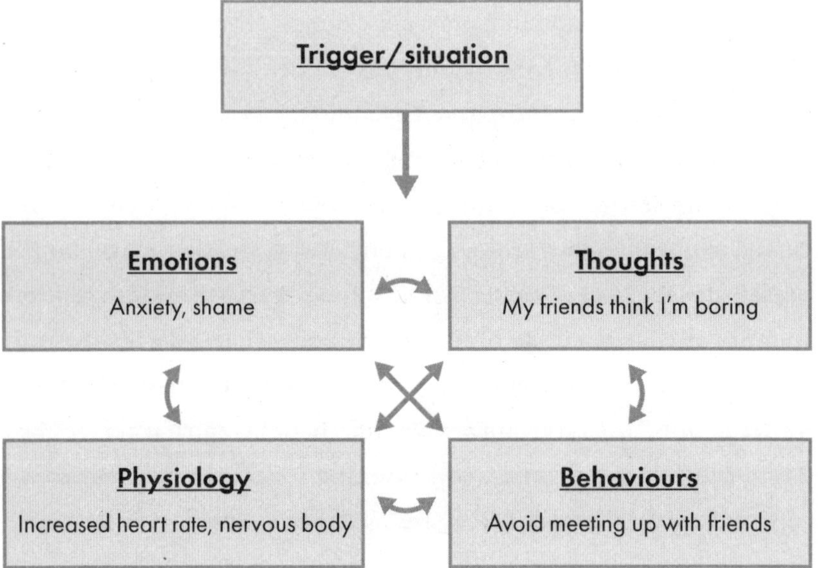

As you can see in the mind map:

- Overthinking can be triggered by either how we are feeling (emotionally or physically) or by our behaviour (what we are doing).
- Our thoughts and beliefs can also amplify or trigger overthinking if there is an expectation gap and we believe we shouldn't be feeling like this, or if our expectations are not met.
- Overthinking changes how we feel physically, as it activates our fight-or-flight response, releasing cortisol and increasing cardiovascular activity, so heart rate and blood pressure increase. It can also push us into freeze mode, where it's difficult to do anything and we feel overwhelmed.
- Overthinking changes our behaviours: we're more likely to avoid the things we feel fearful of and not do the things that

could make us feel better. Avoiding means that we don't have a chance to break the cycle and prove our thoughts wrong.

All this means that how we experience the world corresponds with our state of mind and how we feel in our bodies. When we feel good, the world feels good, but when we feel bad, our feelings colour our thoughts and shape our behaviour.

I call these vicious cycles 'doom spirals' – when you're stuck in a negative mood state that spirals on a loop, out of control. In a doom spiral, you are imprisoned by overthinking or caught in 'analysis paralysis'.

Doom spiral

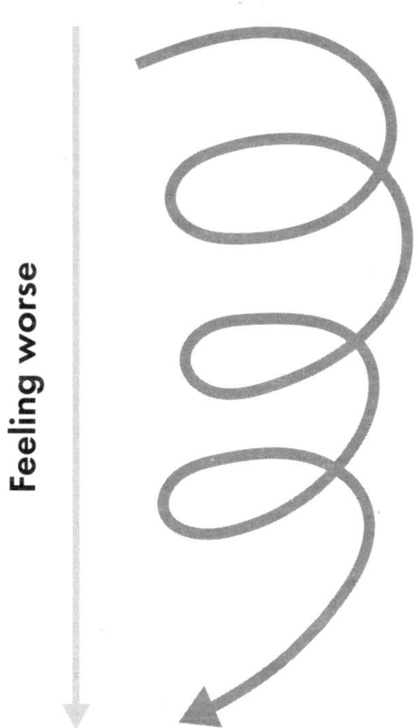

Overthinking is the problem, not the solution! 31

Once you're in this type of mood state, it's hard to get out of, as the link between our thoughts, feelings, how we feel physically and our behaviours works against us. All these factors feed into each other, driving our mood lower or pushing our anxiety into overdrive. We're no longer just feeling bad; we're raking through the hot coals of our past problems and conjuring up future worries.

The worse we feel, the worse our thinking becomes. When we become trapped in the doom spiral, it feels impossible to get out – and it doesn't help when people tell us to just stop overthinking.

Overthinking doesn't work!

This type of thinking will not help you to process what happened. It is the second arrow. As the Buddhist parable tells us, we can't avoid pain and suffering, but we do have a choice in how we react to them.

It might feel like you're trying to work things out by thinking them through, but while this is an understandable thought, I hope you're beginning to see that it's simply not true. When you're in a doom spiral, the abstract questions you ask yourself **do not** have an answer. This type of analysis has a negative effect on mood, increases negative thinking and is a predisposing factor for depression. Rather than helping you work things out, it impairs problem-solving, saps motivation and makes it very difficult for you to enjoy your life.

I will teach you to recognize these negative habitual thinking patterns. When you **notice** the thoughts, you can begin to make changes. Once you become aware of these thoughts, you are giving yourself a choice. Rather than let overthinking drag you down a path that doesn't take you where you want or need to go, you can **choose** an alternative response and break the overthinking habit.

Remember:

- Overthinking is when you get stuck on certain thoughts and feelings, usually negative.
- Overthinking starts off as a way to try to cope, but shifts from an intentional response to an automatic behaviour.
- Overthinking shifts you to abstract thinking, moving from what's happened to overgeneralizations, imagined scenarios and unsolvable thoughts.
- Overthinking is not helpful, and it does not help you gain important insights.
- You can't think your way out of a negative feeling; that would be like digging to get out of a hole.
- Overthinking drags you away from the initial issue and into problems that you don't need to be thinking about.
- Overthinking can become uncontrollable and can lead to doom spirals.
- The mood you're in when you overthink is a magnet for similar experiences and feelings.

Chapter 2
The root of overthinking

By the end of this chapter, you will:
- Understand the root causes of overthinking.
- Know your overthinking triggers and the common topics of your overthinking.
- Understand the research on overthinking and the problems it can cause.

Overthinking is best seen as a faulty coping mechanism, developed in response to feeling vulnerable or exposed. It starts as a way to manage how you're feeling and to try to work things out, but instead it makes your problems mutate and grow. It becomes a reflexive, habitual response to emotional distress, triggered not just by goal discrepancies but any time you're feeling bad.

Overthinking runs on a continuum from the occasional bout to full-blown overwhelm.

It starts off at a low level, with us being pulled back into thinking repeatedly about something. As overthinking increases, the thoughts start to crop up regularly; for example, when you're waiting to hear from somebody and you're left in limbo. You think it's going to be fine, but there's a difference between thinking it and *knowing* it.

Next, overthinking becomes all-consuming, with your mind constantly returning to the thoughts. Maybe your boss emails you on Friday and one indecipherable comment ruins your whole weekend. Maybe a date hasn't replied to your message and, with each passing day, their silence becomes harder to ignore. These thoughts feel important

The overthinking continuum

and pressing. Imaginary conversations or other people's comments play in your mind. It's like your nose is pushed up against a window: there's no room for other perspectives or a different view.

At the extreme end of the continuum is overwhelm: regret, self-criticism and shame are all mixed together, with thoughts echoing in your head all the time. Overthinking can become paralysing. This is when you are pushed into freeze mode. At this point, you feel unable to do anything else, and feel completely convinced your thoughts are reality or are definitely going to happen. As you move along the continuum, emotions also increase in intensity, as Ananya described in one of her therapy sessions with me.

It was a very bad day. In that moment I thought it was ground zero. I literally thought it was the end of the world. I went totally nuts. A day later, it was fine – I could see I'd created a full-blown drama in my mind – but it was so difficult to keep hold of any perspective in the moment. It felt horrendous and I couldn't snap out of it. I was swallowed up in a hole.

What triggers overthinking?

The number-one trigger to overthinking is discomfort: either the discomfort itself (emotional or physical) or the thoughts you have in response to experiencing discomfort. As you read through the table opposite, make a note of your hotspots (the topics and emotions you are most sensitive to) for discomfort and overthinking.

When I talk about discomfort in this book, I'm thinking about:

Feeling vulnerable or exposed	Being open and honest about your feelings, thoughts and needs. Sharing parts of yourself that you might usually keep hidden.
Negative emotions and distress	Sadness, upset, low mood, depression, irritability, anger, frustration, anxiety, worry, shame, guilt, resentment.
Fear	Fear of how you'll do, how things are going to go, what might happen, judgement or rejection.
Physical discomfort	Feeling on edge, increased heart rate, butterflies, sweating, stomach ache, illness, nausea.
Uncertainty and the unknown	Anything that involves waiting to hear about something (health problems, whether you got the job, hearing back from a date). Particularly difficult when there isn't a quick resolution or clear answer.
Anticipatory anxiety	The lead-up to doing something that feels scary or out of your comfort zone.
Avoidance	Suppressing your thoughts or not doing the things that you want to or should do.
Pain	Anything that hurts (physical and emotional). Things going wrong or not happening as you expect.
Periods of growth	Stepping out of your comfort zone and doing things you're less familiar with or that you find challenging.
Stress	Life stressors (new job, relationship breakdown, money worries) or current challenges. Can be chronic or acute.
Conflict	Disagreements, arguments, communication breakdown, passive aggressive behaviour or emotional withdrawal.
Feeling powerless	A lack of autonomy, agency or control over your current situation or a power imbalance.

Triggers can range from minor annoyances (maybe a driver beeps at you) to major life issues (a relationship breakdown). We can also be triggered by associations: we might be more sensitive to overthinking at certain times of day, or when we're in certain places. Even specific people can trigger the thoughts, like comments your sister makes or criticism from a friend. You're also more likely to overthink if you are over-capacity, tired or rundown.

It can take only a tiny event to spark off a spiral of overthinking. When overthinking blows up in your mind, it doesn't matter how big or small the problem is, it can take over your life and feel incredibly distressing. Even if a small part of you knows it's OK, it can feel impossible to hold on to the thought.

– **Note down your own triggers and associations.**

Overthinking's favourite topics

You may have noticed that overthinking loves to prey on the things that really matter to us, because these things loom bigger in our minds. Here are some very common overthinking topics:

- **Relationships:** Friends, partner, children, parents, wider family, exes, dating, sex, conflicts, loneliness.
- **How we view ourselves:** Anything that links to self-worth, self-esteem and identity.
- **Sense of control:** Work, physical and mental health, finances, debt, relationships, loss, trauma, bereavement.
- **Our values:** Anything that clashes with our beliefs, religion, expectations or the way we think about life. Our values are also shaped by the social, cultural and historical context in which we find ourselves.

We really care about these things and the people attached to them, so any issues in these areas are more emotive and *feel* more threatening. This makes us more sensitive and reactive. We may have favourite topics that we return to again and again. For example, we may think, 'I'm so tired, what's wrong with me?' as soon as we feel tired (even though it's normal to feel tired sometimes). The stronger the habit becomes, the more difficult it feels to control it, and overthinking continues even when it isn't wanted.

These topics are often tied to our self-concept, that is, how we view ourselves. If your self-worth is pinned to one area of your life, such as work, relationships or your role as a parent, it can feel like your whole world collapses when you struggle in this area. This can be particularly challenging when you are stuck in a situation that is outside of your control. It also makes the thoughts more sticky – we become more entangled in the overthinking web because we care so much.

This was certainly true for Sam, who was struggling with imposter syndrome. He was having difficulties with his confidence at work and felt anxious about his performance. It had left him questioning himself, and he felt full of insecurity and self-doubt. It had negatively changed his self-concept and was also affecting his home life.

Work is causing me so much anxiety. I have a good manager, but I feel guilty that I'm not doing justice to my work. I'm forever questioning myself: 'Can I do this, should I be doing this? Have I bitten off more than I can chew?' I feel like I need to prove myself, as I worry my boss doesn't think I'm good enough. Everything feels like a source of stress. I'm in a constant brain fog and it's stopped me being able to get on with stuff. I don't feel productive, then I feel guilty and question what I've done. I worry I haven't used my time well and that everyone will think badly of me.

Meetings create even more anxiety in me. Especially when they're online and my manager is on the call. I run through all the worst-case scenarios beforehand. I find it hard to concentrate as I'm thinking so much about what other people are thinking about me.

When I'm sitting there, I'm thinking, 'What shall I say?' I think about it so much and I know what I want to say, but then I say nothing. I leave it so long that the pressure builds and I feel like it's been so long since I've spoken that I need to say something really good. Then someone else says what I was going to and gets positive feedback, and I feel so cross with myself that I didn't just speak up. Other people say I come across well on the calls, but it's hard to believe when I'm always panicking. If I do speak up, I feel like what I'm saying is trivial and isn't adding any value to the conversation. I feel like a fraud and that I'll be found out at any moment. I just want to hide. Afterwards I think, 'Why didn't I just shut up and stay quiet?' I regret speaking up.

If it gets too much, I end up tuning out from what's being said or turning my camera off, but then I worry that I've not heard something important.

Then it spills into my personal life. I'm so tired that I end up taking it out on my partner. Then I watch TV until I fall asleep. Anything to zone out from it all. I did a call recently and it went so badly that I couldn't get to sleep that night; I just kept going over and over it in my head. I felt so embarrassed. Other people seem so much more fluent and seem to speak with ease.

I wanted to look for jobs, but I just keep thinking, 'What's the point?' Everything has become a chore. Sometimes I just wish I could escape it all, and I imagine an easy job. When I look at the good points, I know that I'm in a good team, that this is a job I have always wanted to do, that it's a good opportunity. I said to myself I'd work harder on my projects and do additional learning, but I haven't. I can't find the energy. Everyone else copes with these things. It's made me realize I'm not the person I thought I was.

     Understanding the problem

As you can see for Sam, when overthinking takes hold, it can spill into all areas of your life. This makes it very difficult to see yourself in a positive light. Perhaps you can also see that the overthinking is obscuring his view of himself, and that overthinking what he wants to say isn't actually helping as he hopes – it's making everything harder.

– Take a moment to think about which topics tend to be your go-tos for overthinking and note them down. Knowing your favourite topics, triggers and hotspots allows you to get to know yourself better. You'll then be more likely to see your overthinking in action, so rather than blindly going along with it, you can note what your brain is up to. This gives you a chance to break the habit and think differently, so you can choose how you respond.

What does the research say?

In 2019, researchers Watkins and Roberts conducted a research review on rumination.[8] They found that overthinking was moderately genetic, and that environmental factors (essentially the environment you live in, including work, social, economic and physical factors) can be associated with overthinking, as well as early adversity, over-controlling parenting, feeling like the victim, interpersonal stress and difficult life circumstances.

They also found that overthinking is both a symptom and a cause of multiple mental health problems, including depression, eating disorders and anxiety disorders (social anxiety, health anxiety, OCD and GAD). Overthinking is also a common trauma response. (If you're looking for a book specific to trauma, then have a look at my book *How to Overcome Trauma and Find Yourself Again: Seven Steps to Grow from Pain.*[9])

When we experience adversity or face difficult life events, I think of it as opening up a gap between the life we thought we knew (and all the expectations that ran alongside this) and our new reality – or how life is now, as a result of what has happened. This gap represents the loss of what we thought our life was going to be like – or, if you've never known this safety or were born into a life of abuse, it represents the loss of what you didn't have.

Trauma affects our lives now, but also the future we imagine. With any loss, we have to grieve for what has happened and for the change to the life we thought we knew. These experiences cause anguish, confusion and struggle, making us feel powerless or helpless. They can make us question *everything*, irreversibly altering how we see our lives. They can threaten our sense of who we are, our self-worth, meaning and identity. It's no wonder that it can leave us stuck in overthinking, questioning or ruminating on what's happened or obsessing about the future. We do this to try to make sense of what's happened and to find meaning. However, if you become stuck in this process, it can lead to PTSD.

(If you think you might be suffering from PTSD, or if you are struggling to cope, it's important to see your doctor.)

In 2011, the BBC's Lab UK and the University of Liverpool ran the biggest ever online test into stress.[10] Nearly 40,000 people from 172 countries took part. It revealed that rumination is the biggest predictor of depression and anxiety, and also determines the level of stress that people experience.

Causes of overthinking

It's not just that we get depressed or anxious and start overthinking; we get depressed and anxious *because* of overthinking. It is part of the development of these problems as well as a result of them.

The study found that traumatic life events, such as abuse or childhood bullying, were the biggest cause of anxiety and depression when dwelled upon, followed by family history, income and education. Next comes relationship status and social inclusion. However, the study also found that those who didn't ruminate or blame themselves for their difficulties had much lower levels of depression and anxiety, even if they had experienced many negative events in their lives. This is a key idea that we'll come back to in the next chapter.

Another study carried out by the University of Exeter found that, while no overthinking is good, it's worse when you negatively evaluate your emotions and are self-critical and judgemental of how you're feeling.[11] There is also a strong association between perfectionism and rumination.[12] Several studies show that overthinking is common if you are neurodivergent.[13,14,15] Read on for more on neurodivergence and overthinking.

Causes of overthinking that I see in my clinic

In my clinic, I find a common root of overthinking is low self-esteem or a fragile sense of self. If you consider overthinking's favourite topics, many stem from a wish to be acceptable to others or a fear of not being good enough. Overthinking erodes your confidence and, when your self-esteem is low, you're more likely to connect things back to what you have done wrong, to blame yourself or to feel a sense of failure.

As I mentioned above, overthinking is also more common if you are neurodivergent. There are multiple reasons why (and this list is by no means exhaustive). Neurodiversity is characterized by a busy mind that is liable to get caught in a cycle of repetitive thoughts or analysis, as well as being prone to mental restlessness or overactivity. It is often accompanied by a heightened sensitivity to the world or to emotions, leading to high levels of anxiety. Everyday activities can be a cause of anxiety, and this can result in a build-up of stress and shame spirals. It can be harder to get the things you want done, and it can leave you feeling different, misunderstood or useless, wrestling with a neurotypical world. Added to which, if you're neurodivergent, you are often subjected to more criticism than your neurotypical peers, which negatively impacts self-worth and wellbeing. Rejection sensitivity dysphoria (RSD) commonly accompanies ADHD, and can provide huge reams of material for overthinking. RSD can make you highly sensitive to rejection (or perceived rejection) or criticism, which can trigger overthinking and feelings of self-doubt and guilt, intensifying feelings of shame.

Rose explained to me how it sometimes felt with ADHD:

Even though every day is the same, getting ready always causes me problems. It's so hard to do the things I want to and I frequently forget stuff. My family just don't get it, they think that because I find other things easy, I should be able to do this, and that I'm just not trying, but I'm trying so hard and it makes me feel useless and incompetent. It's like my brain is on three different channels, so when someone is talking to me, I sometimes zone out. I then have no idea what they've said and feel like an awful person.

I spend my whole day trying to get myself to do what I'm meant to be doing. I try not to let anyone down, but as soon as it's not urgent or it's a chore, it feels impossible to start. It's only when the panic sets in and I know that the deadline is close that I manage to begin working, so I'm in a constant state of stress about not doing it or having to do it in time. Even though I know my diagnosis makes sense and it's been a relief to understand myself better, I can't help but question it with all the talk that 'everyone's got ADHD these days'.

It's been like this all my life. When I was younger, I was seen as the problem child, always getting told off for overreacting or being too loud or losing things. I still feel constantly anxious about getting things wrong – and then I frequently do. When someone gives me feedback, especially if I think they don't like something I've done or said, my RSD means that even if they're trying to say it nicely, I hear 'How could you have possibly thought that?' or 'I don't like you' or 'You're not good

---

Rejection sensitivity doesn't just apply to ADHD. Many people I work with tell me they fear being rejected by others if they show themselves as they truly are. This insecurity puts how we come across under greater pressure. We might believe that, to be acceptable to others, we have to be a certain way – and this can lead to people-pleasing. It can make us more socially anxious, like Xiang, whom we met on page 27, as we fear judgement and feel overly sensitive to what others are thinking. It can also make it difficult to communicate with others, to speak up or share how we feel.

When your self-confidence is low, it makes it harder to trust in yourself and your instincts. Mistakes and failure feel more terrifying, so you are more likely to be avoidant, like Sam (see page 39). You might set unrealistically high standards for how you should come across and seek out external validation from others, but the effects are only brief and it doesn't change how you feel inside.

Another common reason people give me for overthinking is the idea that, if they're not thinking about a problem, they're not taking it seriously. They see worry as a 'better safe than sorry' approach, and believe – like Olive (see page 2) – that, if they don't worry about things, they are tempting fate. They say things to me like, 'If I don't think about the worst-case scenarios, I'm jinxing it and it won't work out.' They might worry that, if something good happens, they are due something bad, or that they shouldn't enjoy it when things go well as good times don't last.

These superstitious thoughts are often referred to as magical thinking: the belief that thoughts, emotions, words or rituals can influence the external world. By worrying, you imagine that you are preventing bad things from happening or protecting yourself against them. This is a bit like the idea that, if you don't bring an umbrella, it's more likely to rain. Cultural ideas can also feed into these thoughts, such as traditions like the 'evil eye'. I know that I can fall prey to these beliefs sometimes. I was hiring a car recently and, when they told me about the added insurance I could take out, I had a thought that if I didn't take out the insurance, I'd be more likely to crash.

In a funny way, this type of thinking allows us to believe that we can have control over every outcome in our lives, rather than facing the reality that we don't have ultimate power over whether things work out. These thoughts can also be used as a way to avoid potential disappointment: we might think that, if we risk confidence and things don't work out, it will hurt all the more. Yet, this just isn't true. When we try to avoid potential disappointment by worrying, we are not protecting ourselves: we are just making ourselves suffer unnecessarily. If it does go OK, the worry was pointless and if it doesn't, then you've suffered twice. Thoughts have no influence on real-world events. Having the thought, 'If I don't take out insurance I am more likely to crash', does not make you more likely to crash, just like thinking, 'I'm going to win the lottery' doesn't make that event any more likely (sadly).

In Part Three of this book, we'll be looking at ways you can future-proof against this kind of overthinking and build confidence. The better you feel about yourself, the easier it will be to disengage from overthinking in the longer term and to regain trust in yourself.

– Make a note of potential causal factors of overthinking for you.

A quick history lesson

To understand why overthinking loves these topics so much, we need to take a quick look back in time. This is helpful not only to understand why we are so prone to getting stuck on these topics, but also to help you gain some distance from them.

The human brain is the product of many millions of years of evolution, based around one simple goal – survival. We were designed to function in a world where there was always danger, there were no second chances, and we had to rely on others to stay alive. We had to be hyper-aware of threats and automatically recognize and evaluate potential dangers or risks. Negative emotions can be viewed as evolved adaptations that helped us survive in life-threatening situations. They spark what are called 'specific action tendencies': an automatic threat response – fight, flight, freeze or fawn – helping us to survive. For example, anger creates the urge to attack (fight), fear creates the urge to escape (flight), an overwhelming threat triggers the urge to shut down (freeze) and powerlessness triggers the urge to appease (fawn). These action tendencies infuse the mind and body. Negative emotions narrow our attention to focus on the threat and our body automatically responds to flee or attack.

We are fundamentally social and relational in nature, and have a deep need for social inclusion. We are born ready to relate to others and, as we evolved, we had to be self-aware to succeed. Early humans needed to live together and get on in a group to ensure survival, as being cut off from the group would have resulted in death.

Getting on with others was a necessary life skill: we had to be tuned in to what they might be thinking, form useful alliances, avoid enemies and find suitable mates. The group also supplied care and support, while helping to regulate our emotions. Social mistakes or isolation would have been a threat to our relationships or reputation, and so they needed to be avoided. As a result, we are programmed to notice social hierarchy and to compare ourselves to others. This is why we care so much about our relationships, our acceptance in a group and what others think of us. (If you'd like to read more on this subject, I recommend Dan Siegel's[16] work in this area, as well as Lee Kirkpatrick and Bruce Ellis's research[17] on evolutionary psychology and self-esteem.)

We also have a basic need for agency and certainty. The brain is constantly trying to predict what will happen next, allowing it to prepare the body and mind in the most effective way possible. In our evolutionary past, agency gave us a sense of control, autonomy and competence. Our drive for certainty made life more predictable, and treating unknowns as potential threats would have been adaptive and protected us from surprises. In uncertain situations, that planning is a lot harder, which explains our dislike of uncertainty. It is better to be cautious and avoid the uncertainty altogether or to be ready to respond, putting the brain and body in an aroused state. All this explains why uncertainty can make us feel anxious.

Much of our behaviour from childhood onward is an expression of this wish for control. 'No' and 'I want that' quickly become part of a toddler's vocabulary when they start experimenting with cause and effect – and they want to control the effect. The teenage years are often characterized by trying to wrest control from parents. If you've ever been in a job with a controlling manager, you'll know how horrible it feels to not have control as an adult. We like to be effective in influencing things. When we lose that sense of control, we feel helpless and hopeless, and can become unhappy and depressed.[18] The desire for control can be so strong and feel so rewarding, that it's no wonder we sometimes try to control the uncontrollable.

These innate needs are still within us and, while they've helped us to survive as a species, they have primed our minds to avoid threats, to want control and certainty, and to crave acceptance from others. In modern times, our shift from doing to thinking means that these fundamental needs are now feeding comparison, indecision, insecurity and self-doubt. These feelings are a recipe for overthinking.

How bad can it be?

You might believe that overthinking doesn't do much harm, because, come on: you're only thinking, after all! But it's important to recognize that, whether threats are real or imagined, the brain is triggered in the same way.

Think about this for a moment: when you smell your favourite food, your mouth starts watering, but you could also imagine your favourite food and trigger the same response. Consider that, when you're at the cinema watching a scary or emotive movie, you know that you're in the cinema safely watching a film, but that doesn't stop you feeling terrified or emotional. This can leave you drained and tired afterward, even though you haven't moved. Thoughts and mental images have a powerful effect on the brain and body.

Life now demands less from our bodies and more from our minds. Our lives have never been so free of immediate physical threats, and yet we've never felt so threatened. Our brains are increasingly overloaded with cognitive demands as we juggle work, family, study, technology, finances, friends, and looking after ourselves. Most jobs involve complex decision-making, information-processing and tight deadlines, alongside constant demands on our attention from phone calls, WhatsApp messages, emails, social media notifications and Teams calls. In addition, our personal lives and work lives are now deeply intertwined. This can lead to mental exhaustion, chronic stress, anxiety and burnout.

Ivanka Savic and colleagues at Sweden's Karolinska Institute and Stockholm University compared the brains of people suffering from work-related chronic stress to those of healthy, less-stressed counterparts using structural magnetic resonance imaging (MRI) techniques.[19] They found a difference in regions active in decision-making, emotion-processing, memory and attention allocation. In the stressed group, the prefrontal cortex also appeared thinner, which correlated with worse emotion regulation. The researchers then scanned the participants' brains again after a three-month-long stress-rehabilitation programme that incorporated cognitive therapy and breathing techniques. They found the thinning in the prefrontal cortex was reversed. These positive changes may partly be thanks to the plastic nature of our brains and their ability to adapt. We'll be looking at this in more detail in Chapter Six.

Overthinking is another weight on our mental load, as it exacerbates and maintains psychological stress. The mental strain of overthinking and replaying the memory of a stressful experience after it's over can stimulate similar pathways in the brain as the actual experience. The amygdala plays a key role in both our emotions and our decision-making, and it is especially sensitive to negative information. This can make decisions that feel big or threatening much harder to take, and can leave us stuck in a cycle of doubt and indecision.

If we sense something that is threatening, the amygdala activates the fight-or-flight response. It activates the nervous system, increasing the stress hormone cortisol. Our heart rate quickens, blood pressure increases and adrenaline lights up the body, putting us on high alert. When we think about or imagine a threatening scenario or go back over past hurts, even though they are not happening to us now, the amygdala still activates the nervous system, shifting our moods. This can leave your body chronically activated, meaning the response continues long after the initial event, keeping the stress reaction switched on. This can even cause the experience to be perceived as more distressing than it was.

The same thing happens when we are self-critical: we trigger the threat system, which depresses our mood, turns down positive feelings and increases stressful and unpleasant feelings. It releases cortisol, weakens the immune system, increases blood pressure and can change the pathways in the brain.

When we overthink, we are living through the very thing we are worried about or trying to avoid, or reliving the past hurts that made us feel so terrible! Again and again and again. No wonder overthinking is so exhausting.

– Take a moment to note down the evolutionary arguments about why we are so prone to overthinking. When we remember that this is how the brain is programmed, it's easier to step back from self-critical thoughts and self-blame.

The negative impact of 'threat mode' on our thinking

Once we're in a fight-or-flight state, we experience the world differently. It becomes threatening, so we become more reactive and hypervigilant to any potential problems. We are more likely to misread social cues, such as seeing a neutral face as angry or jumping to negative conclusions. We don't sleep well, as we are more prone to nightmares and are sensitized to pain.

It is much harder for us to engage the rational brain in this mode, and we do not have access to higher-conscious states such as planning. It reduces our attention. There is no room for love, nurture or care. It can leave us feeling frazzled or out of sorts, and push us to a point where our problems feel insurmountable. We might wish to escape or avoid the situations that trigger these thoughts, or it can push us into freeze mode as we end up flooded and overwhelmed. In this state, we feel unable to do anything. We are paralysed by our thoughts.

To cope well, we need our executive functioning (the cognitive processes and mental skills that help us plan, monitor and successfully execute our goals) to be working well. Yet, overthinking impairs our executive functioning and makes it harder to concentrate. This makes it difficult to stop overthinking, and shifts us from the concrete style of thinking, which is proven to help us feel better, to abstract thinking, which makes us overgeneralize and feel worse.

In one study,[20] an overthinking group and a non-overthinking group were given a list of activities to help them take control of their lives (e.g. meeting a friend for dinner or playing sport). When the groups were asked if they thought the activities would be helpful, all participants stated that the activities would lift their mood. When each group was asked how willing and motivated they were to engage in the activity if they had the opportunity, the group who had been overthinking were considerably less willing, even though they'd said moments before that it would lift their mood.

These findings suggest that, even when we intellectually know something is helpful, overthinking gets in the way of doing the things that could make us feel better. In a second study,[21] one group was asked to ruminate while the other group was distracted with other activities. They were then presented with a task to problem-solve – for example, what would you do if a friend avoided you? The group that had been overthinking came up with solutions that were significantly lower in quality. Not only is it harder to take action when you're overthinking, it's also more difficult to come up with ideas.

Even when we know that overthinking is negatively affecting us, it can feel impossible to stop. Overthinking makes us believe that this is how life is, and that we don't have any choice other than to think about these things. I hope you're starting to see that this isn't the whole story. When we understand that this is how the brain and body are programmed to work, it helps make sense of why we are more likely to get stuck in overthinking. When we're stuck in a negative circuit, it is much harder to have access to thinking that can help us feel better. It's not our fault! In Step Two (see Chapter Eleven) I'll be introducing you to polyvagal theory. I'll show you how to use the mind–body link to calm your body and tend to your nervous system, so you can learn to override this evolved reaction and choose your response.

When we scrutinize our overthinking, and see it for what it really is, it's easy to see that it isn't useful at all. Since overthinking solves nothing in our minds, it would be better named 'the quick route to misery and feeling stuck'. It's this habitual negative thinking that needs to stop. In the next chapter, I want to help you consider your reality and show you that you *do* have a choice in where you place your attention and what you bring into your life.

Remember:

- Overthinking is best seen as a faulty coping mechanism that amplifies any problem.
- It is both a cause and a symptom of a number of mental health problems.
- Overthinking damages self-worth and can be linked to low confidence.
- It can leave you feeling overwhelmed, angry or sad.
- There are evolutionary reasons for why we overthink, and these reasons show us why we find it so difficult to stop.

Chapter 3
The spotlight of attention

By the end of this chapter, you will:

- Understand what your spotlight of attention is.
- Recognize that your reality is dependent on what you choose to focus on.
- Begin to see how your mindset and emotions shape your experience of the world, and how you can use this to your advantage.
- Understand that your mind makes up stories to fit how you're feeling, but that it doesn't always tell the truth.

Imagine that you are a lighting technician at a theatre. You get to decide how the stage is lit and what everyone in the audience sees. You can light the stage with a broad beam, so you see the full scene and all the characters in the play, or you can use a narrow beam to pick out one actor or one part of the scene. You can also use the colour of the lighting to subtly manipulate the mood of the scene to change how the audience feels as they watch the play unfold. Warmer lights can create a cozy, happy feeling, while cooler lights can evoke feelings of detachment or melancholy.

Now imagine that the stage is your mind and the beam is the spotlight of your attention. What you choose to focus on is your field of awareness. Sometimes we have a broad beam of attention, which allows us to take in the full picture of our life. At other times, we have a narrow awareness because we are focusing on a specific issue. There are times when a narrow focus is useful – such as when you need to be really detail-orientated or if you're breaking down a larger project into more manageable steps – but in most cases, a narrow focus to our thinking leads us towards negative thought patterns.

Our emotions colour our thoughts like the stage lighting in a theatre, and this also affects what we see. Negative emotions, such as fear and anger, narrow our focus of attention to the immediate and spark the specific action tendencies we once needed to ensure survival. If we feel anxious, our mind constricts and focuses on the threat so we can flee. Our emotions also influence our 'thought-action tendencies' – how we think and act. Low mood brings a negative bias, limiting our ability to be open to new ideas and other people and narrowing the range of options available to us. Positive emotions broaden our focus of attention, expanding our thinking so it becomes more efficient, flexible and creative. We are open to information, better at integrating it and able to come up with a greater range of thoughts and potential solutions or actions to pursue.

A narrow spotlight of attention

Leisure

Positive thoughts

Positive feedback

'Other people say I come across well'   Friends   Family

Positive emotions   Exercise   Small improvements

Projects that have gone well   Hobbies   Daily activities

I see overthinking as a problem with our spotlight of attention. It's as if the beam has got stuck on a setting that is too narrow, which changes how we see the world. The beam sits firmly on one tiny detail in our life, casting everything else into darkness. We notice the things that fit with our view and any counter ideas fall out of awareness. This detailed analytical focus takes more effort and energy, as well as missing the wider picture. It shifts our focus of attention to all that's wrong in our lives, and leads to a higher likelihood of problematic coping strategies such as avoidance and reactive behaviour.

To stop overthinking, we need to **notice** what is in our awareness and **choose** what we let into our spotlight of attention so we can understand how our mood manipulates what we see. It's important to consider how we're feeling and reflect on our lives, but we don't want negative thoughts and emotions to rule our lives or take centre stage.

A key part of all the strategies we will cover in Part Three is to learn to recognize what you are letting into your field of awareness and create a broader focus of attention. Freedom comes from increasing our awareness so we begin to recognize the repetitive thoughts and see them for what they are – overthinking. We can then choose what we do and *don't* want in our spotlight of attention.

Creating your own reality

We think of our minds and the world as separate, but when we look at the outside world, we are looking at only a small part that interests us. Rather than one objective reality, our experience of the world is subjective. Our reality is dependent on our perception, thoughts and feelings – and what our brains choose to focus on will impact how we experience the world.

We create our world through our spotlight of attention. Our spotlight of attention invites the outside world into our inner world and magnifies

Widening your spotlight of attention

it, bringing it into our awareness and causing it to take up more space in our minds. What we focus on is our reality. Haemin Sunim, a Zen Buddhist teacher, beautifully describes this:

> *The world we see is not the entire universe but a limited one that the mind cares about. However, to our minds, that small world is the entire universe. Our reality is not the infinitely stretching cosmos but the small part we choose to focus on. Reality exists because our minds exist. Without the mind, there would be no universe.*[22]

We can see this in our everyday. A few years ago, I was cycling on a new route and I passed a huge sign that said 'R. J. Meaker Fencing'. Before this, I had never knowingly seen any fencing put up by R. J. Meaker, but for some reason it stuck in my head. Despite not consciously deciding to, I began to see their signs all the time. This selective attention now means I see the signs everywhere!

You've probably experienced something similar if you've been deciding whether to buy a particular brand of car or bag. You start to see that brand everywhere. It's not that these items weren't there before, it's that they weren't in your awareness. Now that this brand has become something relevant to you, your brain is on the lookout for it. Your brain is seeking out information that it thinks is useful, but your awareness changes *what* and *how* you see things and, as a result, it changes your approach to life.

This is problematic when we get stuck overthinking. When we look at the world through the lens of an overthinking mind, it changes what's in our awareness. Our current reality is shaped by our spotlight of attention, but unlike the lighting technician, we don't see it as a stage or one part of our life, we see it as the truth of our life at that moment in time. It's difficult to see an alternative view, as our thinking becomes so narrow and our mood shapes what we see. Our perception becomes selective (just like me noticing the fencing signs everywhere). We see problems that don't exist or aren't as big as they seem and, when our brains offer up these different scenarios and we spend time thinking about them, we are telling our brains that this is useful. As with a social media algorithm, you've paused on the thought, and now your brain is sending you as many related thoughts as it can, confirming what you think as the truth.

The more often this happens, the more likely we are to think in this way the next time we feel bad. This is where habitual thinking comes in – making it harder and harder to pull the beam back to a broader focus, which maintains and exacerbates the problem. This shifts our reality and we see the world differently, but it's not the whole truth of what's going on; it's one small part of your life that you're thinking about – and you may not even be right about it!

If you've ever watched the TV show *The Traitors*, you'll have seen many good examples of how we can get things so wrong. *The Traitors* is a reality show in which contestants compete to win prize money. Some contestants are loyal, called the Faithfuls, and some are secretly made Traitors, which gives them the power to expel the Faithfuls. In order to win the prize, the Faithfuls must identify who the Traitors are. Once they suspect that a person in the game is a Traitor, they put a spotlight on them and interpret everything through that lens. They build up a story that confirms their belief and see all of that person's behaviour as a potential clue to the fact they are not onside. They frequently pick the wrong people, but they become completely convinced they are correct. As the viewer, it's easy to see how wrong they are because we know the truth.

Where you choose to focus your attention influences what you bring into your life, but we have more influence and agency over our lives than we believe. I'll show you how to use this to your advantage as we work through the steps in Part Three.

How our mindset shapes our experience of the world

When I talk about the truth of what's going on, I'm thinking about how we interpret the things that happen to us. It's this interpretation that influences how we feel, much more than the event itself. It's our appraisal of what's happened and the meaning we give to it that gives the event its emotional impact.

Imagine you're walking down the street and you tread in some dog poo. If you think:

- *This is just my luck, why do these things always happen to me? I can never do anything right* – you're likely to feel sad or low.
- *Oh no, if I go home and change my shoes, I'll be late for my meeting, but what if the poo smells at work? My boss will think badly of me and I'm going to get germs everywhere* – you're likely to feel anxious.
- *What kind of world am I living in? People have no decency or consideration for anyone these days* – you're likely to feel angry.
- *These things happen, it's just bad luck, and in the grand scheme of things it's not worth getting annoyed over* – you'll probably feel OK.

Our thinking drives our behaviour and how we feel in our lives (physically and emotionally), which shapes our beliefs and feeds into our sense of who we are. These all combine to create our reality.

The study in stress[23] that we discussed on page 43 demonstrated this. Those who didn't ruminate or blame themselves for their difficulties had much lower levels of depression and anxiety, even if they *had* experienced many negative events in their lives. How they *thought* about events made a difference to how they felt.

When we bring this back to our field of awareness, it's not just what's in our spotlight of attention that matters, it's also how much we believe this view at the time. When it comes to overthinking, the brain can be very convinced by a belief, but it doesn't always have our best interests in mind, and sometimes our interpretations can be problematic.

Chloe had just been through a breakup, and her overthinking meant she couldn't get away from the idea that there was something wrong with her.

I thought it was different this time, and it just makes it worse as I didn't expect it. Everyone leaves me. I open up or try to trust, but I'm always let down. I thought this time it was going to work out, but every time it goes wrong, and I can't help but feel like it's something to do with me. I just keep thinking, 'Is it ever going to happen? Will I ever be in a relationship?' I feel like I'll never find someone and, even if I do, how can I ever trust them?

I've been going over and over what happened. It's making me doubt my own sanity. Did I imagine how well we got on and the interest he showed me? We were planning things together for the future, but now I can see we're on completely different pages. I feel so stupid. When I think back over everything that he said, I find it hard to know if any of it was ever true, whether he meant anything he said. I hate that I wasn't enough for him. I feel like an idiot. I'm so annoyed with myself; I just feel sick when I think about it.

I asked him, 'Why have you done this?' But he just said it's him, not me. I really want to understand if I've done anything wrong. It feels so hurtful. He's discarded me. I was so open with him, I risked opening up – and

---

Breakups are unbelievably tough. To be in a relationship, you have to allow yourself to be vulnerable with another person, so when it doesn't work out, it's incredibly painful. It can feel impossible to move your spotlight of attention away from what's happened. But, while it's important to allow yourself to feel upset and to grieve the relationship, it's also important not to get stuck overthinking. From Chloe's example, we can see how overthinking stops you from seeing that there's nothing wrong with you, it's just that this relationship isn't right.

How our emotions shape our experience of the world

As you saw in the overthinking mind map in Chapter One (see page 29), the link between our thoughts and emotions works in both directions. It becomes a chicken-and-egg paradox where a thought might come first that influences our mood, but our mood also massively influences our thoughts.

If you think of the dog-poo example on page 62, you might have started the day feeling angry, and this feeling shapes your experience, making you more likely to think in an angry way. When you step in the dog poo, it becomes another thing to feel annoyed about – and it's used as evidence of all that's wrong with life. But, if you were lucky enough to be in a good mood, it will be much easier to see that the dog poo is not worth wasting your energy on. So we can begin to see that:

- Negative emotions, such as fear, anger or low mood, narrow our awareness. Like a con artist or a master manipulator, negative emotions show us only what they want us to see, distorting our view.
- Positive emotions, such as happiness, joy and gratitude, help to broaden our awareness, opening us up to new possibilities, ideas and other people.

We know overthinking is both triggered by negative moods and a cause of them, so when you're overthinking, you're guaranteed to be at a disadvantage in terms of what you see and how you see it. And it's rarely just one emotion that we are experiencing. When we overthink, we tend to move between these moods and the thoughts linked to them, like a pinball in a machine, pinging around from one problem to the next. From anger to hurt, from sadness to shame and guilt, our feelings become mixed up like a lethal cocktail of all our different moods. With that narrow beam, negative emotions keep us away from all the good stuff, so instead of seeing a fair view, we see anything that matches our mood or current thinking.

How each emotion shapes our view

As you'll see in the list below, each mood tends to have key themes. Take a moment to look at the impacts of the different negative emotions we tend to be stuck in when we're overthinking. It's clear how much these feelings will shape your view of life and your reality.

- **Low mood** links to themes of loss, defeat, failure, worthlessness and unlovability. When we're in a low mood, we're more likely to turn in on ourselves, focus on our own faults and mistakes, and feel a sense of loss and failure. Low mood feels heavy, slowing you down and stealing motivation. It casts a gloom over everything, making it harder to concentrate, make decisions or complete the things you need to do. Overthinking magnifies these feelings and, if we dwell on them, it can lead to hopelessness, paralysis, self-hate and overwhelm.
- **Anxiety** is linked to a deep sense of threat, fear, danger and vulnerability. It makes us think about times in the past when we felt threatened, or about future worries and fears. It can leave us feeling like we are not safe, or it can make us hyper-fixate. We're also more likely to see threats that may not even exist as we become hypersensitive, like a faulty burglar alarm that goes off too easily. We're more likely to think the worst and to catastrophize. Anxiety sets off the fight-or-flight reaction in

the body and can push us into freeze. In the longer term, it can lead to chronic arousal and burnout, and make us more prone to panic attacks.

- **Anger** links to themes of unfairness, feeling a situation is unjust or a violation, or feeling that someone has broken your personal rules. Anger makes you the victim of what has happened and can lead to resentment, frustration, blaming and rage. It sets off the fight-or-flight reaction and can make you tight with tension. It often presents as a secondary emotion, acting as an emotional cover-up, protecting you from vulnerable feelings of fear, upset, hurt or frustration. It allows you to pretend that how you're feeling is no longer the issue, but that other people or other things are the problem – if they had got this right, or that hadn't happened, you'd feel fine!

- **Guilt** is often described as a self-conscious emotion. It's a sense that we've done or thought something we shouldn't have, or not done something we should have. It comes with a wish to put things right and is linked to our sense of morality – a set of values or standards that we want to live up to. We feel guilty when we fall short of these values. When we hold very high standards, guilt can lead us to feel excessive responsibility. Guilt can make us withdraw from others or shroud our thoughts in secrecy. It also has a tendency to linger, so it's no surprise that it often accompanies overthinking as we go over and over events in our minds.

- **Shame** is a corrosive emotion, making us believe our actions or thoughts make us bad people. It can make us feel there is something deeply wrong with us. This fear is a heavy secret and it makes us hide away, believing our whole selves are flawed. Shame is often described as burning because it feels so awful. It's another of overthinking's favourite emotions, linking to painful feelings of humiliation, regret, inferiority, helplessness and despair. It has a negative effect on self-esteem and relationships. When we keep this feeling in the dark, there's no chance to see the cracks in it.

Whether you're low, anxious, angry or feeling guilty or ashamed, when you overthink in these mood states, the brain puts a spotlight on the thoughts created by its mood. The thoughts feel real at these times, so you take them seriously and they influence you and your decisions, tricking you into believing that things are worse than they are.

The more you take your thoughts as reality, the more deeply lodged they become in your mind, and the doom spiral means you become stuck with these continuously critical, fearful, attacking or self-doubting thoughts. Due to the habitual nature of overthinking, this can happen both consciously and outside of your awareness: it might be a commentary that follows you around just outside of awareness, or something you consciously think about. Some thoughts may have been going through your head for years.

Be careful of creating stories around your feelings

Our minds are constantly ticking away in the background, making up stories to fit our moods and trying to find an explanation for why we are feeling the way we do. When we create a story around how we're feeling, we often believe our thoughts and don't question them. For example, we create a story when we tell ourselves things like 'I've been wronged', 'Nothing works out' or 'Everything is my fault'. Instead of holding these ideas lightly and checking they are correct, the thoughts feel plausible and true, which narrows our awareness.

Our spotlight of attention lights up any evidence that supports our belief, while ignoring any positive information. It also makes us more likely to interpret ambiguous information negatively and to recall perceived problems. It's not the emotion that lingers, but the story you attach to it. Replaying what happened over and over in your mind can

Doom spiral: 'I'm not good enough'

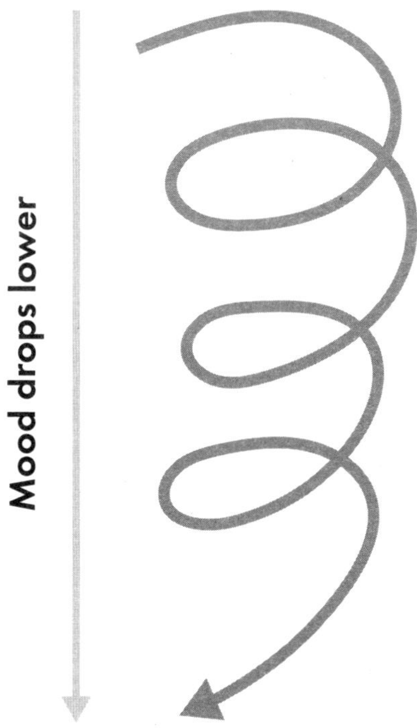

make you believe that things never change. Your brain conjures up every setback you've experienced, and uses that information to support your current thinking. That's why emotions can feel like they last a long time, as we keep feeding them with our thoughts and reinforcing the feeling.

The story we tell ourselves can become a self-fulfilling prophecy. If we think 'I'm not good enough', we have low self-regard, which perpetuates this negative thinking about ourselves, the future and the world. This is a confirmation bias[24] that keeps the story going, driving our low emotions down further and extending the life of the emotion we are experiencing.

We forget that this story is just one interpretation of what might be going on. It is not the truth of what is happening. These thoughts are only a small part of our reality that we are focusing on at that moment, thanks to our spotlight of attention. When we stop ourselves from being pulled into creating a story about where our emotions come from, we shorten the life cycle of the emotion and have a chance to see that our feelings pass.

In preparation for Step One (see Chapter Ten), it is important to simply recognize that your thoughts and feelings are not facts. Of course, your thoughts and feelings are useful (I wouldn't be much of a psychologist if I told you otherwise!), but they form only one part of the picture. There is always more than one perspective, *especially* when it comes to overthinking. Rather than identifying with the thought, I want you to see it as just a thought.

You are not your thoughts; you are the awareness. By becoming more aware of what's going on in your mind and body, you can stop your thoughts and feelings from taking over and carrying you along a pathway to anxiety, low mood or stress. If you get caught up in your thoughts and feelings, you could try saying to yourself: 'I am not my thoughts and feelings.' You can also remind yourself that you have a choice in what you think about. Ask yourself: 'Is this what I want in my awareness?'

Remember:

- Overthinking is a problem with your spotlight of attention.

- Negative emotions narrow your focus of attention, while positive emotions broaden your focus.

- When your brain offers up different negative scenarios and you spend time thinking about them, you are telling your brain that it is being useful and increasing the likelihood that this thinking will become automatic.

- It is not what happens to you, but how you interpret events that is key.

- Don't believe everything you think or feel.

Chapter 4
Classic overthinking traps

By the end of this chapter, you will:
- Understand the difference between self-reflection and overthinking.
- Know how to tell if you are overthinking.
- Begin to identify which thinking traps you fall into.

By now, you will be well versed in how overthinking operates. Going over things, getting angry or deeply analysing what's happened in your life might feel like the right thing to do, but as you have seen, this line of behaviour is like putting on sunglasses to try to see at night: the world just ends up even darker.

While self-reflection is important (there wouldn't be much point in my job if it wasn't!), when introspection goes awry and thoughts get stuck on repeat, it becomes a problem. I want to show you that there is a big difference between reflection and overthinking. As you'll see in the table, overthinking is *never* helpful.

REFLECTION	OVERTHINKING
Moves you forward	Leaves you stuck
Increases capacity and helps you feel better	Steals your capacity and lowers your mood
Looks at concrete issues that you can action	Looks at abstract, unsolvable issues
Lets you unpack what has happened and refine your thoughts	Creates a doom spiral of snowballing negative thoughts
Helps you evaluate your capabilities and increase your coping capacity	Interferes with problem-solving
Lets you use your emotions as information and take action to meet your needs	Leaves you stuck going over and over the problem and ignores what you really need
Allows you to feel your emotions and then let them pass	Creates a story around your emotions and extends the life of the emotion you are experiencing
Lets you consciously choose how you want your future to be	Keeps you in automatic patterns of habitual thinking

REFLECTION	OVERTHINKING
Gives you greater agency in your life and the confidence to make changes	Makes you feel the victim of your circumstances and powerless to change
Allows you to review your life, reflect on what you have learned and take responsibility	Pulls you into corrosive cycles of shame, blame, resentment and anger

I am not suggesting that you never think about the things that are worrying you or getting you down. Avoidance of feelings and thinking about what's going on in your life causes its own set of problems. I'm suggesting that you are selective about how and when you do it, and that you don't get pulled into the same old traps again and again without making any progress. If you're overthinking, you're spending far too much time thinking about your negative thoughts and emotions.

By becoming aware of our habitual overthinking, we can begin to make intentional choices instead of automatically reacting. In this chapter, I'll be introducing you to a simple check to tell if you're overthinking, as well as the seven most common overthinking traps. The better you get at noticing overthinking, the greater your opportunity to make changes.

How can you tell if it's overthinking?

The clue is in the name: overthinking means to think *too much* about something. It's most likely overthinking when you are:

- Preoccupied by something and keep coming back to it again and again.

- In a bad mood, distressed or overwhelmed.

- Jumping from topic to topic without a break.

- Moving from something specific that's happened to a general feeling about yourself or your life.

- Feeling worse rather than better as a result of thinking about an issue.

- Worrying or becoming self-critical about the very fact that you're overthinking.

How to recognize overthinking

To catch overthinking in action, try asking yourself these three questions:

1. **'Is this thinking helping me to take action?'** If you're not getting anywhere or you're feeling lost, there's no point continuing. Be aware of going over the same topics again and again without making progress. Watch out for abstract thinking and trying to answer unanswerable questions.
2. **'How am I feeling during and after thinking?'** If you're feeling worse, it's not helpful. Be careful of purposely hurting yourself and going back to a problem that's upsetting you.
3. **'Do I feel more or less sure as a result of this thinking?'** If you feel less certain or stuck, it's overthinking.

The seven overthinking styles

When we are trapped in overthinking, we over-analyse and go through our problems with a fine-tooth comb, examining every small detail, but we don't all overthink in the same way. Different people have different overthinking styles, and different topics lend themselves to different types of thinking.

Understanding which traps you fall into can be really helpful, as it will increase your awareness. This will enable you to notice when you fall into negative thinking patterns. You can then make a conscious choice to change.

As you read through the seven thinking traps below, think about which you identify with the most. You may fit multiple categories.

The Dweller

Instead of letting go of a loss or setback, you replay it repeatedly in your mind, reliving the experience blow by blow and feeling the whole thing as if it's happening again. One moment you're daydreaming, and the next you're thinking about negative feedback or the things that have gone wrong in your life. Or perhaps you're about to fall asleep and then suddenly you're reliving an embarrassing moment that happened three years ago. We might become stuck thinking about a breakup, as Chloe did (see page 63), or a relationship that's not working out.

Your brain's analysis takes you into the intricacies of what happened, the lost opportunities, mistakes and failures. You find yourself analysing every part of your life and thinking about how you could have done things differently, thinking about the things you're getting wrong and where you need to improve. You can remember in detail the pain and humiliation you've suffered; and regret, self-criticism and blame feed your anger and upset. You beat yourself up, thinking about how bad or worthless you are, how everything is your fault, leaving you feeling hopeless and driving down your self-esteem. Or sometimes you may blame others and take the victim role.

Mateo's reaction to his work appraisal is a good example of this thinking trap. In the review, his manager (Issa) ran through all the feedback, which was overwhelmingly positive. As a focus for improvement, it was suggested Mateo attend a management course.

> *I spiralled after the meeting; I couldn't stop thinking about what Issa had said to me. I ended up picking everything apart and kept replaying the meeting in my head. I feel really defensive. I'm still questioning why I need to do this management course. Do they think I'm not managing the team well enough? Did one of my team say I wasn't a good boss? Did I say something wrong in the meeting? I can't believe I'm in this situation. I try and look at everything I'm doing and think of ways to improve, especially the things I'm not doing well enough on. I'm hypercritical of my work: I can't make mistakes and I waste hours on it, editing and reworking it.*

The Interrogator

You try to understand yourself by focusing on your negative feelings and questioning why you are feeling this way. It begins innocently, as you notice you're feeling off: 'What's wrong with me? Why am I feeling like this? Why aren't I feeling OK?' It quickly slides into abstract thinking: 'Why am I always so upset? I'm not happy enough. Where am I going wrong?' Or perhaps you start thinking about why you're feeling so passive and unmotivated: 'Why don't I feel up to doing things anymore? Why do I feel so tired?'

We might even compare ourselves to a previous version of ourselves, saying things like: 'This never used to be a problem for me.' We entertain all the possible causes for why we might be feeling like this: 'Maybe I'm depressed? Maybe it's because I haven't lost any weight? Maybe it's because I don't have any close friends who really know me?' When we overthink, we accept all the explanations as equally plausible. You may also criticize yourself for feeling this way: 'I'm weak and pathetic for feeling like this, no one else finds things this hard.' Before you know it, you're feeling like you need to completely overhaul your life and change everything in it. This is how Rika felt.

the bare minimum. I'm trying to detox – no sugar, no coffee, no alcohol and less time online. I've been going to the gym again and journalling. But I still feel awful. I don't know what I want to do, I just don't enjoy things in the same way anymore. I don't know where I want to live. Should I be doing something else? Is it my friends? Sometimes I feel like I don't really have proper friends who truly understand me. I just can't see the point. I don't know what's wrong with me. I'm just wasting my time. I don't look forward to anything anymore, and there's nothing that excites me. I don't even know what I like anymore. I feel so frustrated with myself when I feel like this. I want to be free and happy. It just doesn't make sense. I feel so low and exhausted by life.

The Catastrophizer

Worry can be obvious. For example, it may take the form of imagining every worst-case scenario and all the terrible eventualities that could happen, dramatic self-assessments, worrying about our health, or even thinking about dying. We don't just worry about the things that we have control over: we also worry about the things we have no control over at all. What ifs and catastrophizing can take on a life of their own until they don't even feel like worries anymore: they feel completely true. The anxiety spirals can leave your body filled with cortisol and adrenaline, stopping you sleeping at night or waking you up early. Worrying can even lead to panic attacks.

Worry can also be more subtle, dressed up as helpful, pretending to keep you safe. It makes you believe that, if you cover every eventuality, you'll feel more prepared and able to cope better if anything does go wrong. It demands you pay attention to potential threats, but this anticipatory anxiety can make you dread upcoming commitments. It can make you act on fear instead of staying true to what matters to you, leading to you saying no to something you were looking forward to, quitting a job or giving up on a degree. Aubrey's fears about his health were a good example of this. He kept getting headaches and, after hearing about a friend who'd had a brain tumour, he couldn't stop worrying.

I'd had headaches all week, so I went to the doctor. She said she could see no reason to be concerned, but decided to run some tests. After I left, I couldn't stop thinking it could be something really serious. If she really thought I was fine, why did she bother with the tests? I knew I shouldn't do it, but I googled my symptoms and then I felt so much worse. I couldn't get the idea out of my head that it was a tumour. I kept checking to see if I felt OK, but I couldn't reassure myself. Over the next few days, while I was waiting for the test results, I didn't have any bandwidth for anything else. I was really irritable and distracted, and I couldn't concentrate on anything. I just wanted everyone to go away and leave me alone. When I got the results and they were fine, I was so relieved, but I felt so stupid that I'd wasted so much time and energy. I'm wasting my life worrying about these things and they haven't even happened. If they ever do, I'll have spent so much time thinking about it that I won't have even enjoyed my life as much as I could. Sometimes I feel like I'm going insane.

The Wobbler

A wobbler often gets stuck trying to make the 'right' or 'best' decision. We fear making the wrong choice or missing out on a better option, so we check every single review before booking dinner, or we can't decide on a new phone deal or whether to take a job. In the modern world, we are faced with more choices than ever before, and the quest for the perfect decision adds pressure and expectation.

We also get stuck in the 'will I, won't I?' web, debating whether we'll commit to our plans (which, when we made them, we were excited about) or cancelling as the prospect now feels too much. As soon as this door is open, there's room for a huge amount of feeling to rush in, such as anxiety about going, tiredness, questioning if we feel up to it, and the hassle of what's ahead.

We second-guess our decisions, going over and over what we should do, considering every variable of a situation. It can make us overly cautious or leave us so drained from all our research that we feel completely unable to make a decision and end up doing nothing. More choice leads to greater anxiety, dissatisfaction, regret and analysis paralysis. Yet it's important to remember that what's best for us is completely subjective, so there's no exact science to it and no perfect answer. If you haven't already, you need to watch the brilliant TED Talk by Barry Schwartz, which sums up 'the paradox of choice'.[25]

A good example of this thinking trap is Poppy, who had spent days questioning whether she should go out with her friends. The more she thought about it, the more unsure she became. Her indecision left her agitated and restless, pushing her down the doom spiral and into a heightened state, making it even harder for her to work out what she wanted to do.

My social battery feels like it's on minus 55 per cent because I've been so busy. I can't face doing anything except collapsing and zoning out on YouTube. I just don't have the energy to go. I promised I was going to do it, and at the time I was really looking forward to it, but I'm dreading it now. I can't even remember why I thought I'd want to do it, but I'm also really worried about letting them down, and I'm worried that they'll be annoyed with me. There are so many emotions swirling in my mind that I can't hang on to the reason I'd said yes in the first place. I don't want to make the effort; I'm on terrible form and I won't even be good company. On the other side of it, I don't want to miss out, and I know I'm always glad when I do go. It feels like it's lose–lose because, even if I don't go, I'll still feel bad about it. I've been thinking about it for the past three days, but the more I think about it, the less sure I feel about what to do. Maybe I should message and say I can't make it, but what if I change my mind and do want to go later?

The Over–Analyser

You've had what felt like a slightly awkward conversation with someone, and now you can't stop thinking about it, cringing as you go over it again and again. You run through a post-mortem of what happened, replaying each word and gesture, analysing their body language, the look they gave you or their tone of voice. You wonder if you said something wrong and made yourself look stupid or accidentally offended the person, imagining what others who witnessed it were thinking (and, of course, in your mind they weren't thinking anything good).

Alternatively, before seeing people, you might run through different scenarios in your head and prepare what you're going to say, making sure you're up to date on what everyone's been up to, or coming up with some witty anecdotes to tell. Overthinking makes you see problems that don't really exist, or at least aren't as big as your thoughts make them out to be. This thinking creates anxiety and leaves you feeling embarrassed or ashamed. Worse, it creates the impression you're trying to avoid, as being stuck in your head can leave you seeming aloof, shy or even rude. These thoughts can take on a life of their own and lead you to act impulsively or make bad decisions about the problems you have. You might cancel seeing friends or confront others, even though the perceived problems are based on guesswork and there may be no clear evidence to support your belief.

Jude had fallen into this thinking trap after seeing friends. He hated the idea of coming across as underconfident and, any time he felt uncomfortable, he'd spend hours afterwards going over what had happened. Even if he felt good after an event, he'd think about it for ages and, by the time he'd overthought it, he was left completely unsure of how he had come across.

I keep thinking about what I said and it's stuck in my brain. I feel like I came across really weirdly when I was speaking to them. Normally, I try to control things, but I couldn't with this. It's so difficult as you don't have any control over what they're going to ask you. It's so hard talking about myself; I feel so nervous. I don't want to be seen as anxious. I really want people to like me. I'm trying to project an image of being confident, but under it I feel like I'm shy and awkward. I hate it when the focus is on me. It freaks me out and I end up over-dramatizing everything in my head. A tiny comment and I think they don't like me anymore. People say that others won't even notice these tiny things, but I notice things instantly in other people, so I'm sure they will, too. I'm really analytical, so I'm hyper-aware of everyone else. It means I'm always thinking about what people are thinking of me. It doesn't need to be a big thing: something small can set me off for the rest of the week. I worry about what they're thinking and wonder how I'm being perceived. It's getting in the way of me being myself. I know I'm being ridiculous, but I can't help it.

The Victim

This type of thinking usually centres around a wrong we believe has been done to us, leaving us obsessing over past arguments, conflicts, clashes with our values, perceived criticisms and slights. We focus on injustices we have suffered and feel wounded by what's happened. We become self-righteous, internally blaming others in our rage: 'I can't believe she did that to me', 'I'm going to get him back for that', 'She'll regret it, I'll make her pay'. We find ourselves rehearsing mental arguments, going over what we wish we'd said to call the other person out or to defend and justify ourselves. We may think about what we will say when we see them next.

Overthinking amplifies our thoughts so we feel overwhelmed with questions about whether we or others are to blame, whether we should get our own back or just withdraw. We might be partially right in our thinking, as the people who have inflicted harm may have been wrong, but it's like swallowing poison and hoping the other person dies. Overthinking only lets you see one side of the story, without considering what else might be going on. It can lead us to act impulsively, as we act out our bad moods and exaggerated concerns, or to seek retribution against others and get our own back, which can seriously backfire. Once the anger subsides, it can leave us feeling guilty or ashamed, wishing we hadn't lost our temper.

Evelyn felt let down by her family and, after an argument with her sister, fell into the victim trap. The problem with anger isn't anger itself, but the combination of anger and overthinking. It amplified the feeling that she had been wronged and hurt, leaving her as the victim and fuelling resentment and shame.

> *I can't believe my sister is annoyed with me. I keep replaying it in my head and what I should have said. I feel like I have to look after*

*my entire family. When something happens, the first thing I think
is, 'How are they feeling?' I'm always the one in charge, the safe
pair of hands. I'm the one everyone comes to to fix things and sort
stuff out, but I don't want to be that person. What do I get in return?
My siblings don't do anything; they've always left me to deal with
things. The truth is no one ever thinks about me. I don't think I've
ever learned to think about myself, as no one has ever done it for me.
If I say something, people don't listen because it's me. I could never
tell anyone how I was feeling. No one in the family ever talked about
emotions, they just shouted and screamed. I've spent so much time
dealing with everyone else's problems that I don't even know how
to talk about my own. I feel awful and I've got no one to turn to. I'm
so full of resentment. I used to dream of being in a different family.*

The Overwhelmed

This type of thinking feels inescapable as we jump from problem
to problem and cannot find our way to a solution. We dredge up
any concern, often unrelated, so a tidal wave of problems hits us at
the same time. It all feels so believable that it's impossible to gain any
distance from it, and we become consumed by what's going on. 'I'm
sick of my family never appreciating me, my job is a nightmare, my
partner has lost interest in me, I feel so alone, everything is a mess,
I don't know what to do.' Next, we're reviewing our shortcomings,
failings and faults.

This type of overthinking is particularly immobilizing as there are
so many conflicting thoughts that it becomes difficult to identify what
we feel or think, making us want to shut down or run away. Overwhelm

also pushes us into problem behaviours, such as drinking, to escape these thoughts.

When I first met Fatima, it was clear she was stuck in overwhelm. She talked about 'dwelling on the past' and focusing on various 'arguments and upsets'. As you'll see when you read about her experiences, how she felt was completely valid. She had created a whole new division for the business she worked for, but she discovered that, despite all her hard work, she would not be rewarded. The long hours of work and sacrifice no longer felt worth it. The outcome had broken her personal rules and values about fairness.

Fatima's work was entwined with her sense of self, so it had a huge impact on the rest of her life. She had always done well in work, and this external validation had made her feel good about herself and meant that she rarely experienced discomfort. Yet, this experience fundamentally challenged everything she thought about herself and her work. It was the first time since her childhood that she'd been put in touch with feeling vulnerable, which felt terrifying. Instead of seeing that the company had failed her, overthinking left Fatima herself feeling like a failure.

I've always worked hard and done well in the business. I worked so hard to set up a new division. I did it because I believed in the idea, but I expected to be financially rewarded for it. The time and energy I've put into it has come at a cost to the rest of my life. I put up with so much with the expectation I'd be rewarded and, even more stupidly, I was under the impression that it was appreciated and I was valued.

I believed in a meritocracy. I have always worked hard, kept my head down, done the right thing. It's so unfair. I felt blindsided when they told me my renumeration. When I spoke to management, they said they can't reward me this year, but that they'll look again next year and it should be a promising year. But when I set up the division, my boss hinted strongly that it would be worth my while. Now I feel like they don't value me and that I've been an idiot to believe they did.

I couldn't help but get upset in the meeting, and now I'm wondering, 'What are management saying behind my back? How will they view me now?' I've never been upset at work before, and I'm worried that now they won't think I'm capable of more responsibility. I also feel really humiliated. I'm not seen by my managers in the way I thought I was. My reputation is called into question. I feel a huge sense of shame. It feels so personal. Why haven't they chosen me? Why aren't I good enough? Did I do something wrong? Don't they see me as an asset to hold on to? I've always been so loyal to the company as I believed in it, but now I see that I'm just someone to get as much from as they can, and that when I stop being useful, they'll just replace me with someone else. I believed the company was about the people as much as the outcomes, but how they've acted over this shows me that all they care about is how much money the company makes.

It's completely changed how I see my future. I'd imagined working for this firm until retirement. I'd always prided myself on being someone who was a company person, someone everyone could come to. I used to love work, but now I just feel resentful. I regret not pushing harder for this. I regret being so naive. I regret wasting so many hours of my life in a place where I'm not even valued. Now I feel completely out of control and I can't even see the future. My mind is running so quickly I can't keep up with it. If I leave, I've failed; it's like I'm running away and I'm letting my family down, and I don't want to leave everything I've worked so hard on. But at the same time, I don't want to stay if they're going to treat me like this. Maybe I should do something else entirely.

What are your traps for overthinking?

Which thinking traps do you most commonly fall into? Which overthinking themes are you particularly sensitive to? Can you see how, when you're in a trap, it changes your thinking and can leave you feeling powerless? If it's hard to see the impact of these thinking traps in yourself, use the case studies in this chapter as a template. Fatima is clearly a huge asset to the company she works for, but the thinking traps she's stuck in prevent her from seeing this. What's happened is understandably upsetting, but thinking so critically of herself is making it even harder and leaves her in the victim role, leading to feelings of resentment, blaming and anger.

As you read through Part Two of this book, I want you to notice when you're falling into these traps. So, now, make a note of each type of thinking trap and how it applies to you. Get to know your overthinking style and your sensitive spots. Note down any triggers so you gain an even better insight into what your brain is up to. All this will increase your awareness of overthinking, and will be useful information for when we begin Step One.

Once you notice your automatic response, you can check what's going on, disrupt the thoughts and choose what you do next. It's only once you notice the habit that you can break it. I'll also be introducing you to lots of strategies to overcome these traps as you work through the book.

For now, when you notice yourself overthinking, hold on to the idea that *this is overthinking*. You can even say it to yourself. This is a way to begin to externalize the thoughts, to see them as separate from you and to remember that these are thoughts, not facts. The better you get at noticing the thoughts in action, the more successfully the strategies will work.

Remember:

- Reflection moves you forward, looks at concrete issues that you can action, and helps you to feel better.
- Overthinking leaves you stuck, looks at abstract, unsolvable issues and makes you feel worse.
- By paying attention to what, when and where tends to trigger you into overthinking, you can learn to identify when you are overthinking.
- There are a number of different overthinking traps or styles, and we all experience overthinking differently. You might be a dweller, an interrogator, a catastrophizer, a wobbler, an over-analyser, a victim or an overwhelmed thinker – or a mix of more than one. Identifying your own overthinking tendencies will help you to overcome them.

PART II

WHY WE OVERTHINK

Chapter 5
Why is overthinking so prevalent?

By the end of this chapter, you will:
- Have an understanding of the current mental health landscape and the prevalence of overthinking.
- Understand the different reasons for overthinking, which include escapism, fear of discomfort and phone use.

The better you understand overthinking, the easier it becomes to tackle. In Part Two, we will take a step back to understand why we overthink, before we begin on the steps to curing it.

As we've seen again and again in the media, we are in the middle of a mental health crisis. Mental health disorders are on the up: one in four people will experience a mental health problem of some kind each year in England, and one in six English adults has experienced a common mental disorder, such as depression or anxiety, in the past week.[26] Nearly one in five American adults will have a diagnosable mental health condition in any given year, and 46 per cent of Americans will meet the criteria for a diagnosable mental health condition sometime in their life, half of whom will have developed it by the age of 14.[27] Over 12 years, antidepressant prescriptions almost doubled in England, from 47 million in 2011 to 89 million in 2023, and nearly one in five people over 18 in England is now prescribed them annually.[28]

Mental health is a particular concern for teenagers and young adults. Since the 1940s, there have been hundreds of research studies that showed a U-shaped curve in human wellbeing: happiness rose initially to a peak at around 30, then declined in midlife and rose again after retirement. The happiest people were the young and old, with emotional crises most likely to hit during midlife. Recently, however, there has been a shift – and now young people (aged 18–25) report being the unhappiest age group of all.

A study from 2022[29] showed that happiness for people under 40 is significantly lower than it has been in recent decades, with unhappiness increasing as you move down the age groups. In the graph overleaf,[30] you can see how life satisfaction changes with age now, compared to the U-shaped curve of the past.

Depression[31] and anxiety are rapidly increasing among young people, and research published in the journal *Lancet Child & Adolescent Health*

How life satisfaction changes with age

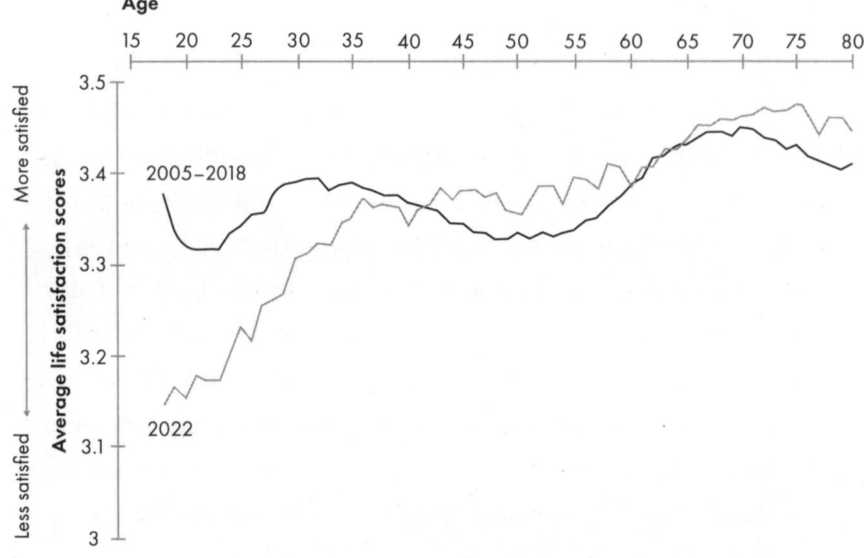

Blanchflower, David G. and Bryson, Alex and Xu, Xiaowei, The Declining Mental Health of the Young and the Global Disappearance of the Hump Shape in Age in Unhappiness (April 2024). NBER Working Paper No. w32337, Available at SSRN: https://ssrn.com/abstract=4794387

showed a 65 per cent increase in children and young people admitted to acute hospital wards.[32] We are heading to an all-time record for health-related benefits claims, according to recent forecasts,[33] and there has been a huge rise in young people taking time off work due to mental health issues.

We have never been as prone to overthinking as we are now and, while overthinking affects pretty much everyone at one point or another in their lives, I've noticed a pattern of it becoming increasingly common and problematic in the younger people I see. Alongside the prevalent reasons for overthinking outlined in Chapter Two, I see some new potential causes.

Reasons for overthinking

Expectations vs escape

Today, there is so much more emphasis on the importance of being happy than there was in the past. One of the biggest problems for overthinkers is the idea that we should always feel in a positive, content frame of mind.

We are sold the idea that we can have an incredible life. I think that, in previous generations, there was an expectation that life was difficult. This meant you expected things to go wrong, and when they did, you knew it was normal. You didn't personalize the problems you faced, so you didn't think that the world was against you, or that you'd done something wrong, or that you weren't getting what you deserved.

But the modern world is scary – wars, climate change, pandemics, political upheaval, the cost-of-living crisis and AI threats – and these problems are so much bigger than us. Reality isn't very appealing, and it's easy to escape from it by going online. When we use social media, we know it's not real life, but the images and lives portrayed are so much more attractive. The pictures and stories make us believe we could have something better than real life.

As awful and horrible as overthinking can be, in a strange way it allows us to keep alive the idea that life *can* be perfect and everything can work out well. The future can remain filled with possibility, and imagining future scenarios allows them to remain perfect in our minds. Real life is sometimes hard, occasionally boring and often just *average*. The imagination is a pretty nice break from how tough life can feel at times.

In our heads, our dreams can remain untouched by the reality of life and all it entails. We don't have to face the hard work that goes into achieving great things, or the reality that we might make mistakes or not succeed. While having dreams might feel like a good thing, when we hold these unrealistic ideals, real life can rarely live up to them. Even if we do dare to try, reality can feel disappointing compared to what we'd imagined.

Instead of accepting this as normal, we can often be triggered into overthinking, questioning why we don't have the life we imagined or why we're falling short. It can make us focus on what we don't have, rather than what we do have. We can end up focusing on all the things we feel are wrong in our lives.

So instead of *doing* these things we dream of, we just keep thinking about them – and this brings us to the second problem.

No natural inoculation to cope with difficulty

The human brain has evolved over millions of years to be shaped by experience. It's our experiences (not thinking about things) that are key to emotional development. As a result of our evolution, humans are amazing at adapting. If we'd been knocked down by difficulty, we wouldn't have lasted long as a species.

Yet think how many of our experiences have been displaced by time on our phones. The virtual world takes us away from seeing friends in person and from doing things in real life. All the activities that used to enrich our lives are being replaced with a worse alternative and, more importantly, we are also losing all the psychological benefits that these experiences bring.

Technology has also massively reduced how much we have to physically do. We don't even need to leave the house if we don't want to; there is very little we have to wait for and fewer unknowns. Many of us are working from home, with no commute, and university has moved much of its teaching online.

Physically doing things gave us more opportunity to naturally experience and manage struggle on a smaller scale. It's the discomfort that comes from small struggles that leads to growth, as we learn that we can tolerate frustration and uncertainty, and that we can cope when things don't go to plan.

Stepping out of our comfort zones can feel really unsettling, as it opens up a small gap of uncertainty – and being in this space can leave us feeling vulnerable, as we struggle with not being able to do things so easily or dealing with the unknown. Avoiding uncertainty and trying to keep a tight control of our lives gives us little practice when a bigger change happens.

It sounds basic, but having to wait to find out something, even if it's just the outcome of the next episode of a TV show, gives you a chance to get used to uncertainty. Getting lost, or making the wrong choice, gives you experience of things going wrong and shows you that you can cope. Asking someone something and being unsure of their response, or putting yourself in uncomfortable situations, teaches you that you don't need to have an exact idea of how everything will go – and that, even if things don't go perfectly, it's not such a big deal.

Working hard at something and getting over setbacks teaches you that you can overcome difficulty when you persevere. It also shows you the importance of tolerating discomfort as a way to get to the outcomes you want.

Rather than trying to avoid discomfort and uncertainty, which is ultimately impossible, we need to learn to tolerate them and see that nothing terrible happens when we feel this way. Once we are more accepting of discomfort, we are less likely to overthink.

Unfortunately, I've seen the reverse happening. Many people I speak to have become increasingly fearful of discomfort, which brings me neatly to the next problem.

More time thinking makes you overly tuned in to your feelings

If we believe discomfort is something to fear, it makes us hypervigilant when it comes to our feelings. As a result, we are thinking more about our feelings than ever before. We are constantly noticing, questioning and validating our internal experiences. This is great for some things, but thinking is not a blanket response for everything that happens to us. How we feel fluctuates and changes, so it's not something we need to be in tune with at all times.

When we combine being overly focused on our feelings with a false expectation that we should feel good all the time, our goal discrepancy will be regularly triggered whenever we experience negative emotions. In addition, there is now a great deal of misinformation and bad advice online that fuels this. Four out of five doctors in the UK are worried about the over-medicalization of mental health, and believe that the stresses and strains of everyday life are being too readily labelled as mental health disorders. Over-diagnosis and over-treatment with medication has also been widely reported in the US.[34] Concerns have been raised over broadening diagnostic categories and the adding of new conditions, especially when these decisions are made by people with financial ties to the pharmaceutical industry. By pathologizing our feelings and diagnosing our differences or distress as disorders, we are in danger of medicalizing ordinary or understandable reactions and behaviours.

Of course, these experiences are very real, and there is no doubt that many people are severely struggling, but when we don't see this in context as a reaction to our circumstances, it takes away our power to change things. As you've seen in Part One of this book, thinking about our emotions more, and focusing on them, will certainly not help. No one sails through life without incident; our relationships, social experiences and life difficulties are inherently linked to our emotions. It's better to recognize that these responses are understandable when you consider what is going on in your life rather than thinking that there is something wrong with you.

This hypervigilance, alongside the fact that we're getting less natural inoculation against life's difficulties, makes it understandable that people might find it harder to cope. The recommended first-line treatment is 'talking therapy' (such as cognitive behavioural therapy), but this is poorly available and waiting times are long. Therefore, antidepressants are more commonly prescribed. I've seen what a difference medication can make, but they deal with the symptoms rather than the cause. They don't give you the skills to cope. This is why it's extremely important to have the opportunity to learn coping strategies.

Feeling distressed is hard enough, without adding worry about what's wrong with you or feeling bad about it. The focus needs to be on what you can do to manage, but a focus on feelings does the opposite and increases fear and avoidance. This makes you feel disengaged from life, and means you are more likely not to do things.

Increased self-scrutiny

The natural move towards avoidance really shrinks our lives. Not only do we miss out on a chance to prove our fears wrong, but there are also fewer opportunities to disrupt overthinking or to gain a different view. Instead, we've created more time and space to overthink, which can lead to increased self-scrutiny.

Our commute, office chats, seeing friends or getting outside our comfort zones by trying new things all offer us a chance to gain perspective and shift problematic thinking. Going out and doing things, even if it is just running errands, also keeps our minds engaged. It's very difficult to be both fully engaged in a task and overthinking things.

Therefore, when we're immersed in something, our mood is also boosted, which is the perfect antidote to overthinking.

We're naturally prone to comparison, but social media turbocharges this tendency in a way that can be unforgiving and cruel. It stipulates how we need to look and the trends we need to follow, and reminds us of all the ways we're falling short. In addition, social media use can give rise to online disputes, or can create the fear of missing out, as you can see your friends going out without you, look at what your ex is up to, or realise you have been excluded from a WhatsApp group. This all gives us much more room for overthinking and self-scrutiny to creep in.

It feels as if there is an ever-widening gap between what we show on the outside and how we feel on the inside. It feels as if our inner and outer lives are split – who we are online, in person, at home, with certain friends – and all these different selves are not joined up. This can also mean that we don't express our feelings. Instead, questions, fears and upsets all whir round our heads without an outlet.

In addition, we fear not being accepted, so mistakes and failures can feel catastrophic. This tendency makes us lose touch with our instincts and just being ourselves. Many of the people I see worry so much about saying or doing the wrong thing that they spend hours thinking, planning and analysing. This leads me on to the next issue.

We are trying to be in control of life

An increasing number of people feel a deep sense of responsibility for the outcomes in their lives. They find it difficult to manage uncertainty and they adopt a perfectionistic approach. It can make them rigid and inflexible, as they over-plan, seek order and believe they need to be in control of every aspect of their lives. Overthinking pretends to be a way to decide what to do, but it is really a way to try to control the outcome and eliminate the risks or consequences. We might consider every decision in minute detail instead of just seeing what happens or working things out as we go.

Trying to be in control can also have a negative impact on our relationships. It makes it harder to trust or rely on those close to us, and we are more likely to blame others. It can also inadvertently make parenting styles more controlling (another risk factor for overthinking) as we are so much more involved in our children's lives.

If we put ourselves at the centre of everything that happens, we can become too self-focused and hold a level of responsibility that just doesn't add up. When things go wrong, we don't just have to deal with disappointment but also with regret: we blame ourselves, believing that if we'd tried harder, things would have been OK. This self-criticism causes increased suffering and pain. This then fuels a cycle, as we believe we need to try harder and take tighter control to avoid ever making a mistake again, instead of recognizing these experiences as normal.

Overthinking is not inevitable

Despite the prevalence of overthinking, it is not inevitable. You can live in the present, experience life without worry or fear, and be in control of your day-to-day feelings and emotions. Even if you do slip into overthinking, this book will give you the tools you need to break free and live your life the way you want to.

Remember:
- Overthinking is more prevalent than ever in these times.
- There are problems with placing an extreme value on happiness, fearing discomfort, being hypervigilant of your feelings and trying to control life.

- The move from doing to thinking about things amplifies overthinking – it's our experiences (not thinking about things) that are important for emotional development.
- Increased self-scrutiny and avoidance make us feel worse.
- There are many reasons for overthinking in the modern world, but we can overcome overthinking once we are aware of it.

Chapter 6
Blame your brain!

By the end of this chapter, you will:
- Understand why overthinking is not your fault and how it becomes a hardwired habit.
- Have a basic understanding of our brain networks and how they affect overthinking.
- Recognize the impact of mood on our brain networks.
- See that our brains are malleable and can be reshaped to form better habits.
- Learn to never think about your problems when you are in a negative mood.

To understand why it's so easy to overthink, and how quickly it can become habitual, it's helpful to know more about how the brain is organized and our network of thoughts. For me, this was a lightbulb moment, as I realized why it can be so hard to get out of a bad mood, as well as understanding the importance of boosting your mood before thinking about any problems.

When we understand what's going on in our brains, we can make sense of why we react and behave as we do. The brain is a complex web, in which our thoughts, memories and emotions are interlaced in intricate networks of associations. When we think, different networks work together, communicating through a fast-paced, synchronized set of signals. These neural pathways are important for a number of reasons:

- They allow us to think, and to be incredibly efficient at doing it.
- They enable us to interact.
- They allow us to experience emotions and sensations.
- They create memories and help us to learn new things.
- They decode situations and help us make sense of the world.

I think of the neural pathways as a mental map that helps us to navigate our lives. When information fits our mental map or we are in situations we know, our brains can run on autopilot – a mode they like to be in. If we tried to process everything as if we were encountering it for the first time, we wouldn't get much done. These shortcuts allow us to follow routines without thinking too much about them, and to filter our environment for what's relevant. This takes up less energy and frees up mental space for other things. Familiarity feels safe, as we know what to expect and experience less internal discomfort. These shortcuts also allow us to quickly see connections and similarities, and to recognize patterns in our daily life, which helps us make sense of the world around us. We can see this happening in others: I remember when I had my first child, I was amazed that he could see categories so easily – that he knew a picture of a car was the same thing as a toy car and a real car. This is all a healthy part of the brain's functioning.

However, these intricate networks are also at the root of overthinking.

How the brain's wiring causes us problems

There's a well-known saying in psychology: 'Neurons that fire together, wire together.' This is a fundamental principle in neuroscience and psychology known as Hebb's Law.[35] Repeated and persistent stimulation of a neural pathway strengthens the connection between the neurons. The brain develops preferred communication pathways that link together different brain circuits to quickly and efficiently complete specific tasks.

These pathways can be imagined a bit like real pathways – a web of connections taking you between thought networks, emotions and memories. To imagine this, I want you to think for a moment about your local park. When I walk my daughters to school through my park, we walk past the tennis courts and football pitches, the café, the climbing boulders and the playground. At the far end of the park, there's a finger maze.

Concrete pathways run throughout the park, connecting the different areas. There are several pathways through the middle so you don't have to walk all the way round to get from one side to the other, but there are also foot-worn routes in the grass, which offer shortcuts, carved out slowly over time for increased efficiency at getting between points.

The different areas of the park can be imagined as different thought networks. The tennis courts might represent your family and the football pitches your friends. The café could be your romantic relationships and the climbing boulders your education, while the playground could represent your health.

Like the different areas in the park, our thoughts, memories and emotions are not independent of each other. Many networks are connected to each other, and there are dominant well-formed pathways, like the concrete routes, and lesser, more fragile new pathways like the foot-worn routes in the grass.

In my clinic, Mia was chatting to me about a recent episode of overthinking that sums up how these pathways work in the brain.

> *I made a mistake at work and began to think about all the things that have gone wrong since I started my job. I feel like I don't have the ability to do this role, and it reminded me of all the times I've fallen short in the past. A 2:2 at uni, not getting the A-levels I wanted at school. I just wish I found these things as easy as other people do. I don't know what's wrong with me, why I can't just get on with the job. I'm not doing a good job at work and I'm not doing a good job at home either. I just feel like I'm failing at everything. I'm hardly ever there for the kids – and when I am, I'm short-tempered.*
>
> *I don't feel like I make the most of my time with them and enjoy my kids enough. I don't even remember their childhoods clearly. I'm not sure I cherished those important moments or enjoyed each day enough. It's not how I thought I'd be as a mum, and I really worry about the impact me being like this will have on their self-esteem and their futures.*

Mia jumped from a mistake at work to other problems at work, to memories of falling short in the past at uni and A-levels, then back to work and a global sense of failure. This led her on to her home life, her role as a mother and her children's futures. Work, uni, school, home, parenting and children are all linked to each other in Mia's thought network, so they're easy to move between. As she thought about her failures, her brain linked her up to other times she believed she had failed.

From one specific incident, Mia's brain had connected her to a cascade of other thoughts and memories, via these networks. The more her mind ran these routes, like the foot-worn routes in the park, the more dominant these routes became and the more likely she was to run along them and link them up again the next time she felt the same way. You can also see how this thinking limited her ability to take action. The negative thoughts went from a specific issue at work (which it might have been possible to improve or think differently about) to a sense of failure in life that felt all-consuming and impossible to overcome.

The impact of our emotions

Our thought networks are also connected by our emotions. Positive thoughts, memories and emotions tend to be connected in a different network from negative thoughts, feelings and emotions. It's like the brain has the run of two different routes. It's much harder to move between negative thoughts and positive thoughts, or between negative moods and positive moods, because they're on different tracks. You could imagine it like the two ends of the park I've described. Although you can get from the finger maze to the café, it's a bit of a walk, so it's less easy to go between these places.

When we feel happy, we are more likely to recall happy thoughts and memories, but negative moods connect us to negative thoughts and memories. This can be seen in the overthinking mind map we looked at in Chapter One (see page 29).

What this means from a brain perspective is that your brain has greater access to the thoughts and memories that are congruent with your mood. It's not just that our mood influences our thoughts: our mood actually changes which pathways we have access to along the network. When we are in a negative mood, it's as if the links to the good memories are broken. The road to positive thoughts and feelings is not only closed, they're completely blocked off, and we will also be more likely to interpret anything that is happening through the lens of the negative mood. No wonder it's so difficult to get out of a bad mood: at these times, our thinking is stacked against us.

When our negative mood network is activated and we ask ourselves why we're feeling so awful, the brain comes up with all the reasons it can think of that match our mood, activating our negative *thought* network and linking to similar thoughts and memories. An argument with your father, hurtful comments from your partner, or worries about your weight – all are pulled into your spotlight of attention, and it becomes very difficult to change track.

These thoughts may only be loosely connected to what you're going through, or may even have nothing to do with each other or what you are currently facing. All they have in common is that you *felt* a similar way.

If we go back to Mia, her mood meant that she had access only to thoughts that matched her negative feelings. She didn't remember all the times she'd done well at work, that she had a good job despite not doing as well as she wanted in her studies, how normal it is not to have a perfect memory of your children growing up, or all the good parts of her parenting. When we think of this in terms of her spotlight of attention, we can see that her brain's focus was narrowed to this issue and anything that matched it.

Since overthinking is both triggered by and causes negative mood, it's not good news for leaving the negative brain track we're on. This also explains why it can be so difficult to change how we're feeling and to shift our thinking, as we don't have the same access to more positive thoughts when we're not feeling good.

A good example of this phenomenon in my life is the mornings before school. I can wake up in a good mood, with the promise of a good morning, but despite my best intentions, by the time I've repeated the same instructions to my children again and again (and again!), my mood shifts to one of annoyance and frustration and, before I know it, I'm noticing everything that everyone is doing wrong. I start the day as Dr Jekyll on my positive mood network, but before I know it, I'm Mr Hyde and stuck on the negative. Even though, rationally, I know this is not how I want to be, in that moment it's very difficult to see things differently.

Hardwired habits

There's another reason this brain wiring can cause us problems. Every time we feel bad and overthink, we strengthen the association between the two, carving out a path between feeling bad and overthinking, just like those shortcuts in the park. The more frequently this pathway is followed, intentionally or not, the faster those neural pathways become, making synaptic transmission more efficient and making future activation of the pathway easier and quicker.

In simple terms, the more often you go down a pathway and create a link between feeling bad and overthinking, the more likely you are to go down it in the future. Just like real pathways, the routes used most frequently are the easiest routes to move along quickly and efficiently.

This association is why overthinking becomes habitual. These pathways become the default system in the brain, hardwired over time. Instead of being triggered by a goal discrepancy, we become so practised at this type of thinking that it becomes an automatic response to feeling bad. It's a bit like addiction when, if you repeatedly respond to feeling bad by using alcohol, drugs, sex or shopping, you begin to desire those things whenever you feel distressed.

Dan had grown up in a family where there was always conflict. His father was frequently angry and made life at home scary. As an adult, every time Dan had an argument, he'd start to think about his short temper and worry he was like his dad.

I hate it when I'm angry. I feel like I'm being just like my dad, and I swore that I'd never be anything like him as he made our lives so miserable. Dad was always so good with other people, they'd say what a great guy he was, but it's not how he was at home. We were all scared of him. It felt like we were always walking on eggshells, afraid to say anything that might upset him. The slightest thing would set him off. He and my mum were always arguing, and then he'd take it out on me and my sisters too. I was the only one that stood up to him, but it never made any difference.

I've worked so hard to change things and to ensure my relationships are different, but I hate conflict as it reminds me so much of when I was younger. Whenever I have an argument, I feel myself shift into angry mode. If I lose my temper, I feel like I'm turning into my dad. I wish I could control it. Then I start thinking about growing up – no one protected us, and I wish my mum had left my dad sooner so we didn't have to be exposed to that. I had to grow up so young. My parents brought nothing but misery to us, but for some reason my siblings are OK and I've ended up being the one who is alone. I feel so let down, and now I feel like history is repeating itself.

Many people I work with worry about history repeating itself, but as I'm sure you can see when considering Dan's story, feeling angry sometimes is not the same as being that person all the time. Dan's efforts to change already make him different from his father. It's not surprising that when he feels angry it brings up memories of what he's experienced in the past and puts him in touch with those old feelings. It's important for Dan to see it is understandable to feel upset. When he understands why the old feelings return, he can acknowledge how hard it was to grow up in that situation, without adding shame on top.

When Dan was growing up, he felt afraid and upset in response to his father's anger, and the feelings and experience were twinned together again and again, carving a link between conflict and the memory of arguments. Even with the positive changes Dan has made, these pathways are easy to go back to, as the old habits were so entrenched. When Dan felt upset, the old thoughts were fresh and ready to go, making the thoughts more conscious and accessible in his brain. What was once a conscious process was now happening all the time, often without Dan even realizing it.

You might be actively making these links between your thoughts, such as when your focus on health triggers thoughts about ageing and your appearance. Or perhaps it's passive, like when you wake up in the night from a nightmare and your brain starts racing. Without consciously making the link, you remember an argument you had with your work colleague that day, or you recall that text from your friend that made you feel sure she's unhappy with you. Suddenly you're mired in all the different things that haven't been working out recently, and you're the opposite of sleepy.

The final nail in the coffin is that, in these negative mood states, we don't have the same access to higher-level thinking, organization and planning – so it really is harder to make good decisions. Prolonged stress can even shrink the hippocampus,[36] the part of the brain that is responsible for learning, memory and problem-solving. So just when you need your best thinking, you're unable to access it!

Breaking the habit

Don't worry, there's good news, too. Our experiences shape the brain's structure and function over time, but although these networks link up, they are not fixed.[37] The brain is malleable: it can change. This plasticity means it can reshape and rewire. Think back to those pathways in the park. Even if a pathway is overgrown, the more often it gets walked down, the clearer the path becomes and the easier it gets to walk along. It's the same for the brain.

- Every time we overcome the urge to overthink, the weaker those negative pathways become, helping us to stop this bad habit.
- We can then build a healthier habit, strengthening a new response using coping strategies that work.

On the days when I'm stuck noticing everything that is wrong in my life, I find it helpful to remember these facts about neural networks. I *know*, rationally, how fortunate I am, but at the time I don't *feel* it, which makes my mood drop further as I tell myself that I shouldn't be feeling like this with all I have. When I recognize that I am on a different neural network, one which is blocking my view of the good things, it allows me to take a step back and see that the negativity is just how my brain is working at that time. I can pause rather than blindly following the thinking.

In this way, when I notice that I'm stuck on a negative track, I can gain a small bit of distance from what's happening – if you think back to that overthinking continuum in Chapter Two (see page 35), I'm no longer pressing my nose against the glass, unable to see anything else. Rather than being pulled along the different pathways into more doom and gloom, noticing keeps a connection to a different view and widens my spotlight of attention.

I now have a choice that didn't exist before: I can remind myself that I don't have to continue with this thinking, and that I can change paths. Rather than automatically responding, I can disrupt the thought and intentionally choose my response: I can do a quick check of the beliefs that might be driving it and question if these add up; or I can make a choice to redirect and do something that will help me to feel better.

Every time I make an intentional choice to not automatically follow the old pathways, I am changing the association and breaking the overthinking habit, and I am building a new pathway in my brain that will lead me to a better place.

– **Make a note of the reasons why overthinking is not your fault.** Store this as useful information so you can show yourself self-compassion, which is a key ingredient for change. The good news is that our brain networks can change, which is something I'll be telling you more about in Part Three.

Broadening our spotlight of attention

When we link this information about neural networks with what we have discussed in previous chapters, we know that the following things occur when we overthink:

- Our negative mood keeps our awareness stuck.
- We are limited in the thoughts that are activated and accessible – a result of how our brains are set up – which makes it much harder to shift tracks.

- High negative or low positive moods narrow our spotlight of attention, which increases the likelihood that we will continue to focus on the same topic over time.

This is why it's so important *not* to think about things when you are feeling negative!

The good news is that we can learn to steer our spotlight of attention and regain a broader focus by boosting mood. It's actually really simple: shifting our mood changes the habitual pathways in the brain, gives us access to different thinking, and makes it less likely that thoughts will become repetitive. I'll be teaching you how to do this in more detail in Part Three.

Being in a positive mood is the best place to make decisions, problem-solve or have access to multiple perspectives.

I'm not suggesting you don't think about your problems or that you try to turn everything into a positive, but it is important to consider *when* you choose to think about issues. Studies show that helping distressed people even momentarily experience positive emotions helps their bodies and minds recover faster from stress.

In one of these studies[38] participants were told they would be given 60 seconds to prepare a three-minute speech, that there was a 50 per cent chance 'the computer' would select them to deliver their speech, and that the speech would be videotaped and shown to students to be evaluated. If they were not selected to deliver their speech, they were told that a film clip would begin on the video monitor. In fact, no participants delivered a speech and each viewed a film clip. The cover story was simply used to make participants anxious and to justify the switch to an unrelated film clip!

Two of the possible film clips were meant to elicit positive emotions while one was intended to be neutral and the last to invoke negative emotions:

1. Waves breaking on a beach to induce contentment.
2. A puppy playing to elicit amusement.
3. Sticks piling up to elicit no emotion.
4. A young boy crying as he watches his father die to elicit sadness.

While participants watched one of the film clips, their bodily reactions were monitored using physiological sensors to monitor cardiovascular reactivity. After the initial inducement of stress to the participants, the researchers found that the positive emotions generated from the positive film clips were able to undo the effects of stress on the cardiovascular system and help regulate negative emotions. The 'cry' film, however, lengthened recovery time. Positive emotions broadened participants' thought-action tendencies (how we think and act; see page 56), moving from the negative emotions' 'specific action tendencies' (such as fight or flight) to being able to consider a wider range of thoughts and actions. The researchers concluded that positive emotions 'undo' the aftereffects of negative emotions.

Therefore, if you do need to re-evaluate or look in more detail at certain areas of your life, the best time to do so is when you're feeling better. Positive emotions positively alter our thinking, actions and physical response, while helping us maintain wellbeing.

When our mood is higher, we have access to higher-level thinking, organization and planning. We make better decisions, come up with better ideas to manage, and can connect to others for support or to help us think things through. It's like lighting up the stage with that wide beam: it gives us a better view of what's going on and takes in the full picture. It broadens our spotlight of attention and increases our awareness so we can break the habit.

Going forward, I want you to put this rule in place as non-negotiable: *I will not think about how I'm feeling or about my problems when my mood is negative*. I know it's harder than it sounds, but you'll be an expert at this by the end of the book!

Remember:
- Your current thinking links to similar thoughts, which impacts your mood and what you do.
- Your current mood links to similar thoughts and memories linked to that mood. When you feel happy, you are more likely to recall happy thoughts and memories, but negative moods connect to negative thoughts and memories.
- When you are in a negative mood, you don't have the same access to higher-level thinking, organization and planning, so it is harder to make good decisions.
- A positive mood will increase your array of accessible thoughts and actions, so your spotlight of attention is broader and you are less likely to get stuck in overthinking.

Chapter 7
Self-criticism

By the end of this chapter, you will:
- Understand the problems that self-criticism causes and why it's toxic for overthinking.
- Recognize your negative thought bias.
- Understand the importance of self-compassion and why you need it to beat overthinking.
- Learn to speak to yourself more kindly.

Now that we've looked at how our brains work when we're overthinking, we need to do some behavioural work to equip us for the steps in Part Three of this book. In the next chapters, I'll be looking at the problems that feed overthinking – self-criticism, comparison and our capacity to cope – and how best to manage them.

One of the biggest causes of overthinking that I come across is the way we perceive ourselves. Sometimes, we can be our worst critics. If someone followed you around, saying you were useless, always pointing out your mistakes, and reminding you of all the things you were unhappy with, how would you feel emotionally? Anxious, upset, unhappy? How would you feel in your body? Small, insignificant, deflated? If the criticism was constant, it would feel hard to find the motivation to do the things you want, and you might even feel depressed. It's no different when this criticism is coming from within you.

This negative internal monologue doesn't just make you feel bad about yourself, it also feeds overthinking and leads to feelings of shame and inadequacy. Our own thoughts are often far harsher than anyone else's feedback, as we can be incredibly critical or even punitive to ourselves. What makes self-criticism even harder is the negative bias created by our evolved threat focus (see page 48). Try this exercise to see what I mean:

- Take a moment to think about something good that happened to you. Perhaps you passed an exam, completed a project, reached a goal or were given a compliment. How long did you think about the good thing? How much did you go over the event in your head? How long did you keep the good feeling?

- Now think about something difficult or bad that happened to you, or something you felt you did wrong or could have done better. Perhaps you received some criticism, did less well than you hoped on an exam, or failed to meet a goal.

How long did you spend going over that event in your head?

How long did the negative feelings last?

I'm guessing you spent longer thinking about the negative event than the positive one. This exercise is a really simple way to see how we think about and attend to information. From a survival standpoint, it makes sense, as a strong recollection of bad experiences means we're more likely to learn from mistakes and avoid a life-threatening situation. However, this means that smaller, day-to-day stressors and irritations tend to take centre stage in our spotlight, which leaves less space for the good stuff.

When things don't go according to plan, it's all we can think about: self-criticism weighs in as we repeatedly replay what went wrong in our minds. It can be the obvious critical commentary of self-doubt, ruminating over mistakes and failures, or, more subtly, it could be imagining what your mum would think or your friend would say. This behaviour tends to occur under the misguided belief that we need to be self-critical to ensure we do our best and keep ourselves in check; that we need to suffer in order to succeed. Yet self-criticism has the opposite effect, as it makes everything harder: it makes you less likely to achieve your goals, it puts you at higher risk of depression and stress, it will make you less effective at implementing coping strategies and it's a recipe for overthinking.[39,40]

Think back to Chapter Two and the impact of negative thoughts. As discussed in that chapter, research shows that critical thoughts stimulate the body's threat system and increase cortisol, just as thinking about food stimulates your digestive system or sexual thoughts stimulate your sexual system. Remember that your brain reacts in the same way to threats whether they're from an external source or your own self-criticism, stimulating your body to produce a physical response. Overthinking exacerbates and maintains psychological stress – it activates the nervous system, increasing cortisol, adrenaline, heart rate and blood pressure.

Most overthinkers feel a strong sense of shame over getting stuck in these overthinking patterns. This exacerbates self-criticism: you might be cross with yourself or feel foolish for overthinking, or be hard on yourself about why overthinking took over and why a different view was so difficult to see at the time. This increases stress, stops you trusting in yourself and leaves you feeling even worse. It's hard enough overthinking, without adding self-criticism and shame on top. In my clinic, people say things like: 'These aren't even proper problems; other people have much worse things to deal with and they don't worry like this.' Or they say: 'Anyone else could handle this; I don't know why I can't take it in my stride.'

Shame also makes you keep things quiet, so you don't tell others how much you're struggling or how overwhelmed you feel. The negative thoughts remain stuck in your head, without others to support or reassure you.

It's important to recognize that you do not deserve to feel bad, and that punishing yourself by going over what's happened is not the answer. Getting upset or angry with yourself, demanding that you do better, will only amplify the problem. It will make you more likely to give up and will pave the way for negative moods and low self-esteem. Self-criticism is not helpful; it's a problem to overcome. It's time to switch self-criticism for self-compassion.

A compassionate mind

Now I want to introduce you to your new best friend on this journey: self-compassion. A huge volume of research[41] shows how important compassion is – and that it's compassion, not criticism, that gets results.

Self-compassionate people are more resilient and more likely to meet their potential. They bounce back more easily from setbacks, take steps to improve themselves and are more likely to learn from their mistakes. Developing compassion is a vital tool to help us get through our difficulties and avoid the second arrow.

I think the simplest way to approach compassion is to remember what it means to be human. It's human to feel a range of emotions. No human is perfect, and we all make mistakes. Yet it's surprising how many people find self-compassion difficult. They feel wary of it, believing they don't deserve it or fearing it will make them weak. Most people I meet are compassionate towards others, but lack self-compassion. It can feel easier to be kind to those we care about, but it doesn't always come naturally when we think of ourselves. We struggle to operate the same rules for ourselves that we automatically use for others. I'm guessing you're the same. But we can learn to make a change.

– Take a moment to think about why you believe compassion is important when you're supporting others. Doesn't this apply to you, too? There shouldn't be one rule for you and a different one for everyone else.

How to have a compassionate approach

A compassionate approach means being thoughtful, curious, open and wise. It comes from a place of warmth, support and kindness. Professor Paul Gilbert,[42] the Founder and President of the Compassionate Mind Foundation,[43] outlines seven key attributes to compassion. As you read through the list, think about each one and how to incorporate it into your life.

1. **Make a decision** to be compassionate towards yourself. It sounds strange, but you need to decide this is how you are going to be going forward.

2. **Become sensitive to your feelings** and thoughts, and learn to become sensitive to what you might need.

3. **Be emotionally open** and sympathetic to your own and other people's suffering. Only then can you bring understanding rather than criticism to what you're going through.

4. **Don't fear your feelings**, as being compassionate towards yourself means getting to know your feelings and learning to tolerate them.

5. **Don't be critical of your feelings** or try to avoid them, which is a common habit of overthinkers. Whether you feel anxious, sad, angry, jealous or happy, you can learn to be kind, open, tolerant and accepting of your feelings. Although you may wish to change how you are feeling, this is best done from a compassionate position, rather than in the old way (self-criticism or avoiding). This means kindly facing your feelings, as you would for a friend. This allows you to be more reflective and to develop empathy for what you're going through.

6. **Find empathy** for yourself. The way you come to understand and think about your feelings and thoughts is also key. It's important to be open-hearted and to curiously explore how you're feeling. When we have empathy for others, we try to understand that they may think and feel differently from us. For example, if your partner snaps at you, empathy means recognizing the context of what's going on for them. If you know they've been under a huge amount of stress, then

you forgive them – this is showing empathy. It's the same for yourself. If you make a mistake or feel nervous about doing something, it's important to acknowledge your feelings and to bring empathy to your situation rather than blame or self-criticism.

7. **Do not condemn, judge or put yourself or others down**. This can be an easy habit to fall into when you are depressed or angry. Being compassionate means giving this up. We want to be aware of our thoughts and feelings, but without judging, suppressing or trying to push them out of our minds. Instead, try to notice critical thoughts without acting on them – and bring kindness.

Speak to yourself differently

Developing compassion is a way to bring our emotions into balance. It's the perfect antidote to self-criticism, and it's proven to make us more able to cope with life's stresses.

View the process of developing self-compassion as ongoing. Change is hard, but you're doing your best. It's OK that you won't manage it every time, that on the harder days you might slip back into the old patterns and habits. Taking this approach is a compassionate approach.

It might feel strange as you learn to speak to yourself differently. It's a bit like learning a new language – you have to get over the uncomfortable beginning, when your attempts feel clunky, but you'll slowly become more fluent and you'll find that a more compassionate approach becomes natural.

This process can be particularly difficult if you weren't shown compassion growing up. Our childhood experiences are the foundation on which the rest of our lives are built, influencing the adults we become. What you learned as a child shapes your thoughts, feelings and behaviours. It influences how you see and experience things now and gives you a sense of who you are. The way we are spoken to as children helps us to develop the language we use internally. If you weren't given positive encouragement and reassurance or taught positive self-motivation and to take on board your achievements, you will find it harder to develop that language now. If you had a critical care-giver or were negatively compared to others, it's likely that you have internalized these ways of relating to yourself. The good news is that this can change.

Do not get cross with yourself for overthinking. Do not tell yourself you're stupid or weak, or that other people cope better than you. We all go through difficulties in life and find things hard. Other people aren't out there coping with everything and finding life easy. You are definitely not alone! You could say to yourself:

It's OK to feel like this. It's not surprising, what with everything that has been going on, but overthinking isn't helpful. I'm fortunate not to be going through some of the difficulties I know others face, but that doesn't mean that I will feel happy every day or never feel bad. I still have a right to feel tired, anxious, low, worried, uncertain, sad or angry, because it's an understandable reaction to what I'm going through.

I think about the movement between good days and bad days as two rooms, with an interconnecting door. There's the good room where we like to spend as much time as possible. This is where we are when life goes well and we are managing; when we feel capable and connected to others. The room next door is the struggle room, where we go when we overthink or when life feels unmanageable and we are threatened with negative emotions such as anxiety, fear, frustration, anger or sadness.

In each room, we think and feel differently, and we relate and speak to ourselves differently too. When we're in one room, it's hard to remember that the room next door exists. In the good room, it's tempting to imagine that all's well, and that we are safe and will never come to any harm, but this can lead us to denying parts of ourselves or suppressing negative emotions. When we're in the struggle room, we feel overwhelmed and our problems can feel insurmountable. This can overspill from what we're currently facing into other areas: for example, we might end up feeling that everything is wrong in our lives.

I want you to try to keep the door between the two rooms open. This is hard, but it's important to remember that both rooms exist. Moving between these rooms is part of life and how we process our experiences. We want to use the good room to shore up our resources, but we also need to remember that the negative emotions of the struggle room are a normal response to difficulty. We won't be in that room forever; in time, we will move back into the good room.

A simple way to keep the two rooms in mind and to find compassion can be to reflect on how much things can differ day to day or week to week. We're different on different days, for different reasons. We can have a horrible day or week, but the next week can be much better. When we keep hold of this thread to things improving, it is easier to weather the darker days, speak to ourselves more kindly, and remind ourselves that – as bad as things might feel right now – this is not a permanent state. This idea will become particularly important when you get to Step Four.

– If the self-critical voice is hard to shift, I want you to name it and shame it. Whose voice is the critical voice? Does it stem from someone in your past? If so, take a moment to reflect. Would you take advice from this person on anything else? If the answer is no, don't take their thoughts as the truth of who you are. If the voice is yours, remind yourself that self-criticism is never helpful; it only ever leaves you feeling worse.

– Notice when it's difficult to have compassion. What is it about those times? Why do they pose such a trap?

Building a compassionate voice or image

Before you read on, take a moment to think about someone you know who is compassionate. It could be someone in your life now, from your past or even someone famous. What is it about this person that is compassionate? What do they say and do that shows you their compassion?

Now I want to help you build a compassionate image or presence. This is your own personal idea of what being cared about feels like. Give your image the qualities of compassion:

- Wisdom
- Strength
- Warmth
- Non-judgement

Close your eyes and imagine how this compassionate presence would look, feel and sound. Slow your breathing and bring your face into a half-smile. Allow an image to come to mind. Now fill out the table opposite, which will help you to think more about your compassionate image:

How would you like your ideal caring, compassionate image to feel, look and seem? How do they sound? Is it someone you know? Are they old or young? What is their gender? Are they non-human – an animal, the sea, a home, colour or light?	
What colours and sounds do you associate with the qualities of wisdom, strength, warmth and non-judgement?	
Has your image gone through similar experiences to you?	
Are they like a friend or part of a group that welcomes you to belong? Or is your image a place you could go to or an animal you can be with?	
How would you like your ideal caring, compassionate image to relate to you?	
How will you relate to your compassionate image?	
Are there any other sensory qualities you wish to give them or it?	

As you will discover in the next chapter, a compassionate approach is also essential for managing and overcoming comparison, which is another major factor in overthinking.

Remember:

- We can often be our own worst critics, which causes more harm than good.
- Self-compassion is a key tool on your journey towards beating overthinking.
- You can develop a voice to speak differently to yourself – practise it!

Chapter 8
Unfairly comparing

By the end of this chapter, you will:
- Recognize the negative impact of comparison on overthinking.
- See why social media is problematic and how much of your life you are losing to it.
- Be ready to put a stop to unintentional phone use and reduce time online.
- Learn a simple technique that will change your life.
- Understand that it's experience that counts because experience, not information, is the key to emotional development.

In this chapter we'll be exploring comparison, one of the biggest triggers I see to overthinking. It is important to have a good understanding of why comparison causes so many problems and to limit its impact, in order to embrace the steps we'll be taking in Part Three.

It's all very well saying 'Don't compare yourself to others', but it's human nature to do this. We have a natural drive towards comparison. This comes back to our evolutionary history of social interaction. We thrive in groups; it's what we're programmed for. Thanks to survival of the fittest, and the necessity of getting on in a group (think back to Chapter Two), human beings have an inherent need for social inclusion and belonging. Since, throughout our history as a species, social acceptance provided security and access to resources, we have a fundamental need to be valued by others. Social rejection threatened this need.

The need to belong is central to our behaviour and identity, pushing us to form and maintain close, lasting and positive relationships. Good relationships help us to manage stress and self-esteem, and to avoid loneliness. As a result, we are highly motivated to seek acceptance and avoid social exclusion. We evaluate our own abilities and opinions by comparing ourselves, and are constantly monitoring how others value and accept us.[44] This is intimately linked to our self-esteem and our sense of belonging – and goes to the core of who we are.

Unfortunately, we tend to be drawn into comparing ourselves to people we see as better off than us (this is called 'upward social comparison'),[45] especially when we're feeling bad. We cherry-pick their best bits, without taking in the whole picture of their lives. We believe that others are coping more easily with life – that they are managing to do all the things we 'should' be doing *and* that they are doing it better. We might even compare ourselves to a previous version of ourselves, a time when we were less tired, more social or more productive.

We are not only trying to live up to our own expectations, we're also trying to live up to an imagined version of what other people are doing. This fuels many of our beliefs and expectations, and we use these unfair and unrealistic ideas to set our standards for how we believe we should be living. It's an alternate reality that doesn't actually exist, but in spite of this we use this information against ourselves, and our lives are set up to ensure we always feel second-rate.

When we don't feel we measure up, an alarm goes off that motivates us to try to change our behaviour. This happens automatically and outside of our awareness (it is not something we think about and choose to do), but it affects how we evaluate ourselves.

A research study randomly assigned participants (women aged between 18 and 25) to watch TikTok videos featuring thin dancers, large dancers or animals (the control condition). After watching the videos, participants rated their weight satisfaction, overall appearance satisfaction, and body-shape satisfaction. Body satisfaction significantly increased after watching videos featuring large dancers or control videos. However, after watching videos of thin dancers (upward social comparison), body satisfaction decreased. These findings have been repeatedly demonstrated in English-speaking Western countries[46] and in Southern Europe.[47]

Another study, in which young women were shown photographs of either very thin women or average-sized women found even more interesting results.[48] This time the images were flashed on a screen for just 20 milliseconds, too fast for the women to become consciously aware of what they had seen. Yet the results were the same. Young women exposed to images of very thin women became more anxious about their own bodies and appearance.

We might *know* that it's a bad idea to compare ourselves with people we see on social media, for example, but this knowledge has a limited effect. The part of the brain doing the comparison is not governed by the part of the brain that knows, consciously, that these are people's highlight reels. We are then pulled into relating to ourselves in problematic ways, as this part of the brain doesn't respond to rational thought.

And this comparison game happens to all of us. While I was writing this book, I'd catch myself on a bad day questioning why I was finding it so difficult. I'd be pulled down a rabbit warren of thoughts without even being fully aware. I'd have people in my mind who I believed could just sit down in front of their computers and effortlessly write. I'd imagine them making time to do it in a sensible and calm way without it spilling into the rest of their lives. I'd have to consciously rein myself back in and remind myself that this was an illusion my mind was conjuring up to make me feel bad. I'd also remind myself of all the people I'd heard saying that they struggled with and hated parts of the writing process!

The not-so-wondrous web

In the past, direct comparison was made with a narrow group of people with whom we had day-to-day contact. Now, thanks to the internet, we've never been exposed to more information and we have a much wider pool of comparison. This information overload provides us with so many potential triggers for overthinking. It changes our expectations and sets standards that are impossible to achieve.

We are bombarded with messages of how to be happy and reach our potential (if we just take time to meditate, exercise, parent well, journal, eat right, save the planet, visit friends, clean our homes, declutter, do our jobs, and be good children, siblings and friends).

Consumer culture promotes the idea that wealth, status, physical attractiveness and being ridiculously busy are measures of a successful life. The culture encourages us to think only about ourselves and what we need. It manipulates us into thinking we don't have enough and hooks us into comparison. However, the external markers that are promoted by society – such as social recognition, physical attractiveness and financial success – are *negatively* related to wellbeing. Instead of making us happy, they are linked to increased depression, anxiety, narcissism and physical illness.[49,50]

Mobile apps are designed to be addictive, so we stay on them rather than engaging in the things that will truly connect us to others. Social media is the worst for stealing time and pulling you into negative comparisons. These removed relationships push us into social anxiety, checking, worrying, insecurity and self-doubt. We constantly question ourselves: are we parenting right, taking enough exercise, being a good enough partner? Are we attractive or successful enough?

While we think that we're just looking at pictures, our internal psychological system is monitoring our sense of belonging in the moment and our internalized experience of acceptance and rejection over time. Even with a work account, I found Instagram demoralizing and realized that it changed how I looked at my life. I started to see things as an opportunity for a good photo or a potential quote or post. Social media combined with front-facing cameras means that many people's phones are now filled with photos predominately of themselves. This shifts our perspective and increases self-focus. It's a very different way of looking at our lives from even twenty years ago.

Even if our lives are comparatively good, if we see people around us with a great family, successful job, nicer house or better holidays, it's easy to look at ourselves as falling short. This is how Najwa felt.

I'm not where I thought I'd be. I haven't done the things I expected to or wanted to in life and now it feels too late. My kids have grown up and left home, and I'm left with all this empty space. I feel like I've been so unlucky. I haven't reached my potential or been as successful as I wanted to be. I dread it when I'm out and people ask me what I do. I feel a deep sense of failure.

I can't help looking on Instagram at other people and thinking how good their lives are. It makes me feel sick. I have to take it off my phone to stop myself looking at it, but then I'm back on it again. I see other people who have fulfilled professional lives and I see people I was at school with doing much better than me – and they weren't even bright. I don't see how they've managed to do it and I haven't. I'm scared I'm not going to attain the future I deserve.

When I see other people doing well, I can't help but feel awful. I'm happy for my friends when they get promotions or new jobs, but I also feel really jealous and resentful that it's not the same for me. I have to go to their celebration drinks and hear all their good news, while internally I feel so envious. I hate myself for feeling like that, but I can't help it. Then I beat myself up for being a horrible person and not being gracious enough to enjoy their success. Maybe I'm a terrible person, only thinking about myself, but I feel completely demotivated and disillusioned. Sometimes I feel tired of life.

Najwa found it really helpful to see that comparison was her critical voice in disguise. It's a bit like a wolf dressed up in sheep's clothing. It might appear innocent, but when you believe you are not coping as well as others or see your friends' achievements and believe you're not doing well enough, it's self-criticism. It can even come in the form of seeing someone else going through a tough time – such as bereavement or a serious illness – and belittling your own experience or worrying that you're not making the most of your own life.

It's important that we don't compare how we feel inside with how other people's lives appear to us from the outside. We presume that because they look OK from the outside, they must feel OK, but we forget that we can only hear what's going on inside our own heads. It's easy to imagine that everyone else has got it together and they don't have the same insecurities, worries or fears, but we are all similar under the surface. No one is on top of everything.

It's also important to watch out for the urge to compare yourself to a previous version of yourself. It might seem like a helpful thought to motivate you, but it's another overthinking trap. The more aware of it you are, the quicker you can disrupt the thinking and redirect. Adopt a more compassionate view and remember you're seeing only part of the picture.

Get off your phone (please)

I love being able to work from home, FaceTime my extended family, giggle at a funny meme or find my way on Google Maps (I have no sense of direction), but you don't need me to tell you that, after doom-scrolling, you're left feeling worse.

I'm sure it won't come as a surprise to hear that an increasing addiction to our phones is linked to overthinking. Scrolling pulls us automatically into comparison and steals our time and energy. Even worse, it distracts us from doing the things that matter to us and that make our lives feel meaningful. It cuts out the parts of life most important for health and happiness, as well as the things that can help us overcome overthinking.

How we're living now is not how the human brain was designed to live. From an evolutionary perspective, phone-use interferes with our wiring and the production of the brain chemicals that make us feel good. The human brain has evolved to earn dopamine with hard work, not to get quick fixes from a phone. We are programmed for human connection, which gives us oxytocin. We need time outdoors in nature, nutritious food and good sleep for serotonin. We need to move to release endorphins.

Since 2007 (the year that Apple introduced the iPhone), the free time we used to spend on the important things like our relationships, hobbies, creativity, community, giving back and reflecting on our lives has gradually been replaced by phone time. I find it pretty depressing that for most people, their phone is the first thing they look at in the morning and the last thing they look at at night. You know you're addicted (though you're in the majority) if you can't even be separated from it when you go to the toilet.

Now, we do practically everything through a screen, and we spend less time in the presence of other people. We like our friends' photos, or text them, but we don't see them or speak to them as much. We don't have the same opportunities to bump into friends, or to say hello to the person who operates the till in a local shop.

We don't have to put ourselves out there in the same way we used to – we can work from home, avoid phone calls, or arrange a date through an app. We spend hours looking at all the amazing things we could do or see, but we don't actually do them. We are in nature less, read fewer books, sleep less and move less. Phones also take us away from experiences that teach us to manage discomfort and show us normal life is nothing to fear. We can get stuck imagining that someone is unhappy with us or that we've been rejected by a friend, without a chance to see them and realize that all's OK. We have little chance to gain perspective or check out our fears.

Seeing life through your phone is not the same as experiencing life. You miss out on so much!

Ideas for reducing phone use

Comparison is automatic, so the only solution is to minimize your time online, *especially* if you are not feeling good. Whether it's TikTok, YouTube, Snapchat, Instagram or Facebook, it will make you feel worse.

There are very few benefits of phone use for anyone – and even less for overthinkers. Use these ideas to stop unintentional phone use and reduce your time online:

- Turn off any notifications on your phone.
- Mute WhatsApp groups.
- Have time when your phone is on 'Do not disturb' or put your phone in a different room when you don't need it.
- Put your phone away in a bag or pocket when you're walking outside so you can take in your surroundings (instead of being led around by your phone).
- Keep your phone on silent and out of view when you're spending time with other people.
- Stop taking photos of yourself. If you have thousands of photos of yourself on your phone, it's pretty difficult not to over-scrutinize. It changes the relationship you have with yourself and your physical appearance.

Most importantly, **move your phone out of your bedroom** and buy an alarm clock to wake yourself up instead. You will be amazed at the difference this makes. It is life-changing (and free, minus the alarm clock). Phones are one of the top triggers to overthinking. If you don't do anything else I suggest in this chapter, please do this.

Seek out true connection

Good relationships offer dependability, security, acceptance and validation, which are all excellent at countering overthinking and something no strategy or money can buy. Spending time with other people is the best fix you can get. It allows you to be attuned to each other so you can understand what someone else is thinking and feeling – the non-verbal cues, their tone of voice, their immediate response – and see empathy, kindness and compassion in their eyes. Spend time with the people you like and love. Don't interact solely through messaging, voice notes or a screen.

Stop taking lessons on how to live and start living. It's the experience that counts – and experience, not information, is the key to emotional development. Don't just watch or be a voyeur online – you need to go out and do it! It is so much better to live life and try things out than go through life just imagining. We'll be focusing on this in Step Five, and as part of moving forward and future-proofing your life against overthinking.

Adam Alter[51] and Jonathan Haidt[52] have done brilliant work on the topic of screentime. In his TED Talk, Adam Alter finished by saying:

> *You've got a choice. You can either glide by, past, say, the beautiful ocean scenes and take snaps out the window – that's the easy thing to do – or you can go out of your way to move the car to the side of the road, to push that brake pedal, to get out, take off your shoes and socks, take a couple of steps on to the sand, feel what the sand feels like under your feet, walk to the ocean, and let the ocean lap at your ankles. Your life will be richer and more meaningful because you breathe in that experience, and because you've left your phone in the car.*[53]

Remember:

- Comparisons are naturally heightened in our modern lives.
- Social media creates unhealthy comparisons.
- Experiences are necessary for development – and this means getting off your phone!

Chapter 9
Take a capacity check

By the end of this chapter, you will:

- Understand capacity and that capacity is finite.
- Recognize when you're over-capacity and identify the impact of capacity on your ability to regulate your emotions.
- Know how to increase your capacity and stimulate dopamine, serotonin, endorphins and oxytocin.
- Be aware of the importance of sleep and have an understanding of simple techniques to ensure you are sleeping well.
- Have a plan for what to do if you go into freeze mode.

When we are over-capacity, it becomes difficult to regulate our emotions. We are more likely to overreact, and even small things that go wrong can have a big impact. When your capacity is stretched, it primes you for overthinking and makes it much, *much* more likely: it's like our thoughts are stickier, so they're easier to become entangled in. The mental exhaustion and the emotional toll of overthinking then takes up even more of our precious capacity, further reducing our ability to cope.

Capacity varies from person to person, but it is always finite. A simple way to think about capacity is to imagine it as a pan sitting on the stove. When life is straightforward, there is a small amount of water in the pan and, when the heat is on, the water can bubble away without a problem. As issues pile up in our lives, whether they are to do with work, our relationships, commitments or the standards we place on ourselves, the water level rises. How we're feeling physically and the emotions we're experiencing also take up space, so if we are tired, stressed or overwhelmed, there's more water in the pan.

As we work through things and deal with various issues, the water level goes down, but sometimes the pan gets so full that it starts to bubble over, and even small things can make it overflow. It's also important to look out for stacking – when multiple issues pile up. You might manage one issue successfully, but it becomes much harder when you look up to see three more ahead.

Understanding the nervous system

It's helpful to understand how the autonomic nervous system (ANS) functions and why it can become dysregulated. It has evolved to keep us alive and is an adaptive response to threat. When we experience stress, the sympathetic nervous system (part of the ANS) is activated, and when the threat passes, the parasympathetic nervous system (also part of the ANS) kicks back in. What follows is a simple explanation of polyvagal theory, which explains how the ANS, in particular the vagus nerve, influences our social behaviour, emotions and stress responses.

The ANS is regulated by the vagus nerve, which is thought to have the widest distribution of nerve fibres within the human body and connects the brain, heart and gut. The vagus nerve operates using neuroception[54] – meaning that it picks up information from the environment and evaluates it on a neurobiological level to determine whether a certain situation, person or place is safe or dangerous. This nerve carries information from the body to the brain and from the brain to the body. This process happens outside of our awareness; in a typical day, we read thousands of cues as we interact with the world and the people in it.

The vagus nerve feels out external situations and sends information to the brain in two ways:

- The ventral side responds to cues about safety in the environment and interactions. It supports feelings of physical safety and being emotionally connected to others.
- The dorsal side responds to cues about danger. It makes us feel less connected to others and puts us in a state of self-protection. If it senses extreme danger, we can shut down and feel frozen.

If the ANS concludes that a situation is safe, the vagus nerve tells the body to relax, engaging the parasympathetic nervous system to calm the body. In this mode, we feel connected to others, grounded and content. We feel present in what we are doing, secure and safe.

If we sense something in our environment that is dangerous, we shift to threat mode. We know this mode as 'fight or flight'. The vagus nerve sends a signal to the sympathetic nervous system, and this arousal system prepares the body to respond. All this happens automatically – the conscious thought comes later. In this state, we experience the world as threatening; it changes our reality and we think and behave differently. We become overly alert to any potential problems (fight), and we are more likely to avoid (flight).

If we become overwhelmed by threat, we can be pushed into freeze mode. In this state, we might look outwardly calm, but internally we have a sense of feeling trapped, out of body or disconnected from the world. We can feel numb, dizzy, dissociated, nauseated, hopeless or ashamed. We do not feel capable and have no sense of agency. We are likely to withdraw, sleeping more or finding other ways to escape how we are feeling.

It's crucial to remember that these responses are not voluntary – the nervous system puts us into these different states. The ANS doesn't run it by us first and check that we agree. When we understand that this is how we evolved, with threat mode helping us find our way to safety, we can begin to find compassion for ourselves. It takes time to build a new response in place of this automatic reaction.

Are you over-capacity?

To feel good, we need a healthy nervous system that is in equilibrium. When the ANS is functioning well, the parasympathetic and sympathetic nervous systems work together, and this helps us to manage our daily stressors and challenges. If your overthinking is on overdrive and your reactions seem out of proportion to what is going on, it's a signal that you're over-capacity. In this state, the nervous system becomes dysregulated and we are pushed into our threat zone – fight, flight, freeze or fawn mode (think back to our evolutionary history in Chapter Two). These modes are part of our evolution but it's problematic if we become stuck in these states.

Being over-capacity and in threat mode causes three problems:

1. It is more difficult to feel connected to other people.
2. We don't have the same access to higher-level thinking, organization and planning, so it's much harder to make good decisions.
3. It is harder to do the things that matter to us, to take in our surroundings or to find enjoyment in our day-to-day lives.

Even though we very much need the support of others, being over-capacity makes us more reactive and it becomes difficult to feel engaged or connected. When we're in threat mode, a rational conversation will not sort things out. We need to focus on bringing the body out of this activated state first, then on boosting our capacity.

Boost your capacity

Before we move on to the steps for curing overthinking in Part Three, I want to ensure you are in the best possible place to make changes. It's important to take care of the basics so you have a solid foundation in place before beginning this work. It's a bit like essential maintenance. You need to care for yourself and do the things that your brain needs to feel good.

Let's look first at the things you can do to increase your capacity and to stimulate dopamine, serotonin, endorphins and oxytocin. These are all essential components of good mental health. For starters, you need:

- **Connection:** See other people in person. You need physical touch, hugs and laughter. If you can't see family and friends, speak to them on the phone so you hear their voices.
- **Nutrition and hydration:** Eat well and drink plenty of water.
- **Nature:** Your body needs sunlight and time outdoors.
- **Movement:** Take some exercise, do some stretching, and try breathing exercises.
- **Mental, physical and sensory rest:** Get good sleep, unplug from screens and from your phone, take breaks from work, and ensure you have quiet and empty time away from bright artificial light and noise, so your mind can wander. Try mindfulness and meditation.
- **Goals:** Give yourself small goals to work towards every day.
- **To avoid problematic coping strategies:** These strategies may include excessive use of alcohol or drugs.

To put yourself in the best place to move forward, try to put as many of these ideas in place as you can. I'll be looking at all of them in more detail as we work through the steps.

Other factors

It is also worth considering whether there are any other contributing factors to your overthinking or your feelings of overwhelm. If you have any concerns, visit your doctor.

- **Thyroid imbalance:** An imbalance in your thyroid gland can cause anxiety or other mood changes as the thyroid hormones are important for regulating neurotransmitters such as serotonin, which can affect mood.

- **Hormonal imbalance:** This is a common cause of anxiety. For women, it's worth considering whether there are certain times in your cycle when you are more prone to overthinking. This can particularly affect women during perimenopause and menopause, when oestrogen and progesterone levels are low. Hormonal imbalances, such as testosterone levels, can also affect a man's mood and play a role in mental health.

- **Stress:** If you are under considerable stress, is there anything you can do to reduce this or gain support? Stress hormones such as adrenaline and cortisol can make overthinking more likely.

- **Autism spectrum condition (ASC) or attention deficit hyperactivity disorder (ADHD):** Anxiety and overthinking are a common experience for people who are neurodivergent. This can include excessive analysis of thoughts, events or situations. Repetitive thoughts such as replaying conversations or obsessing over small details are also common. Some people describe having multiple channels of thought at once. You might have difficulty making decisions, or a tendency to catastrophize or go to worst-case scenarios, or you may experience intrusive thoughts.

- **The pre- and post-natal period:** Motherhood triggers neurological change, and having a baby is a huge transition and adjustment. New parents are primed to be hyperalert to danger so they can physically respond to crying and anticipate their baby's needs.

- **Mental health problems:** Overthinking contributes to the onset, maintenance and recurrence of multiple mental health problems, including depression, anxiety disorders and eating disorders.

Reduce the number of choices you have to make each day

We are bombarded with information and flooded with decisions to take – what to wear, which emails, WhatsApp messages, notifications and comments to respond to – so it's little wonder we can end up with decision fatigue and regret. Many of the choices are small, but each one takes up energy, uses up our attention and requires more cognitive effort.

When you're busy, try to have some things set as a routine. Have specific days or times for what you do: getting up, working, laundry, house-cleaning, exercise and food-planning. Remove choice where you can, so that you have more energy left over for the important stuff. Steve Jobs famously used to wear the same outfit daily to reduce decision fatigue.

If you haven't managed to reduce your phone time yet (see page 135), this is another reason to turn off all your notifications and put your phone on silent. You can then choose when you want to look at it and reduce digital interruptions. I've made a rule with myself that I only check my emails on my computer, so that when I'm out, I'm not worrying about emails. In this way, you are making simple adjustments that will leave you more energy for tackling overthinking.

Sleep well

Sleep is another *big* player in overthinking. It is miserable when you are stuck overthinking at night. In the dark, when you've only got your thoughts to contend with, it can be so much harder to extract yourself from this type of thinking. Overthinking can stop you from falling asleep, or you might be so exhausted that you drop off, but then jolt awake in the night. Your brain moves into overdrive and your body reacts, so you are unable to switch off and go back to sleep.

Not sleeping gives you more time to overthink and is a multiplier of existing issues. Sleep deprivation makes *everything* harder. It leads to a greater risk for depression, irritability and anxiety. It causes problems with learning, focus, reacting and emotional regulation. It makes it harder to make decisions, solve problems and remember things. You're likely to make more mistakes, and it makes it harder to cope with change.

All these things then make you more likely to overthink – and make it harder to stop overthinking once you start. Added to which, when we're forming a new habit (stopping our overthinking), it takes effort and energy, so getting enough sleep will make this easier.

If you're busy all day, it can be easy to fall into the trap of believing it's helpful to run through things in your head at night, but overthinking at night-time is *never* useful. So, as you work through the steps, I need you to sign up to another rule: **No thinking in bed or at night-time. Apply the saying 'sleep on it'. It's always better to decide in the morning.**

Top ten tips for sleep

Each night is a new night and offers an opportunity to sleep better. It's useful to remember that sleep is a process that can't be forced: it happens automatically and should be allowed to unfold. If you ask a good sleeper how they sleep, chances are they just put their head on the pillow and drop off. However, if your sleep is causing you serious problems, it's important to see a doctor or a therapist to get help with it. Treatment is usually very effective.

Try these tips to improve your rest:

1. Keep a fixed bedtime and wake-up time. Sleep loves routine.
2. To set your body clock, get outside and into daylight as early as you can in the day.
3. Avoid alcohol and caffeine for 4–6 hours before bed.
4. Move your phone outside your bedroom, if you haven't already. Use an alarm clock to wake you up instead.
5. Do a brain-dump before bed: write down worries, ideas and things you need to do, so you get everything off your mind.
6. Reserve your bedroom for sleep and sex, so you have a strong association between sleep and your room. Do not work in your room.
7. Create a wind-down routine so you prepare for sleep. This is a signal to your brain and body to relax. Do not use your phone for an hour before bed.
8. Don't automatically judge being awake during the night as negative, as this will stress you out and make it harder to get to sleep.
9. If you've been awake during the night for more than 15 minutes, get up (I know this is hard, but it really works!) and go and do something boring until you feel sleepy again. This keeps the sleep–bedroom association strong. Knowing that short, consolidated sleep often feels more satisfying than longer, fragmented sleep should also help.
10. If you can't sleep, try to accept it (rather than worrying or becoming annoyed). You want your body to stay calm so you are in the best state to drop off. Try to be patient. Change takes time. Getting frustrated with yourself is only going to set you back.

If you're struggling to get to sleep, try these simple techniques:

- Repeat a random (non-emotive) word, like 'the' or 'one'. Doing this stops you thinking of other things.
- Give up on sleep. It might sound strange, but pretend you don't care about sleep – or even try to stay awake. The paradox with sleep is that focusing away from it helps you sleep better. You're not sleeping anyway, so try to take the pressure off and trick yourself into thinking that it doesn't matter. This is called paradoxical intention therapy.
- My current favourite technique is taking the letters of the first word you think of and then choosing new words that start with these letters. You can go for any random word, or have a theme, such as countries: if you thought of Spain, the other words could be Slovenia, Papua New Guinea, Australia, India, Namibia. Namibia then becomes the new word.

Plan ahead for freeze mode

Finally, before moving on to the steps towards the cure, we need to think back to the body's nervous system and consider what to do when we're over-capacity. I want you to think about what you'll do if you get stuck in freeze mode when you're feeling overwhelmed. It's too late to come up with an idea once you are in this mode, so it's important to have a plan in advance. Try out each of the strategies below to consider what might help. Then, I'm going to ask you to write down exactly what you will do, so you can look at the note if you get pushed into freeze.

Use your senses

Focusing on your five senses is a great way to ground yourself in the present moment:

Sight: Look around and say out loud to yourself what you can see. Then take it up a level and name five things of the same colour, then five things of the same shape. It's also good to look at something that reminds you of being loved, supported and safe. This could be an affirmation card, a letter or photograph, or anything you have been given that made you feel cared for.

Sound: Notice and name the sounds that you hear: the birds singing, traffic, a clock ticking. Alternatively, you could tune in to music, a podcast or an audiobook that fits your mood.

Touch: Find an object that feels nice to hold or fiddle with, or has a pleasing texture if you stroke it. Stones can be great, as they can fit in your pocket, or try a tension ball or fidget toy. Stroking your own arm or face can feel soothing.

Smell: Notice the smells around you, or carry a smell you like that makes you feel calm and relaxed, such as an essential oil.

Taste: Strong mints or a really sour sweetie can provide a helpful distraction that can bring you out of freeze mode.

Turn to a friend or family member

Feeling heard and understood can make a huge difference when you're in freeze mode. Phone or meet up with someone to disrupt the thoughts. You could talk about something completely different to take your mind off things, or you might find it useful to discuss how you're feeling. Saying the thoughts out loud can remove some of their power, putting them outside your head so they are no longer swilling around. This makes them more concrete and they feel more manageable. It also helps put you back in control of your thoughts (rather than your thoughts controlling you). When you say them out loud, it's a chance to process them and gain perspective.

Make sure you choose your confidant wisely. It needs to be someone who won't amplify how you're feeling or leave you feeling worse. When you open up about what's going on and allow the right person in, you have a chance to see that you're not alone and that other people feel like you.

Take yourself to a safe space

Imagining a safe space can be a good way to pull out of freeze. Practise visualizing a place where you feel calm, peaceful and safe. It might be somewhere you've been or a place you dream about going. Think about how the place will look; the textures, sounds and smells; and how it feels to be there. Think about whether you'll be there alone or if anyone is with you.

Remember that it's important to visualize your safe space when you feel good, so that you have the image fully formed in your mind. You won't be able to do this for the first time if you're in overwhelm. Practise going there each day and notice how you feel when you are there. It can then be a place to return to if you need it.

Think of what you love

When we are in freeze mode, we often don't feel safe. So think of someone who makes you feel safe and loved. As you bring them to mind, try to think of what they would say, how they would see this situation or what they would do. This could be a time when you use your compassionate image (see page 126), or you could look at a picture that brings these feelings of safety to mind.

– **Before you move on to the first step, write down what you'll do if you become overwhelmed and pushed into freeze mode.**

Well done, you've reached the end of Part Two. Your understanding of why we overthink and what's going on in your brain, combined with reducing the triggers to overthinking – switching self-criticism for self-compassion, avoiding comparison and boosting your capacity – is crucial to overcoming overthinking and will be essential as you work through the steps that follow. You are now in the perfect position to begin.

Remember:

- When you're over-capacity, it is more difficult to feel connected to other people.
- If you are over-capacity, you don't have the same access to higher-level thinking, organization and planning, and it's much harder to make good decisions. It makes it harder to do the things that matter to you, to take in your surroundings or find enjoyment in your day-to-day.
- To boost your capacity, sleep is important!
- You now have a set of techniques to boost your capacity that are ready for use if you go into freeze mode.

PART III

THE CURE

Chapter 10
Step one – notice

By the end of this chapter, you will:

- Notice what is in your spotlight of attention.
- Complete a thought audit and become aware of your overthinking hotspots.
- Externalize your thoughts to gain distance from them.
- Understand your thinking patterns and your triggers.
- Differentiate between productive and unproductive thinking, so you can determine when your thinking is helpful and when it's problematic.

This where the hard work begins. You are ready to embark on the steps and to train your brain to react differently. In the next chapters, you'll develop a greater awareness of your overthinking and gain a better understanding of yourself so you can choose your response and build new, healthier habits. You'll learn to focus on living more intentionally and making active choices about what you want from your life. You *can* stop your overthinking mind from running the show and give up overthinking for good.

The importance of noticing

The first step to overcoming overthinking is to notice what is in your spotlight of attention.

Freedom comes from increasing your awareness, so you begin to recognize your repetitive thoughts and see them for what they are – overthinking. The greater your awareness of this problem, the greater your chance of making changes and getting rid of overthinking for good.

This chapter will build your ability to recognize what you are letting into your field of awareness. You'll start to notice these negative thinking patterns in action and see when you are sliding down a well-worn negative path. You can then move on to Step Two, when you will make an intentional choice to disrupt your habitual overthinking response and choose what you do and *don't* want in your spotlight of attention by broadening your awareness. This will put you in the best position to challenge the thoughts in Step Three, which will allow you to step back from the thoughts and remember that this is your mind making up a story about how you're feeling. You can remind yourself that thoughts aren't facts, and that these stories are just one version of events and not the truth of what is going on. But for now, in Step One, I want you to simply notice the thoughts.

What's on your mind?

Set a timer for one minute. I want you to check in with yourself, to notice what's on your mind right now. Is your mind busy or calm? Is it wandering to other things or not thinking about much at all? Are you thinking about what you've been reading, or is your mind jumping around to what you need to do, an argument you had earlier in the day or something that happened to you? Are you thinking about doing this check-in or something completely different?

You've just noticed what's in your spotlight of attention and become aware of your thoughts and what your mind is doing. It really is that simple. This check-in increases your awareness, so that you can assess your thoughts rather than letting them run the show.

Do a thought audit

Now I want you to carry out a thought audit so you understand your overthinking patterns and triggers. To overcome overthinking, you must become aware of your overthinking habit and have a clear understanding of how it operates.

To do this, you need to really understand your overthinking hotspots. These are the physical feelings and emotions to which you are most sensitive. Top triggers tend to be stress, low mood, anxiety, anger and tiredness. The habit can also become tied to different things in your day. Recognizing your hotspots is the first step towards breaking the habit, regaining control and reducing the frequency and intrusiveness of these thoughts.

Think about all that you have learned so far and read back through the notes you have already made. Chapter Two should have given you a good awareness of how your overthinking operates. Identify as best you can all the things that trigger overthinking and your favoured topics. Maybe going back to a restaurant you visited with your ex stirs up memories. Certain songs might be a trigger, as they remind you of a particular time in your life. If you see your partner chatting with someone, it might trigger jealous overthinking. Perhaps a key overthinking time is social situations – or you might associate overthinking with evenings and time awake in bed.

I'd also like you to consider whether overthinking is serving a particular function for you – is there any part of you that believes overthinking is helpful? If so, what are you using overthinking to try to do? Is it a way to manage feeling angry? When you're nervous, does it feel like a way to prepare? If you can see what you're hoping to gain from overthinking, it will be helpful when we get to Step Four, as we can think about a more helpful response to manage this issue. But, if you're not sure, don't worry. Keep this question in mind as you work through the next steps, so you can consider if there's anything else going on.

To do a full thought audit, note down the answers to these questions:

- **What** are your:

  Emotional and physical discomfort triggers?

  Favourite overthinking topics?

  Thinking traps?

- **Where** are you? Are there specific places that overthinking tends to happen, such as when you're working, at home, alone, in the car, brushing your teeth, cleaning or in bed?

- **When** does it happen? For example, do you overthink when you wake up, in the evening, on your commute or when you're trying new things?

- **Who** are you with? Is overthinking triggered when you're alone or when you're with certain people, such as work colleagues, your parents or friends?

- **Does it serve a function?** Is there anything you still believe that overthinking is helpful for?
- **Is there anything else** that you've noticed about your overthinking?

Keep a diary

Over the next few days, keep a diary to really see your overthinking in action. Any time you start overthinking, write it down. Look back at Chapter Four, if you need some help to identify when it's overthinking. I also want you to notice the function and consequences of overthinking. Use the table on pages 160–61 to keep a note.

When your diary is complete, take a good look at it, and also review your notes from Chapter Two. Give yourself a pat on the back. Noticing overthinking and writing things down has increased your awareness and let you see what is in your spotlight of attention.

Gain some distance

To really see your overthinking in action, I want you to externalize the thoughts by saying them out loud. I know this sounds a bit strange, but you need to see that this is not your voice, but the voice of overthinking, and that overthinking does *not* have your best interests in mind.

This exercise helps you become aware of what's going on in your head and the well-worn paths your brain can take you down. It lets you see that overthinking is usually just the same thought on repeat. This gives you some distance from your thoughts. It teaches you to notice how you feel in your body, and to view thoughts and feelings as passing mental events, so you see that your thoughts are just thoughts and your feelings are just feelings, without getting caught up in them.

To help you, I want you to give a name to your most common overthinking topics so you can step back from them. I've worked with people who have used names like 'the grinch' thoughts, the 'why does no one appreciate me?' thoughts, the 'everyone thinks I'm boring' thoughts, and the classic 'why do these things always happen to me?' thoughts. See if you can spot the topic of Rae's overthinking in the following example, then give it a name.

Rae wanted to see more of her friends and have a better work–life balance, but when she was busy she always ended up cancelling her plans. She'd tell me: 'I'm too tired', 'I've been too busy', 'I need a quiet night in front of the TV'. Rae became more mindful of these thoughts and noticed that, when she was busy, her overthinking talked her out of doing any of the fun bits of life or the things that were important to her life outside work.

When she recognized these thoughts, it allowed her to question them and ask herself if this was what she really wanted: 'I might be tired, but these fun things fill me up and make me feel good. Isn't the whole point of working hard to be able to do the fun bits, like go out for dinner and see friends? These are the things that matter to me and will help me to feel better.' It also let her remember that, when she did meet up with friends, she felt energized and pleased that she'd gone. However, spending every night in front of the TV just allowed life to pass in a blur.

We named Rae's thoughts her 'I'm too tired to do anything fun' thoughts. We used this to externalize them and create distance from them (see the diagram on page 163). Every time she noticed the thoughts, she'd say to herself, 'Here come my "I'm too tired to do anything fun" thoughts again.' Every time they came up, she'd call them out. Seeing these thoughts in action – and their consequences – made a huge difference to Rae.

NOTICE	MONDAY	TUESDAY	WEDNESDAY
Time of day			
Mood (anxiety, worry, fear, low or depressed mood, stress, anger, frustration, irritability, shame, guilt, resentment)			
How does your body feel? (tired, rundown, increased heart rate, nervous stomach, heavy)			
Where are you?			
Who are you with?			
What happened?			
Thoughts and topics			
Which thinking trap is this? (The Dweller, The Interrogator, The Catastrophizer, The Wobbler, The Over-Analyser, The Victim or The Overwhelmed)			
What's the function?			
What's the consequence of overthinking?			

THURSDAY	FRIDAY	SATURDAY	SUNDAY
THURSDAY	FRIDAY	SATURDAY	SUNDAY

It was also helpful to see that these thoughts were the opposite of what she wanted. Rae used the idea of 'opposite action' to combat this – when her mind said 'No' she needed to do the opposite. Stay in on the sofa? What she really needed to do was take opposite action: stick to the original plan and go out. Instead of listening to and believing the stories her mind was telling her, she could remember these were just stories, not facts. It meant she could make an informed choice, rather than listening to her automatic, habitual thoughts.

Externalizing the thoughts can help you notice them, and then you can begin questioning them:

- How am I feeling? If my mood is negative, this is not the time to be thinking about this.
- Is my mood narrowing my spotlight of attention? What is this doing to my awareness?
- Am I in my thoughts or aware of them as an observer?
- Is this something real or imagined? Is it within my control?
- Have I remembered that thoughts and feelings are not facts?

Now, instead of falling down the doom spiral (see page 26) into anxiety, resentment, low mood or stress, you can acknowledge your thoughts and emotions without judgement. They don't define who you are.

Can you change any of your triggers or cues?

Next, I'd like you to think about your cues and triggers to overthinking. Is there anything you can do to change some of these? For example, if you overthink when you wake up, instead of hitting snooze, try doing something different, like making yourself a cup of tea or doing something

Creating distance from your thoughts

I am having the thought that I'm too tired

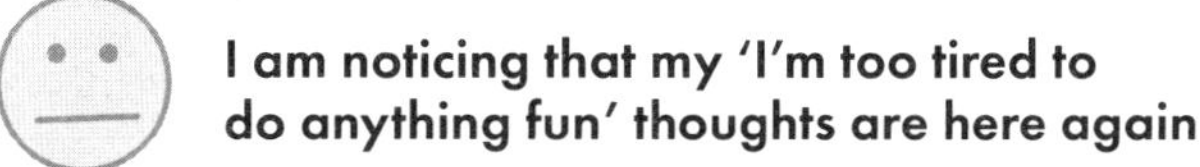

I am noticing that my 'I'm too tired to do anything fun' thoughts are here again

kind for yourself. If certain people trigger overthinking, can you spend less time with them? If you've got into the habit of overthinking at night, can you use the sleep tips from Chapter Nine (see page 147) to make a change?

When Sam (see page 39) completed his diary, he noticed that one of the key places overthinking was triggered was when he was working from home. He found it really hard to understand what his colleagues were thinking when they sent emails or were on video calls. He noticed that this would trigger him to overthink and dissect all his interactions. This could push him on to his negative brain pathways, so he would end up thinking about everything that was wrong. Sam noticed it was particularly difficult to disengage from overthinking if he had several days working from home in a row.

To overcome this, Sam decided to go into work. He noticed that, when he was in the office, he didn't get caught up in so many doom spirals because he was around other people and had a better read on what they were thinking and feeling. He also started to make notes after a day in the office so he could hold on to how he felt when he was around others. Then, on the days he was working from home, he could use this evidence to challenge his overthinking: 'I'm worrying about what Anamaya thinks, but when I saw her she said to me how pleased she was with how I'm doing and I could tell it was genuine.'

Differentiate between productive and unproductive thinking

Finally, I want you to look back at your diary and try to differentiate between whether your thinking is productive or unproductive. It's not that I want you to stop *thinking* altogether, because we know that overthinking is really an attempt to make sense of, understand or resolve something difficult. You just need to learn to discriminate between when your thinking is helpful and when it is unhelpful.

Productive thinking is helpful. It's a way to reflect on something specific that's happened (think back to the table on pages 160–61). Helpful thinking is concrete, detailed and moves you on to problem-solving and a better understanding of what's happening. It lets you take ownership of the situation and choose how you wish to respond. It is the opposite of avoidance, as it lets you concentrate on what you can do. It leads you to taking action, which puts you back in control and moves you forward.

Unproductive thinking is unhelpful. This is overthinking: it moves you to an abstract, general feeling about yourself or your life. It frequently starts with *why?* or *what if?* questions. These generalizations cause your mood to drop, increase distress, make you feel less certain and keep you stuck in the doom spiral with little chance of getting out. Overthinking or unproductive thinking doesn't work. It's like using diesel in a petrol engine; everything grinds to a halt.

I want you to think about the times when you are more likely to do productive thinking. When and where does this type of thinking take place – and when and where doesn't it? Most people tend to think more productively when they're dealing with a specific issue or in a particular zone. We want to find ways for you to use this helpful thinking more often. Consider these questions:

- When are you naturally in a more productive
  thinking mode?
- What are you doing?
- Who are you with?

Change unproductive to productive

Next time you notice yourself overthinking, try to change unproductive thinking to productive thinking. You can do this by expressing the feeling or concern, but aiming to move to problem-solving or letting go. Taking this action puts you back in control of the situation and helps you to regain a sense of control in your life. Try these steps:

- Express the feeling or concern.
- Bring it back to today.
- Shift from why to how. Try asking yourself: How did this happen? How can I do something to help myself?
- Keep your thinking concrete. Review what happened and think about the specifics of the situation.
- Use problem-solving. Ask yourself: What can I do about my situation? Note down anything and everything you can think of. This could include addressing any practical problems that need to be solved; making sure you are looking after yourself; making a plan for how to move forward; or setting yourself future goals and working towards them. Also consider whether there is anything you've been putting off (remember opposite action; see page 162).
- Can you let this go? Much of overthinking is not worth your time and energy. Try not to let the little things get you down.

Moving forward

Don't worry if you weren't able to keep your thinking concrete. Thinking abstractly is a difficult habit to break. If your thinking is stuck on unproductive and doesn't want to change, it's time to move on to Step Two.

You are now up to speed with how overthinking operates in your life, and are an expert at recognizing the familiar pathways your mind will try to lead you down. When you see this thinking as separate from you, you can gain distance from the thoughts. Now you are aware of these habitual patterns, you can see what is in your spotlight of attention and give yourself a choice. This lets you decide what to do next and puts you in the perfect position for Step Two.

Step One: Checklist

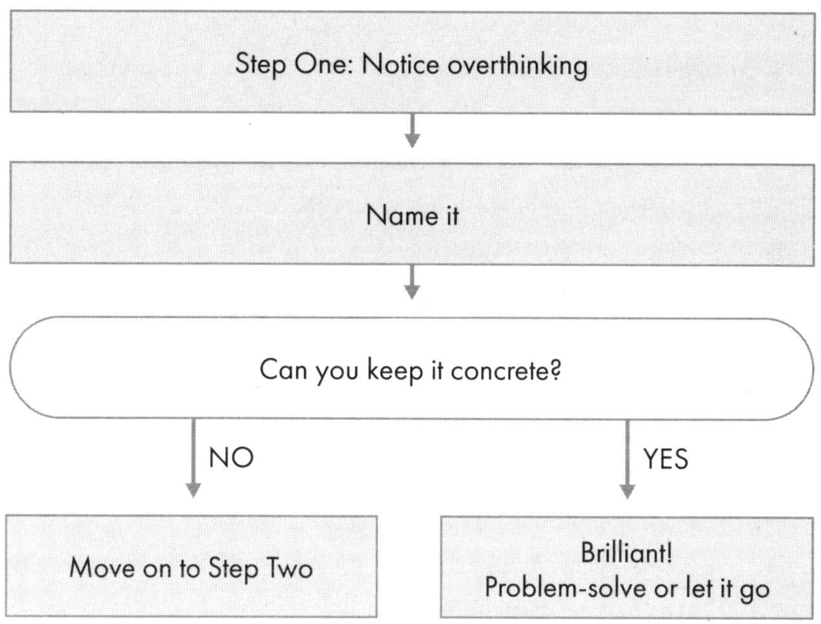

Chapter 11
Step two – choose what you let into your spotlight

By the end of this chapter, you will:

- See that overthinking is under your control.
- Be able to make the choice to stop overthinking.
- Be able to broaden your spotlight of attention and choose what you let into your awareness, using the following techniques:
    1. Mindfulness: Strengthening your attention to the things that matter by using purposeful attention to the present moment, so you get out of your head and back into the world.
    2. Doing something else: Directing your attention to pleasant or neutral activities rather than your negative emotions.
    3. Using the mind–body link: Changing how your body feels to calm your mind.
- Experiment with postponing overthinking.
- Create a list of your favourite tried-and-tested strategies to use when overthinking strikes.

Imagine you are at a train station. You wouldn't jump on the first train you saw and let it carry you off without any idea of where you were going. You would observe the trains, check the route, and choose where you wanted to go. It's the same with your mind. When you automatically react and mindlessly engage with overthinking, it's like stepping on a train without any idea where it's going. In this step, I want you to make a conscious decision not to step on the overthinking train, and to choose instead where you want to go.

The key to this process is learning to control your response to the ups and downs of life. You can't change what happens to you, but you can learn more adaptive ways to cope and a healthier response to distress. Step Two lets you choose what is in your spotlight of attention and expand your awareness, allowing the beam to become unstuck.

When things get difficult, I want you to make an intentional choice *not* to overthink, and to instead use the positive coping strategies in this chapter to broaden your spotlight of attention. You will also put into action the rule from Chapter Six: do not think about important things when your mood is negative.

In this step, you will choose where you focus your time and attention, and decide what you want and *don't* want to let into your awareness. Move yourself from a narrow focus on a problem back to the wider picture of your life. This prevents your thoughts spiralling out of control and lets you step out of the unhappiness and misery these thoughts cause. Crucially, when you choose not to overthink and intentionally choose a new, healthier response, you are creating new pathways in your brain and replacing the old habitual thinking.

Make sure you bring some compassion to this step. Changing your response is possible, but it will be hard to begin with. You could say to yourself: 'When I feel like this, it's really hard to think differently, but it's just my brain stuck on a negative track – and I can change this.

Overthinking never helps, so I can shift my attention and choose what I focus on.'

This step is particularly helpful if your thinking traps are *The Interrogator*, *The Wobbler* or *The Overwhelmed* (see pages 78, 80 or 85). The ideas in this chapter may also be useful additions to your bedtime wind-down routine or techniques to try if you can't sleep.

Overthinking *is* under your control

Think of any times when you have managed to disrupt overthinking. It's easy to fall into the trap of believing that we can't control our thinking, but this just isn't true. What we choose to shine our spotlight of attention on becomes our focus, but you can move that focus and choose not to overthink.

- Can you think of a time when you've been exposed to your overthinking triggers, but you've acted differently?
- Are there times when you haven't engaged with overthinking, or when you've been able to naturally disrupt the thinking?
- What was happening or what did you do to escape your overthinking? Were you too busy to overthink, or were you interrupted or distracted from overthinking? Perhaps you had to go to work, which took your mind off the thoughts? Or maybe someone phoned you when you were in the middle of a doom spiral and you were snapped out of it? It can also be helpful to reflect that overthinking does stop eventually.

– Write a list of the times when you have managed to avoid or stop overthinking. Carry this knowledge with you. You really can stop overthinking, and you have done it before. Channel this ability as we move into Step Two.

Make the choice to stop

The first technique for stopping overthinking is simply to tell your brain to stop when you notice it happening. Tell yourself that you can come back to the topic when your mood has improved. This technique works well to break the thought loop when you're experiencing low-level thoughts. For example, this technique might work if you're having second thoughts about a decision you were previously happy with. You know you want to do it, but *The Wobbler* thinking trap is making you feel anxious about it. When you notice yourself overthinking, try saying to yourself, 'STOP!' Or, if your thinking is more image-based, you could imagine a 'Stop' or 'No entry' sign. You don't need to think about the decision more; it's better to stop thinking about it altogether and to just go with the original plan.

Sadiq struggled with *The Victim* thinking trap and would often get stuck in angry thoughts. He described using this 'Stop' technique when he was out for a walk:

> *A driver wound down his window and shouted abuse at me. I found myself replaying it and feeling really annoyed. It felt so unfair, because I hadn't done anything wrong, and it made me feel vulnerable and unsafe. I found myself rehearsing what I could have done or said. I could feel my body reacting to the thoughts, and at this point I noticed what was happening and made a choice not to be carried away by the thoughts. It was a beautiful day, I was off work and I didn't want to carry this man around with me and further ruin my day. By noticing the thoughts and disrupting them, I could choose to return to enjoying my walk.*

Come up with something you can say to yourself to help you consciously choose to disrupt your thought pattern and shift your attention. Here are some examples:

- No, I don't do that anymore.
- This overthinking is only going to make me feel worse.
- I don't need to be thinking about this.
- Thanks, brain, for trying to be helpful, but I don't want to look at this stuff.
- This isn't helping me right now, so I'll think about this when I'm feeling better.
- It's in the past, what's happened is over and there's nothing I can do to change it.
- I'm stepping out of this.
- I don't want to think about this.
- I'm not getting into this now.

Sometimes, the thinking might not even really belong to you: it might be something that was said to you growing up or that your parents believed. The ideas you grew up with are best thought of as family scripts – and these can influence your reality. Even though you now think differently, you might revert to those old beliefs in stressful moments. When you see the thoughts in action, you can free yourself from these old patterns. Try saying to yourself, 'This thought doesn't belong to me.'

If you have a pressing problem, it is important to look at it, but not when you're feeling at your worst. When your mood is higher, come back to it and ask yourself: 'Does this still feel like a problem that needs my attention?' In my experience, nine times out of ten, the problem is no longer an issue. If it is, move to concrete thinking and take action.

Although effective, this 'Stop' technique won't work for more chronic forms of overthinking. It's a bit like gatecrashers at a party: you can try politely asking them to leave, but if that doesn't work, you need to call the police to forcibly remove them. If you're more entrenched in the thoughts, you'll need to move on to the next strategies and actively push the thoughts out of your spotlight by broadening your awareness and boosting your mood.

Intrusive thoughts

Watch out for intrusive thoughts, urges and images. These are unwanted, often disturbing thoughts, images or impulses that pop into your mind unexpectedly and can feel difficult to control. If you're struggling, there's more information on how to tackle these types of thoughts on page 299. It's also worth seeing your doctor for further help and support.

Broaden your spotlight of attention

As we explored earlier, when you broaden your spotlight of attention, it lets you expand your awareness and consider the full picture of what is going on, which helps you to become more balanced in your views. It also allows you to build on Step One (noticing and creating distance from your thoughts), letting you observe your thoughts and feelings with curiosity and bring the world back in.

When life feels out of control, it can be good to focus on a simple activity that is under your control and straightforward, especially one where you can see progress and improvement. The next techniques push you to physically or mentally move on to such activities, broadening your spotlight of attention, so it's much harder to engage with the thoughts.

You can broaden your spotlight of attention in three ways:

1. Mindfulness

Mindfulness is a practice of awareness that lets you choose what you allow into your spotlight of attention. Being mindful means learning to become an observer of your thoughts. It teaches you to be:

- **Curious** about your thoughts, so you see them rather than taking them as the truth.
- **Non-judgemental**, so you learn to accept yourself. There is no right or wrong, when it comes to your thoughts and feelings or to being mindful.
- **Accepting** of your mind's natural tendency to wander. Each time it wanders, you can notice and bring it back to the present moment.

Mindfulness goes hand in hand with self-compassion and is proven to help with overthinking.[55] It reminds us that we can't think our way into a better future, or think ourselves into changing the past: the only moment we have is now. Instead of being sucked into the rabbit warren of your mind's version of events, it lets you pull the beam wider and become focused on the present, so you can tune back in to your life. This lets you turn your attention away from worrying thoughts and rumination, and gets you out of your head.

Practising mindfulness brings with it a whole host of other benefits, including increased happiness, fulfilment and wellbeing, and improved memory, creativity and mental and physical stamina. People who practise mindfulness regularly report feeling less stressed, depressed, anxious, exhausted and irritable.[56,57]

Pay attention

One mindfulness technique is to simply pay attention to your everyday tasks. This provides a brilliant opportunity to broaden your spotlight of attention, without having to add anything extra into your day. To practise this technique, I want you to think of your attention as a muscle – it's something you can strengthen with practice.

It's unlikely that you'll be fully focused on the task and the present for the duration. It's normal to come back to your negative thoughts, but just gently observe these and then refocus your attention back to the present moment. You are not trying to empty your mind or stop it from wandering; you are simply trying to notice what it does without judgement and bring it back to what you're doing.

Think of yourself as an observer. The aim is to notice common patterns and to be curious. When your mind wanders and you pull it back to the present, you get a chance to see that you can disrupt overthinking and choose your response. Each time you do this, you are overriding your overthinking and breaking down those pathways in your brain.

Here are some tips to help with this mindfulness technique:

- Simply do one thing at a time and focus on what you are doing, whether it's brushing your teeth, cooking, eating, concentrating on what someone is saying, making a cup of tea or listening to the words of a song.
- You can focus on all your senses – touch, sight, hearing, smell and taste – as you accomplish your task. Your mind may wander, but each time you bring it back to what you're doing, you are learning to sustain and strengthen your attention.
- Each time you try this technique, notice how you can change the spotlight of your attention, choose what you let in, and strengthen a different response as you shift your awareness.

A natural reset

Getting outdoors for a walk is a brilliantly simple mindfulness technique. Think of it as your fail-safe strategy for when it all becomes too much and the compassionate voice can't break through. Get into the habit of going for a mindful walk every day. It's a brilliant way to ground you to the present moment, and nature has a measurable effect on our mental health,[58,59] reducing anxiety and depression. Just five minutes of nature exposure can begin to significantly reduce our stress levels and speed up our stress recovery response. It can also improve our sense of wellbeing, and it's good for our physical health and brain functioning, too.

You probably won't want to go for a walk, because it might feel close to impossible to rip your brain away from your thinking, but you can. Make this non-negotiable. It works!

Incorporate your senses as you walk:

- **Sight**: Pay attention to your surroundings: the people, traffic, buildings, plants, animals, sky. What colours and shading can you see?
- **Touch**: Notice the different textures around you. Feel the ground beneath your feet, the sun on your skin, the wind in your hair.
- **Sound**: What can you hear nearby? Which sounds can you hear further away?
- **Smell**: Breathe in the fresh air. Which smells are pleasant? Which are not?

If it helps, count your steps, or say in your mind the different things you see, hear, smell and feel. The rhythmic motion of walking also brings bilateral stimulation (something we'll be looking at later in this chapter).

On those occasions when I'm having a difficult day, getting outdoors can make such a difference – my mantra is 'If in doubt, get out'. Green spaces and blue spaces are particularly good. For me, a walk next to the sea never fails to put things in perspective.

– Before you move on to the next strategy, take a moment to think about how you can live a little more mindfully every day as part of an ongoing practice of broadening your awareness. Whether you're walking your kids to school, sitting on the bus, listening to music or cooking, every time you tune in to what you're doing, you're gaining greater control of your overthinking and learning to disrupt and shift your spotlight of attention.

2. Doing something else

If you're struggling with overthinking, one of the simplest ways to disrupt it is to choose to do something else. It's very difficult to overthink and do something at the same time. When you stop focusing on your negative thoughts and emotions, you stop the doom spiral in its tracks.

Purposely directing your attention to pleasant or neutral activities gives you a temporary shift, so you can pause overthinking and get back in control. This has the added benefit of boosting your mood, shifting you out of your negative brain network and on to a positive track. When your mood is higher, it makes everything easier by increasing capacity, opening you up to new possibilities, ideas and other people, and giving you access to higher states of thinking, such as problem-solving.

You may remember the experiment in Chapter One (see page 24): when participants experiencing low mood, were distracted from how they were feeling for eight minutes, it was effective at lifting their mood and breaking the overthinking cycle. The distraction not only gave them short-term relief from overthinking and negative moods, it also broke the cycle by improving their ability to overcome their problems. In contrast, those who were asked to focus on their emotions and how their lives were going (the overthinking group) felt worse.

When your brain is on a negative track, do anything you enjoy or that distracts you for at least eight minutes. When you're overthinking, it's like carving a deeper and deeper channel as you go over an issue. It can feel impossible to stop and pull yourself out, but remind yourself it will only take eight minutes and will move you to a far better view of what is happening – and in the long run, it will save you hours! Have a think about what activity might work best for you. Set up this activity in advance so it's easy to do the next time you notice yourself overthinking. If you've planned it in advance, you will be much more likely to do it.

Here are a few ideas to get you started, but you could also brainstorm a list of activities to try:

- Focus on a hobby.
- Spend time with someone or something you love.
- Do brain puzzles, such as *Wordle* or sudoku.
- Phone a friend or family member.
- Listen to an engaging podcast or audiobook.
- Play a board game or cards, or work on a jigsaw.
- Put on your favourite songs and sing along.
- Draw or colour.
- Play a musical instrument.

Be careful of the type of 8-minute distraction you use. Problematic coping strategies, such as binge-eating, substance or alcohol misuse, or getting sucked into your phone, might temporarily distract you, but they will increase self-criticism, sap motivation and steal hope. These strategies will make it harder for you to make long-term change or to see yourself differently.

3. Using the mind–body link

Stress is a normal part of life, and in the right amounts it helps us grow and adapt, but as you've seen, overthinking can push us into threat mode (fight, flight, freeze, fawn). When we are stuck in our heads, it's easy to lose touch with how we're feeling physically, creating a disconnect between the body and mind.

It's important to rebuild the connection between the body and mind, becoming aware of how distress resides in the body. This offers a foothold into helping you regulate your emotions. When your body feels safe and calm, you'll feel safe and calm – and this is a brilliant way to improve your mood.

Changing how your body feels is a simple way to calm your nervous system and step back from ruminative, anxious or angry thinking. It gives you more capacity, increases energy, allows you to feel connected to others and, importantly, shifts you out of a negative mood.

The following strategies will teach you to use the bidirectional link between your body and mind to bring your body out of the threat zone. This engages the parasympathetic nervous system (see page 140) to process your emotional pain, calm your body and shift your mood. These strategies are proven to make a difference, and any time you give to them, even if it is just a minute or two to start with, will make a huge difference. Even if you just change your facial expression, it can change how you feel.

Looking after your body needs to be non-negotiable. It takes daily effort, but it is so worth it. Here are some benefits:

- When your body feels calmer, it will calm your mind and stop you from feeling stuck.
- A healthier body has advantages, from improving mood to managing stress.

- You will build a better relationship with your body and become less fearful of physical discomfort.
- Exercise offers a physical way to discharge feelings and can bring some normality back into your life.
- Exercise can move you out of the threat zone, helping you feel more connected to those who might be able to offer support.

Tense and relax

Tense and relax exercises have been proven to reduce stress, anxiety and tension, while also improving your sleep. To start with, try progressive muscle relaxation, which immediately reduces tension: find a quiet place to sit or lie down, then systematically tense and then relax each muscle group in your body, starting with your feet and working all the way up until you reach your head. Really notice how your muscles feel as you move from clenching them tight to releasing.

Take a deep breath

Breathing exercises help your mind focus on something other than rumination or worry, taking the power away from those thoughts. Focusing on your breath is also a great way to be mindful, as it anchors you to the present moment, grounding you in the here and now.

Breathing offers a direct link to the parasympathetic and sympathetic nervous systems. In fight-or-flight mode, our heart rate increases, our breathing gets shorter and shifts into the chest, and our muscles tense. Reversing this reaction with a slow-breathing technique shifts us out of the stress response, activating the parasympathetic nervous system and bringing us back to calm and safety. Breathing exercises are proven to decrease stress, increase optimism, improve sleep, reduce pain, decrease anxiety, lessen impulsivity and strengthen immunity.[60]

Next time you're overthinking, try mindfulness of the breath:

- For the next 2 minutes, I want you to focus your attention on your breath as it enters and leaves your body, noticing any sensations associated with it.
- If your mind wanders, don't worry. The simple act of registering that the mind has wandered, noticing where it has gone and returning to the breath, helps you to become more mindful. Seeing thoughts as thoughts helps you step back from them and avoid the negative spiral.
- If it helps, you can say to yourself: 'Breathing in, I know that I am breathing in . . . breathing out, I know that I am breathing out.'

Alternatively, you can substitute this with counting your breath:

- As you breathe in, count 'one' in your mind, and as you breathe out, count 'one'.
- Breathe in and count 'two'. Breathe out and count 'two'.
- Continue through to 'ten', and then return to 'one' again.
- If you lose count, just return to 'one' and start again.

Create bilateral stimulation

Research suggests that bilateral stimulation (alternating sensory stimulation to the right and left sides of the body) can shift us out of fight-or-flight mode.[61] The practice increases communication between the left and right hemispheres of the brain. There are numerous benefits, including anxiety management, increased happiness and self-esteem, higher levels of creativity and enhanced performance.

A great place to start with bilateral stimulation is the butterfly hug (follow the diagram overleaf). It's a calming and grounding exercise for

Butterfly tapping

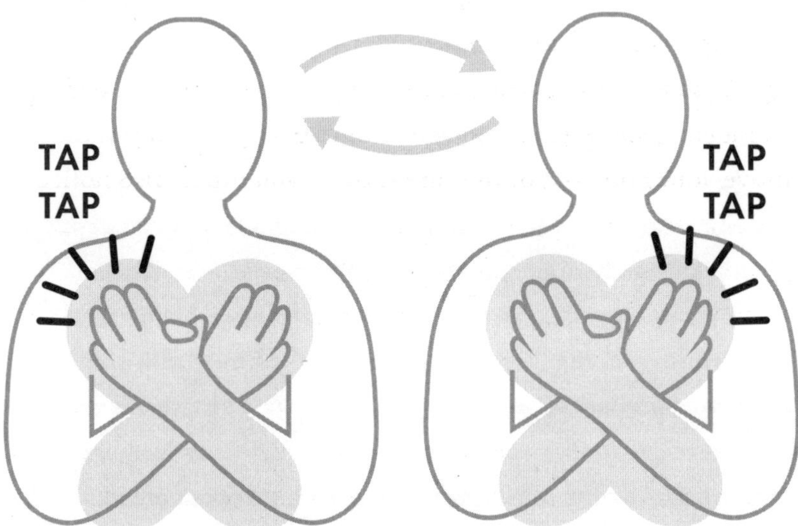

when you're feeling anxious, stressed or stuck in your thoughts, and it only takes a couple of minutes to do:

- Cross your arms over your chest, placing your fingertips on your collarbones or shoulders.
- Hook your thumbs around each other to resemble a butterfly's body, with your thumbs below your neck in the middle of your chest. Spread your hands out to either side like butterfly wings.
- Alternate tapping each hand on your chest, left then right, slowly and rhythmically.
- Breathe deeply while you're tapping.

Try physical exercise

Exercise is one of my personal favourites. It's a brilliant way to disrupt your thinking, taking you out of your current situation so you can return with a fresh perspective. There is a huge literature of research on just how good exercise is for you.[62-5] It's brilliant for stopping overthinking, and all its good effects are generally felt only 15 minutes after starting.

Exercise can be a good distraction and a way to let your thoughts tick over without actively looking at things. It's a brilliant outlet for the physical sensations that can accompany overthinking. It increases confidence, self-esteem and your ability to cope. However, when you move your body out of the threat zone, you might also notice that you feel emotional, as exercise unlocks a part of you that you can't get to through thinking alone. You may find yourself swimming off sadness, running off anger, or getting zen with yoga. The rhythmic pace of exercises like walking, running, cycling and swimming also offers bilateral stimulation. In addition, when you really exert yourself, you breathe more deeply, activating the parasympathetic nervous system.

Exercise also kickstarts a complex chemical and biological process that causes immediate and long-lasting changes in the brain and makes it easier for the brain to grow new neural connections.[66] This is great news for building new habits and stopping the old automatic overthinking.

Exercise can also help you to become more resilient:

- It reframes strong bodily sensations and discomfort so you feel them without fear. A rapid heartbeat and breathlessness from exertion can be something to feel proud of, and this lets you see that being in these states can't hurt or damage you.

- Winning the mental battle to exercise and reaching your goals or coming back from injury teaches you to overcome difficulty in smaller ways, building mental strength. This translates to other areas of your life, as when you push your limits, you see what you are capable of.

- Any movement that gets us out of breath mimics the stress response, which increases our stress tolerance. We'll be experimenting with this further in Step Four.

- When you contract your muscles, they secrete proteins into your blood that make you more resilient, reduce stress and protect against depression.[67]

We all respond to exercise differently, so it's important to find what's right for you. You will rarely feel like doing it beforehand, so choose something that you really enjoy. The more you love it, the easier it will be to convince yourself to do it. Brainstorm a list of activities you want to try, then find out what works for you. This could be anything that gets your body moving, from walking, dancing or running to ice-skating or yoga.

When I don't feel like exercising, instead of debating whether to do it or not, I just tell myself to go. I know I can turn around and come back if I want to. I don't think there's ever been a time I've regretted it.

Like everything, you can have too much of a good thing. Be careful of using exercise to always escape your mood (so much so that you stop tolerating negative moods, or avoid questioning why you feel the way you do), or overexercising, which can leave you feeling stressed and anxious. Exercise is something to enhance your life, not a pass or fail. Try to build an exercise routine without making it so strict that it adds to your stress.

Experiment with postponing overthinking

To test out postponing overthinking and prove this technique works, I want you to do an experiment. Turn down the volume on overthinking on one day, then turn up the volume on overthinking the next day. On the delay days, when your overthinking volume is turned down, I want you to attempt to avoid overthinking entirely (or only do it minimally) for the whole day, using the strategies suggested so far in this chapter.

On the overthinking days, I want you to *increase* your overthinking and allow yourself to excessively overthink all day.

Before you start the experiment, make a prediction about what you think will happen on the days you overthink, and on the days when you delay. If you still think overthinking is helpful (I really hope you don't!), then you should be predicting that on the days you're allowed to overthink, you'll be better at solving problems, feel more motivated and have better outcomes. This experiment is also a good test of magical thinking – if you believe overthinking prevents things from going wrong, then bad things shouldn't happen on the overthinking days.

Complete the worksheet below in as much detail as you can. Make sure you do it as you go, as your memory of how you felt will be most accurate on the day.

	Did anything good happen?	Did anything bad happen?	Did you cope during the day?	Did you solve the problems that arose?	Did you get things done?	How did you feel?
Day 1 – postpone						
Day 2 – overthink						
Day 3 – postpone						
Day 4 – overthink						
Day 5 – postpone						
Day 6 – overthink						
Day 7 – postpone						

At the end of the week, compare what you predicted would happen with what actually happened. Typically, when I do this in my clinic, people are surprised at the results. They find they feel worse on the days they are overthinking. They experience more benefits on the days they don't overthink, and as a result feel much better. Most people find their concentration improves, they are more productive, their mood is higher and they have a much better day when they're *not* overthinking.

– Now you've tried out all the techniques in this chapter, put together a plan that you can look at when overthinking strikes. Next time you feel overthinking coming on, you can action the plan without having to think through what to do.

Moving forward

Well done on saying no to overthinking, broadening your spotlight of attention and boosting your mood. You are now well practised at choosing your response and seeing the benefits of not overthinking. Every time you make an intentional choice to redirect, you are changing the association and breaking the overthinking habit. This creates new neural pathways in your brain and, in time, it becomes easier to take the new paths over the old ones.

If the thoughts are still on your mind, you (and your brain) are now in the best position to move on to Step Three. When your mood is more positive, it puts you on the right brain network to challenge your thoughts, and it will be easier to see more than one perspective. It's time for the next step.

Step Two: Checklist

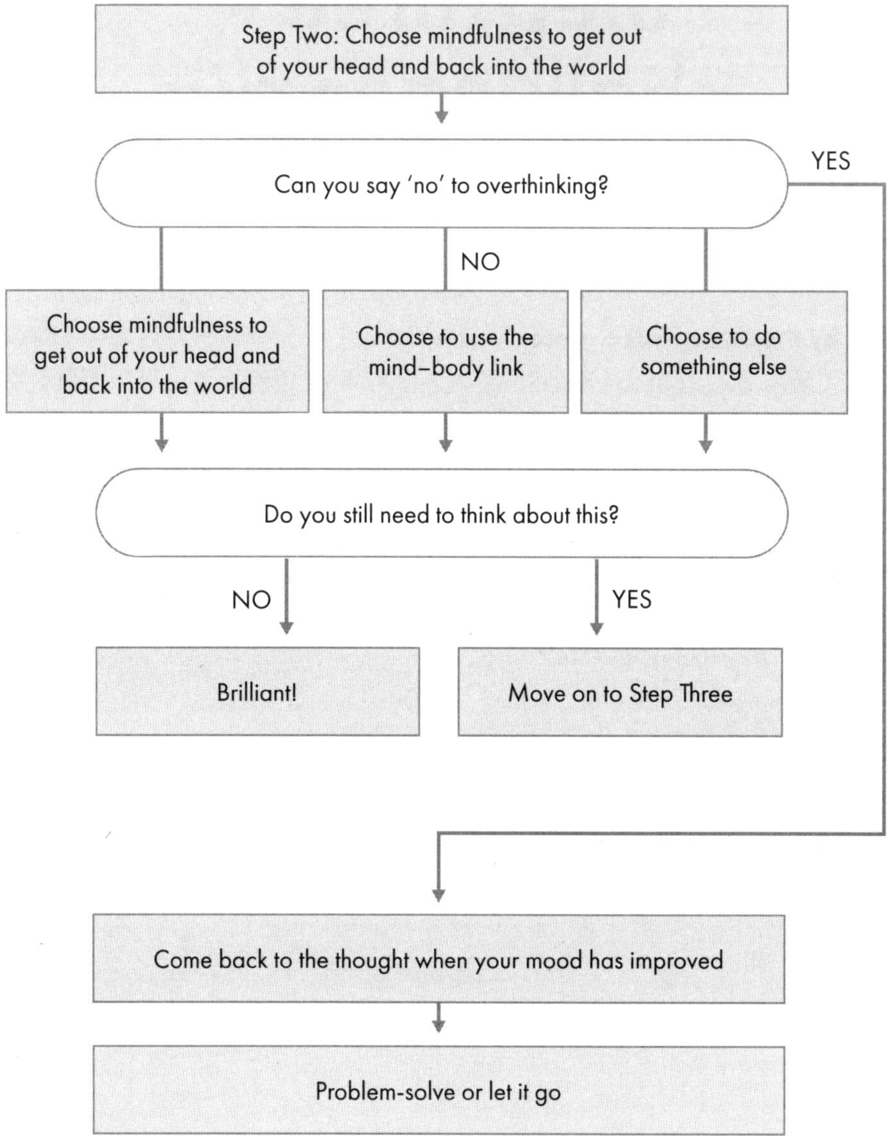

Chapter 12
Step three – challenge your thinking

By the end of this chapter, you will:

- Be able to consciously choose the story you write about your everyday experiences.
- Remember that thoughts aren't facts.
- Know how to challenge your thoughts with the best techniques for your personal overthinking traps.
- Learn to turn overthinking on its head and tune back in to the good stuff.

In this chapter, I am going to show that you can consciously choose the story you write about your everyday experiences. With this choice comes power: the narrative you create shapes the lens through which you see your life. I want you to be intentional about how you frame your experiences, because what you tell yourself today affects how you see yourself tomorrow. You are in control of your narrative and how you see yourself.

I love these words from the ancient Chinese philosopher Lao Tzu, which encapsulate this idea:

Watch your thoughts, they become your words; watch your words, they become your actions; watch your actions, they become your habits; watch your habits, they become your character; watch your character, it becomes your destiny.

Be mindful of the story that you're writing. The stories that we tell ourselves don't just shape our personalities, they become intrinsic to our self-identity.[68] While it feels as though your emotions are happening to you, when you're overthinking, your emotions are actually happening in response to these thoughts. If you think back to Chapter Three, you'll remember that it's not what happens to us, but how we appraise the situation and the meaning we give to the experience that has an impact on how we feel.

Overthinking is the second arrow, and it's this that causes much of our emotional suffering rather than the events themselves.

When we get stuck overthinking, our brains conjure up imagined scenarios. Insecurity, fear, low mood and worry will shine through, distorting what we see. These thoughts are manipulative, coercive and against our best interests. In these moments, it's difficult to do anything but surrender to the thoughts and believe them. We forget it's just our minds taking a familiar shortcut, due to the brain's neural pathways. When we go with this reactive response, we don't leave any room to question our thoughts. And while there might be some truth to them, more often the brain is creating a whole story that bears little resemblance to reality.

In this step, you'll be focusing on your thoughts as a route to broadening your spotlight of attention and learning to reflect before you react. By stepping back from what's happened and considering it from multiple perspectives, you can shape and challenge our thoughts.

As you work through this chapter, you will see that you have more control over your thoughts and feelings than you think. In the first section, I'll introduce you to ways to challenge the overthinking traps, and in the second section, I'll be encouraging you to shift your perspective and turn confirmation bias on its head.

Thoughts aren't facts

The first and most important thing to remember is that your thoughts aren't facts: they are just your interpretation of what you *think* is going on. They would be better named guesses or predictions.

Our experiences can be credibly viewed in many different ways, and you don't have to act on or believe everything you think. When you understand this, you also have the chance to turn down the dial on the emotion and construct your experiences differently.

To challenge your thoughts, make sure you:

- **Detach from the situation** so that you can see it more objectively. How would you see this situation if it was happening to a friend? Or if this were a plot in a movie, what would you want the main character to do? If the answer is obvious, it's likely you've found the right one.

- **Give the benefit of the doubt** when someone's behaviour challenges you. This helps to keep your emotions out of the situation. Think to yourself, 'What's the most generous interpretation I can give so I can try not to blow things out of proportion?' The simplest explanation is usually the most likely: you don't need to look for hidden meanings or become paranoid about what's going on. If your partner was on their phone while talking to you, yes, it's rude, but it doesn't mean they don't care about you. Be careful of where your thoughts take you.

- **Ask yourself, 'Is thinking about this worth my time and energy?'** You don't need to interrogate every thought, feeling or situation. Maybe someone has acted badly or you're unhappy with how something went, but if there's nothing you can do about it, the best thing to do is to step back from it and let it go.

Mindset is crucial when you challenge your thoughts. Try to be open and curious, putting into practice the compassion and mindfulness techniques you have learned so far. Remember that self-criticism is not helpful (in fact, it's a thought to be challenged!). The better you get at spotting negative thoughts in action and hearing what you're saying to yourself, the quicker you can challenge them.

Below, I've listed the seven classic overthinking traps (see page 76) and their solutions. There is overlap in the strategies for each, so read through them all and note down the challenges that resonate or will be most useful to you.

If your overthinking type is 'The Dweller'

If your trap is 'The Dweller' (see page 76) and you get stuck on the past, replaying your losses and setbacks, try the following:

Challenge dwelling

You pick out a single negative detail of your life and dwell on it exclusively, blowing things out of proportion and focusing on (what you see as) your failings and inadequacies, and rejecting any positive views. If something goes wrong, it's your fault, yet if things are going well, you don't take any credit. This magnifies any perceived failures and minimizes anything that goes well.

- Be fair to yourself: if 90 per cent of something was good and 10 per cent of it was not how you wanted, give 90 per cent of your time to thinking about what went well and 10 per cent to what you were unhappy with.

Watch out for overgeneralizing

You see a single negative incident as a never-ending pattern. You think, 'This always happens to me,' or 'Things never work out.'

- Don't use the words 'never' or 'always'. Instead try 'this time'. Nothing lasts forever or doesn't ever change.

Don't let hindsight bias you

You tell yourself that you could have predicted negative events or avoided them. When you replay what's happened, you're living through it again, which keeps you tied to it. But it's only in hindsight that you can view things differently, as you now have new information.

- Let it go and move forward. No one can foresee every eventuality and outcome. Everyone makes mistakes.

Is your thinking black and white?

You're all or nothing. Things are either good or bad: everything's going really well or it's all gone wrong; your friend is amazing or they're driving you mad.

- Life is never that simple: there are always shades of grey. Remember there is always context.

If your overthinking type is 'The Interrogator' or 'The Overwhelmed'

If your trap is 'The Interrogator' (see page 78) and you try to understand yourself by focusing on your negative feelings and questioning why you're feeling them, or 'The Overwhelmed' (see page 85) and your overthinking becomes chaotic, try the following:

Is thinking like this helping you?

When you jump from problem to problem or dredge through all the reasons why you're feeling bad, you're only making yourself feel much, much worse.

- Ask yourself: what are the advantages and disadvantages of thinking this way? And what are the advantages and disadvantages to changing how you think?

Watch out for metacognitive thoughts

You have thoughts about your thoughts (metacognitive thoughts). You worry about overthinking and the effect it is having on you, which leads to a cycle of worry, anxiety and shame. Now you haven't just got the problem to deal with, but you're concerned with your response, too.

- Don't forget that some worry is normal. Interrupt the thinking spiral so that you detach from these thoughts about thoughts.

Use Step Two

The best approach for 'The Interrogator' and 'The Overwhelmed' is to put into action everything you learned in Step Two, which will get you out of your head and back into the world.

- It's *never* good to overthink about how you're feeling. If you're overwhelmed and your mind is racing, the best thing you can do before taking action is to slow things down and bring the world back in. If you've been pushed into freeze mode, make sure you use the plan you put together in Chapter Nine.

If your overthinking type is 'The Catastrophizer'

If your trap is 'The Catastrophizer' (see page 79) and the focus of your overthinking is anxiety and worry, try the following:

Challenge 'what ifs'

You dwell on potential problems that don't exist yet and probably never will. You worry things will turn out badly and behave as if it's a foregone conclusion. You often ask: 'What if I do really badly?'

- If it's a 'what if' and doesn't exist yet, don't think about it. This is a waste of your time and energy. No one can see into the future. You are not a fortune-teller! What alternatives are there to this 'what if' view?

Are your thoughts spiralling?

You predict the worst possible outcome to any situation, even if it's unlikely to happen, making yourself increasingly stressed and anxious.

- What's the best-case scenario? What is the worst? What is the most likely?

Does it really matter?

You are often occupied by problems that are not really problems at all.

- Will this matter in a week, a month, a year, five years, ten years? Asking yourself this question lets you gain some distance from what's happening and put it back in perspective.

What's the most absurd or funny outcome?

Sometimes it can be difficult to even begin to think of alternative scenarios when you're feeling a strong emotion like anxiety or low mood. Try this simple strategy to reduce the perceived seriousness of the situation. When you can see the funny side, it takes away some of the stress.

- Try thinking of the most ridiculously absurd and amazing best-case scenario. If you're worried about money this month, the most ridiculously absurd and amazing best-case scenario might be a penguin waddling over to you with a winning lottery ticket in its beak, and your favourite actor bringing you champagne to celebrate your win. By using your imagination to conjure up some silliness, you escape the grip of the thoughts and bring in some humour.

Challenge your positive beliefs about overthinking

The only way to truly let go of overthinking is to recognize it as a hindrance rather than a help. Use the ideas below[69] to challenge your beliefs and update them:

POSITIVE BELIEF	CHALLENGE
Overthinking helps me problem-solve	Do you actually solve your problems by overthinking, or are you just going over the problem again and again in your head? Do you become so anxious that you delay solving your problems or avoid them altogether? Are you confusing a thought (worry) with an action (problem-solving)?
Overthinking motivates me	Do you know anyone who is successful who doesn't overthink? Are you confusing overthinking with caring? Is it possible that you can want to succeed and not overthink all the time? Does your worry really improve your performance or are there negative repercussions, such as difficulty concentrating or intense anxiety?

POSITIVE BELIEF	CHALLENGE
Overthinking protects me from negative emotions	Has anything bad ever happened that you'd worried about beforehand? If so, did this worrying lessen the emotional pain, or did it make you live through the pain twice? Does overthinking just increase feeling bad in the here and now?
If I don't worry, something bad will happen	Have things ever gone wrong even though you worried? Is your rule about worry – *worry = good outcome, don't worry = bad outcome* – based on real evidence? Can your thoughts really influence the world?
Worrying shows I am a caring person	Are there other ways to show family and friends that you care, instead of worrying? Do you know people who are caring who don't worry excessively? Has anyone ever found your worrying to be negative?
Overthinking is useful	What is overthinking costing you? Does it cause you stress or tire you out? Has it negatively impacted you, your family or friends, or your work? Do you feel your life is better compared to the lives of people who don't overthink? How much time and energy have you lost to overthinking? Wouldn't you prefer to use it for something else?

If your overthinking type is 'The Wobbler'

If your trap is 'The Wobbler' (see page 80) and you get stuck trying to make the 'right' or 'best' decision, try the following:

Stop thinking about it

Think of the game show *Who Wants to Be a Millionaire?*, in which contestants tackle a series of multiple-choice questions for cash prizes. A contestant has confidently chosen an answer and the host asks them, 'Are you sure?' They think about it some more – and the more they think about it, the less certain they become!

- Doubt breeds doubt. Going over and over a problem only increases anxiety and uncertainty.

Don't make a decision based on how you're currently feeling

You often change your mind about decisions that you were once happy with. If you can't decide, then go with your original choice – this was something you wanted.

- Put the feeling to one side and stop over-analysing. Close down the behaviours that feed into indecision: no checking, reassurance-seeking or over-planning. Tell yourself that, if you don't like it, you never have to do it again or you can leave early.

Is this performance anxiety?

You put excessive pressure on yourself to perform well and gain external validation as a route to feeling good about yourself.

- Doing well can be a guard against not feeling good enough. You don't need to prove yourself to others. Take the pressure off yourself.

You don't need to decide yet

You often overthink distant decisions, long before it's necessary. But making the decision now won't be in your best interests if you're not feeling good.

- If you don't need to make a decision yet, put it on hold until you're feeling better.

If your overthinking type is 'The Over-Analyser'

If your trap is 'The Over-Analyser' (see page 82) and you get stuck overthinking interactions, try the following:

Be careful of mindreading

You assume you know what someone else is thinking or feeling, even though you don't have any firm evidence. You conclude that someone is reacting negatively to you without properly investigating that thought.

- Remember that no one can read minds. The only way you can be sure what someone is thinking is if they tell you, or you ask them – otherwise it's just guesswork.

Are you personalizing this?

You take personal responsibility for things going wrong and see negative events as indicative of a negative characteristic in yourself. If someone looks cross, you wonder what you've done, rather than thinking, 'I wonder what's up with them?'

- Very little in life is all down to you, so don't position yourself at the centre of the universe. Events are never just about what you've done. You are one small part and there is so much else going on. Watch out for projection: whose thoughts are these really? Are they your concerns and worries?

Try to be curious

You often jump to conclusions, but instead try to be curious about what is going on. Try to see things for what they are in a more objective way.

- How else could you see this or what other explanations might there be for what's happening? Don't try to over-control; instead, let things happen or play out without having to pin everything down.

Take yourself out of it

More often than not, no one is thinking badly about you. Try to reduce the self-magnification – the scrutiny you put yourself under is so much greater than the scrutiny you put on anyone else.

- Remind yourself it doesn't all come back to you. Other people are much more likely to be thinking about themselves than about you, worrying about how they came across or if they made a bad impression.

If your overthinking type is 'The Victim'

If your trap is 'The Victim' (see page 84) and you are pulled into overthinking arguments and upsets, try the following:

Is this helping or hindering me?

Differentiate between when anger is helpful and when it is unhelpful. When it's helpful, it moves you forward, but it's unhelpful when it leaves you feeling stuck. Anger often gets a bad press, but it is a natural response to threats and gets us ready to defend ourselves. When it works for us, it can highlight an injustice and let us right a wrong. When expressed constructively, it can help us to resolve conflicts and misunderstandings, motivating us and driving us towards our goals, but holding on to resentment and hurt is proven to have a negative effect on your mental and physical health.[70,71]

- Do you feel stuck? If so, challenge your angry thoughts and move from tunnel vision to seeing the bigger picture.

Don't act in anger

When we feel angry, it's like putting on blinkers. It makes you close down on any viewpoint but your own. If two people are arguing, often neither listens to the other person, they just build their own argument more strongly. It's like building a brick wall between you; nothing is solved. Angry decisions tend to be bad ones – we might react impulsively and do things that we regret, such as going volcanic in an argument and throwing everything at the other person to purposely hurt them. Or you may argue with a stranger, which then ruins your day. Or you might become passive aggressive, expressing how you feel indirectly by sulking or using sarcasm, backhanded compliments or the silent treatment.

- Don't let yourself be pulled into arguments. Hurting others or yourself to feel better will make you feel much worse in the long run. Say something to yourself to step back from it: I like to think, 'Don't step on the dance floor, it doesn't get you anywhere.' Fast-forward and play out what you think will happen if you act on your angry feelings. Where will it get you, and will it give you what you want? Think about how you'll feel afterward. There's rarely any gain, and more often it ends in regret.

Who is this hurting the most?

When you carry anger with you, it burrows into your skin, leaving you uncomfortable and unsettled. When someone has upset you, staying in anger and overthinking it keeps that person with you. The situation might have passed, but it's still ongoing while you are thinking about it. Notice what's happening and make the choice not to let them in.

- Try to move away from blaming (yourself or others) or being stuck on what you didn't get. If you were let down, it might feel like you're letting them off the hook, but really you're remembering what it means to be human and that we all make mistakes. Maybe the other person did get it wrong, but perhaps they didn't do it on purpose or intentionally set out to hurt you.

What outcome do you want?

When you feel calmer, think about the outcome you want and work backward to consider the best way to handle the situation. This allows you to think about the bigger picture and come to the issue from a place that is constructive. Give it some time and allow the dust to settle before deciding. When something first happens, it can be difficult to put it away, especially if it comes as a shock, but in time your brain will find a place for it so it no longer affects you.

- Focus on your goals and what's important to you. This helps you to surf smaller problems that are not worth your time and energy. Move to taking personal responsibility. Think about your role in things, take control of what you can and let go of what you can't. Don't let anger define you or run the show. Remember: no response is a response, and saying nothing also carries power. Does the person even warrant a response?

Can you forgive?

If you have been in a situation where you've suffered a grievance at the hands of someone else, then are you in a position to forgive them?[72] I know this isn't easy – it might even feel unjust – but try to do this for your own sake, so you can continue to live your life. Forgiveness doesn't make it go away, but it does stop it from consuming you and free you from carrying resentment.

- Let go of the wish to change what's happened or to call the other person to account. This breaks the ties that bind you to anger. It moves you away from being the victim of what's happened and puts you back into control. The one choice you don't have is rewinding to a time before it happened, but beyond this your choices are infinite.

Track and challenge your thoughts

Over the next week, I want you to put these thought challenges into action and track your thoughts. Use the table overleaf as an example of how to do this. Every time you have a negative thought, write it down and identify which thinking traps you are falling into. When you see your thoughts written out, they become more concrete and it can be easier to see that they are not the whole truth! You can then use the ideas in this chapter to challenge your thoughts. Try following these pointers:

- **Observe your thoughts and feelings and try to externalize them.** When you see them as thoughts and feelings rather than the truth of what's going on, it gives you space to question them.

- **Bring compassion to the situation.** I find it helpful to remember that the mood I'm in changes how I see things and makes me bad at predicting what's really happening or what I might wish to do.

- **What's the evidence?** Remember your thoughts are just one version of what's going on. Recognize your thoughts are not based on real evidence. Make room for more than one perspective. Does what your brain is telling you really add up? Do you have any evidence that supports this viewpoint? Is there any way to check it out? Can you ask someone?

Trigger: What happened?	Thoughts and beliefs: What went through my mind?	Feelings: What emotions did I feel?	Externalize the thought: Which thinking trap is this?	What alternative ways could I see this?	How do I feel now?
Difficult project at work	I can't get it done I'm useless My boss is going to think badly of me	Depressed, frustrated, anxious	The Dweller • All-or-nothing thinking • Discounting positives • Over-generalizing	Notice small wins Focus on what I can do and break it down into smaller tasks Ask for support at work Swap self-criticism for compassion: 'It's a tough project, so it's OK to struggle. I'm doing my best and I'll get there in the end.'	I feel less stuck I was being unfair to myself

Trigger: What happened?	Thoughts and beliefs: What went through my mind?	Feelings: What emotions did I feel?	Externalize the thought: Which thinking trap is this?	What alternative ways could I see this?	How do I feel now?
I haven't heard back from my friend	I must have done something to upset them What if they don't like me?	Anxious and sad	The Over-Analyser • Mind-reading • Personalizing • 'What ifs' • Catastrophizing	I'm making this about me, but I need to take myself out of it This is a 'what if': it doesn't exist yet and may never exist, so it's not worth my time The simplest explanation is that they've been busy or something is going on for them	I'm not thinking about it until I know more
My partner took out all their stress on me	They don't appreciate me They never think about me It will never change	Angry and frustrated	The Victim • Black-and-white thinking • Over-generalizing • Predicting the future	Give the benefit of the doubt, as I know they've got a lot going on Feeling angry is only hurting me I need to keep it concrete: it's one upset, not how they normally are	Calmer, and it feels less personal

Turn overthinking on its head

In this next section, I want you to turn your negative thoughts around by giving time to thinking about things working out and the good stuff in your life. If you focus on the obstacles, then that's what you'll see; but if you focus on the pathway, you'll see a way through. Practising this way of thinking overrides the brain's negative bias and trains it to see the good stuff. Every time you do this, you are strengthening that new neural pathway. It then becomes easier to think in these ways.

What if it works out?

What's the best outcome in this situation? You don't have to convince yourself it will happen, just spend a few minutes thinking about it. You're building a new way of thinking. It can also be helpful to think about what you would do if you knew you couldn't fail. This simplifies your decision and allows you to think without fear, bringing a fresh, optimistic perspective and helping you to move forward more confidently.

Write a letter to yourself

When you're overthinking, it's difficult to see things from a different viewpoint, as your mood stops you from having access to the rational or more positive thinking that could help you. It's not until you feel better that it's possible to put things back in perspective. To keep a connection to this viewpoint, I want you to write down your thoughts when you're feeling good.

You could do this as a letter to yourself that you can come back to the next time you're overthinking. I did this with Aubrey to help with his health anxiety. When he was anxious, he found it impossible to think differently, as fear took over and made him believe something was seriously wrong. Note that, if you are struggling with health anxiety personally, there's more information on how to tackle these types of thoughts at the end of the book (see page 282). It's also worth seeing your doctor for further help and support.

Aubrey wrote:

Aubrey, I want you to remember that when you feel anxious, it changes how you think. I know you're worried that there's something seriously wrong, but this is the pattern that comes when you worry about your health. You only feel like this when you're scared. You're going to want to try to get other people to reassure you, or to go for check-ups and scans, but all that ever happens is you stay stuck in the feeling and feel worse. Afterward, you regret losing days to feeling like this. Reassurance doesn't work – it's never long before you start worrying that someone has missed something important and you're waking up in the night worrying again. You don't need to give these symptoms more attention, you need to give them less attention. Remember, it's always been OK; the worst has never come true. Try to trust in this and do something to take your mind off things. Push yourself to do it; you're always so much happier when you do. I know you won't want to stop thinking about it, but you have to. Focusing more on this will only make you feel worse. Take yourself for a walk, phone Kai and give yourself a break from this worry. Once you feel better, you'll see everything differently and you'll know it's OK.

Turn confirmation bias around

Next, I want you to use confirmation bias to your advantage. Your mind is always searching for proof of what you believe. If you tell yourself that things are always going wrong, your brain will focus on every setback and small inconvenience, and use them as evidence to confirm that narrative. It's not that life is objectively worse, it's that your brain is doing what it's wired to do – finding evidence that supports the reality you believe in and reinforces the story you've chosen to tell.

But confirmation bias doesn't have to be negative. Just like 'what ifs', it works the other way, too. If you start asking yourself, 'How can things get better?' or 'What good is happening in my life?', your brain will begin to look for those answers. It will seek out the small victories, the moments of growth, and the opportunities for change, gradually shifting your perception towards hope and possibility.

This turnaround also allows you to build a positive self-image to replace your old negative view. For example, think of the times you have coped well or of the positive feedback you've been given. We form our identity by integrating our life experiences – when we tell ourselves the story of who we are and what has happened to us, we create a coherent narrative that allows us to make sense of our lives, giving us a feeling of consistency and purpose. Update your self-image so you see the good in yourself and view yourself as someone who can manage difficulty.

The gratitude effect

Finally, I want you to use gratitude to shift your view. You may have heard of the gratitude technique before, but do not underestimate the difference it can make. Gratitude changes how we perceive situations by adjusting our focus to what's important in our lives, so we appreciate what we have. This is another of my favourite strategies; it never fails to make me feel good.

When we think about what we're grateful for, we force our minds to focus on the good things we already have, rather than dwelling on what we don't have or searching for something new. It doesn't mean that you can't talk about what's difficult, but gratitude is helpful in addition to this – it lets you see the full picture of your life, rather than focusing solely on what you're unhappy with. People who are grateful are happier, healthier and more fulfilled.[73] Gratitude improves your relationships and increases happiness, contentment and your long-term wellbeing.

In one study,[74] participants were asked to write a few sentences each week. One group wrote about things they were grateful for that had occurred during the week. A second group wrote about daily irritations or things that had displeased them. The third wrote about events that had affected them (with no emphasis on them being positive or negative). After 10 weeks, those who wrote about gratitude were more optimistic and felt better about their lives. Amazingly, they had also exercised more and made fewer visits to the doctor than those who focused on daily annoyances.

At the end of each day or before you get up in the morning, write down three things you are grateful for:

- Really reflect on your life, acknowledging what you have. Immerse yourself in what's gone well or any good events that have happened.
- Focus on specifics and keep it simple – for example, your first cup of coffee, a walk outdoors, someone holding the door open for you.
- Think about anything that has bought you serenity, joy or awe.
- Focus your gratitude on people, rather than on material items or circumstance – for example, be grateful to your partner for cooking you dinner or to your friend for phoning for a chat.

- Share your grateful thoughts with those you're thinking about, so that they know how much you appreciate them. My husband and I often email our grateful thoughts to each other.
- Finally, consider your contribution,[75] by thinking about what you do for others. Part of our motivation comes from feeling capable of making a difference. Write down three ways you were useful to other people.

Moving forward

When you challenge your beliefs, you are broadening your spotlight of awareness. This creates space to question your thoughts, consider multiple perspectives and see the full picture. This stops us from being pulled into creating a story around our emotions and allows our emotions to pass. While the brain does have a negative bias, we can train it to see the good stuff, by turning overthinking on its head. This is an important way to build resistance against overthinking, which we'll be strengthening in the next steps.

Before you move on to the next step, write down the strategies from this chapter that work best for you. Note how you can use these to address your specific overthinking traps. Take some time to consider the positive changes you can make to your thinking, too.

You should now be an expert at noticing overthinking, choosing what's in your spotlight and challenging your thoughts. You're now ready for the next step – but, just to warn you, it's a big one.

Step Three: Checklist

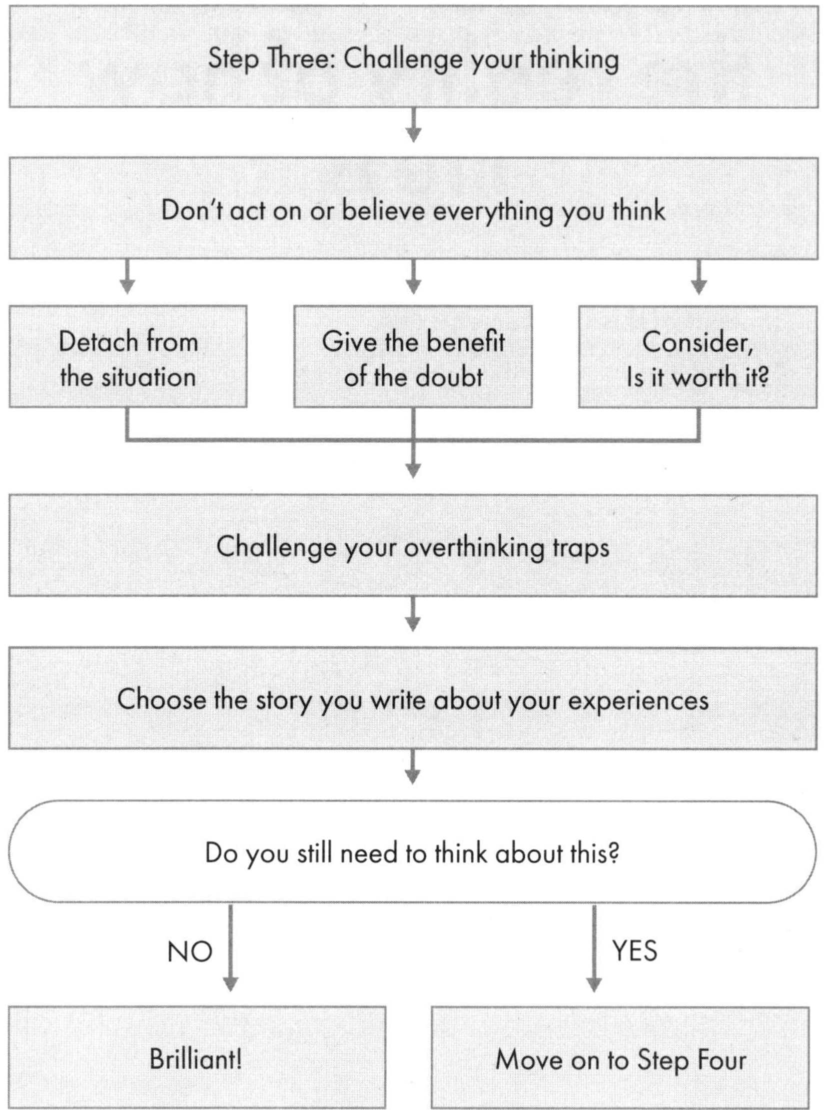

Chapter 13
Step four – accept the reality of how life is

By the end of this chapter, you will:

- Learn to embrace life's positives and negatives.
- Consider your problematic coping strategies.
- Examine how to overcome the expectation gap.

Here's the truth of the matter: the only way to truly let go of overthinking is to accept the reality of how life is.

Our expectations – how we believe we should feel, how we think the world works and the outcomes we expect – are at the root of much of our overthinking. If, for example, we think we're responsible for life going well – that we should be perfect, or that things should never go wrong – then we'll constantly be triggered into overthinking by these impossible standards.

If you think right back to the start of this book, the research told us that personal judgements about our happiness levels were associated with lower overall life satisfaction and psychological wellbeing, as well as greater depressive symptoms. Researchers also found that having high expectations about how happy we *should* be can be detrimental, as it makes it more difficult to achieve the level of happiness that we are expecting from positive events. We need to address the expectation gap in order to accept the reality of things as they are.

As you work through this chapter, use the arguments and practical exercises to re-evaluate your beliefs, rethink your approach to life and update your mental map (see page 29). Make a note of anything that resonates and consider how you will put these ideas into practice.

How to overcome the expectation gap

Overthinking is best seen as a faulty coping mechanism, developed in response to feeling vulnerable or exposed. The goal discrepancy that triggers overthinking is, in fact, an expectation gap. In a funny way, these thoughts are trying to protect us. They give the illusion that we can avoid ever feeling discomfort, pain or vulnerability (the number one trigger to overthinking), but if we expect to feel good all the time or aim for happiness as our default state, we end up permanently disappointed. And more than that, it makes us feel as if we are getting life wrong.

Even when we're living well, there is no avoiding discomfort. We have the full range of emotions because they are all necessary and useful to us. Thinking about this in evolutionary terms, it's also important to remember that, if we didn't feel distress, fear, anxiety and pain, we'd be extinct. Emotions are messages helping us to make sense of what is happening. We shouldn't try to only cultivate the good emotions and repress or avoid the uncomfortable ones. Anger sets a boundary; shame reveals the parts of you that need acceptance and healing; regret invites you to forgive yourself. It is right to feel sad in response to loss, or to feel anxiety if you are worried. These emotions are not something we ever want to lose, as that would make us machines rather than people. Having happiness that little bit out of reach is also adaptive, as it keeps you moving forward and facilitates personal growth.

To close the expectation gap, you need to accept how things are. When you let go of unrealistic expectations, you will no longer be constantly disappointed. You can experience life for what it is and appreciate it without preconceived conditions in your head. **Once you release your expectations, you're free to enjoy things as they are, rather than as you think they should be.**

Addressing negative emotions

Emotions are a bit like children: you don't want them driving your car, as they'll crash it. But you don't want them in the boot, either! The best place for them is in the back seat, so they can be seen and heard and attended to, but they are not in control.

When we're overthinking, we've moved our emotions into the driving seat, but our emotions should not dictate how we think or what we do. We don't need to be in tune with every feeling or analyse everything that happens in our lives, *especially* when we feel bad. This hypervigilance might seem like a way to try to pre-empt and overcome negative feelings, but it only winds up having the opposite effect. When you interrogate every feeling, your brain becomes hypervigilant to any slight change, amplifying everything you feel inside, making you overly sensitive to your emotions.

It's how you interpret a feeling of discomfort that's key. Feeling anxious, low, restless or dissatisfied, is a normal response – not a signal that you are getting things wrong or that there is something wrong with you. We need to bring a mindful approach to our emotions, allowing them to exist without trying to suppress, change, ignore or indulge them too much.

Here are some techniques to try out:

Pass by the feeling

You don't need to react to every change or put every feeling under the microscope. It's like responding to every sound as if there's a burglar in your house: your sensitivity is too high. You can use the mindfulness techniques (see page 174) you've learned so far to help you notice negative thoughts. Observe your thoughts and feelings and see them as external to you, recognizing that you don't need to fix them or make them go away. Think of your thoughts and feelings as people in a parade: you can watch them go by without getting involved. For example, when you first wake, your mood is often low, but it will pick up. Don't judge how the day will go based on how you're feeling. If the feeling keeps coming up, like it's tapping you on the shoulder, then it's worth investigating. Otherwise, wait for it to pass.

Change how you interpret the feeling

There is an increasing assumption that good mental health means we should always be happy, and that uncomfortable feelings and moods shouldn't be part of life. But when you link good mental health with feeling good, you're getting it all wrong. Trying to be happy is what makes us unhappy. It's important to develop emotional flexibility. Good mental health means being able to cope with the difficulties you encounter in life. Instead of interpreting a feeling of discomfort as a problem, you should see it as an expected response. Allow all emotions and remember that they are not a problem to fix, but another language to get to know, understand and use to navigate problems. Your mood naturally fluctuates and, if you're facing something hard or something hasn't gone as you'd hoped, you should treat yourself with compassion.

Remember the idea of two rooms (see page 124). When we're in the struggle room, it's tough enough without believing we've done something wrong to end up there. In the good room, it's tempting to imagine that this is how we should feel all the time, but this can lead to us denying parts of ourselves or repressing negative emotions. Although we might prefer certain parts of ourselves, it is the combination of each part that makes us who we are.

Moving between these rooms is part of life and how we process our experiences. We want to use the good room to shore up our resources, but we also need to remember that the struggle room exists, and that negative emotions are a normal response to difficulty. We won't be there forever; in time, we will move back to the good room.

If you are feeling a strong physical or emotional response, recognize that this is an understandable reaction to what you are going through, and it's OK to feel this way. It's not that you've done something wrong or that you're not making the most of life, it's just that life can be hard sometimes and things don't always go to plan. Don't get hooked into questioning why you're feeling like this or wondering what's wrong with you.

Bear these tips in mind:

- Make sure you bring self-compassion to your experience and consider what you might need. What we require at difficult times is care and understanding. Do you need to see a friendly face or go out for a walk? Refer back to the strategies you've found helpful in Steps One and Two.
- Remind yourself that your emotions have a purpose and no one feels good all the time. You will have good days and bad days, and fluctuations in mood are normal.
- If you find yourself stuck in 'why' questions, make the choice and tell your brain to stop!

Embrace uncertainty

Many people find uncertainty challenging. Waiting to know what's going to happen or waiting for a response can feel unbearable, especially if the outcome really matters to you. You don't know where you stand or how things are going to be. It can feel like you are unable to switch off until you hear. Even when the chance of a negative outcome is tiny, it may be impossible to relax until you feel 100 per cent sure. Instead of considering what's best or letting things unfold, it can make you rush to an answer or act before you're ready, as a way to end the anxiety and so you don't have to think about it anymore. Some people even tell me they'd prefer for something bad to happen rather than continue not knowing what the eventual outcome will be.

In a study at University College London,[76] participants played a computer game in which they turned over rocks while researchers measured their stress response. They had to guess whether or not there would be a snake under the rock, and when there was, they received a mildly painful electric shock on the hand. The researchers found that knowing there was a small chance of getting an electric shock led to significantly more stress (despite there being no objective difference in the intensity of the shock), while knowing they would definitely receive a painful electric shock felt less stressful to the volunteers.

The participants' stress response didn't increase with the certainty of being given an electrical shock; it increased with the uncertainty of this happening. Any element of unpredictability significantly increases people's discomfort.

It's understandable to want certainty: it's one of our innate drives. The brain loves predictability; we're hardwired to crave comfort (think back to the brain's autopilot mode, which we discussed on page 104) and associate the unknown with danger. However, rather than trying to be sure, it's much better to build your tolerance of uncertainty and the discomfort it brings. This builds your natural inoculation to cope with difficulty and gives you a chance to see that you don't always need to know the outcome or have a perfect plan to enjoy something. It also lets you gain greater confidence in your ability to cope. Remember that life would be pretty dull if we knew the outcome of every event in advance!

Try these techniques:

Slowly build your uncertainty-tolerance

Certainty is just an illusion. Even the surest things in life can change in an instant. Accepting that uncertainty is an inevitable part of life is key to getting used to it and managing it. Think of any situations or areas of your life where you are good at managing uncertainty. Ask yourself why (probably because there's nothing you can do about it, so you just move on), then try to foster this approach in other parts of your life.

Try these ideas for small ways to build your tolerance of uncertainty:

- If you're watching a TV series, make yourself wait a day or two between episodes.
- Drive to places you know without using your route planner.
- Go to a restaurant without looking up the menu in advance.
- If you hear a message alert, wait before reading the message.
- Put your phone on airplane mode for parts of the day.
- Reduce the number of times you check your socials.
- Take action even if you don't know the outcome.

Accept that the unknown is neither good nor bad

Uncertainty doesn't mean something bad is going to happen – it means you just don't know yet. Heather Lanier's TED Talk, ' "Good" and "Bad" Are Incomplete Stories We Tell Ourselves',[77] is a brilliant watch to convince yourself of this. I love the old parable she uses at the start of her talk. When I'm struggling with uncertainty, I remind myself of this tale:

Once there was a farmer who owned a beautiful horse, but one day his horse ran away. When his neighbours heard the news, they came to visit. 'That's such bad luck,' they said. 'We'll see,' replied the farmer. Days later, the horse returned, bringing seven wild horses with it. 'Wow,' said the neighbours, 'that's such good luck.' And the farmer shrugged and said, 'We'll see.' The very next day, the farmer's son tried riding one of the wild horses, but it threw him off and he broke his leg. The neighbours said, 'Oh, that's terrible luck.' 'We'll see,' replied the farmer. The next day, soldiers came knocking, looking for men to draft to the army, but they didn't take the farmer's son because his leg was broken. And the neighbours said, 'Ooh, that's good luck!' And the farmer said, 'We'll see.'

Instead of embracing the complexity of life, we are drawn to simplified descriptions of cause and effect. We prefer to think that things happen for a reason and that we are in control of our lives, carefully avoiding the uncertainty of life. When we hastily judge situations as all good or all bad, we oversimplify and miss out on the potential for deeper understanding and learning from the full context. The reality is that life is more complex and nuanced.

Trust that you will work it out

Worrying doesn't prepare you, debating decisions doesn't bring more certainty, and thinking of the worst outcome will not make you any less disappointed if it happens. Is overthinking really worth it for a fake sense of certainty? You can guess my answer.

A research study[78] asked participants to describe a current problem in their lives. They were then divided into three groups. The first group were told to contemplate their problem by worrying about it, while the second group were instructed to think objectively about it. The third group were asked to practise diaphragmatic breathing. Those who were given permission to worry reported lower confidence in their solutions, and the examiners found their solutions were *less* effective compared to the other two groups. The worrying also led to more elevated worry and anxiety, so did nothing to prepare them or make them feel better. This demonstrates how pointless worrying is, as you can only know what to do when you have all the facts and you're in the situation.

Knowing all this should help you to cut down on your worrying. But, most importantly, don't underestimate your ability to cope with whatever the future brings. The following pointers will help you to build confidence in your coping ability:

- Think of times when big things have gone wrong for you, but everything worked out in the end. Remember – and notice – the times when something came out of the blue, but you coped well.

- Try to disengage from the behaviours that feed into uncertainty, such as planning, reassurance-seeking and checking. Although these behaviours might feel good in the moment, they don't change anything or make you more prepared. They're a waste of your time and energy. When you plan, check, control and fix, it only increases anxiety and keeps you focused on your fears.

- Only plan if you have enough information, rather than trying to cover every eventuality. Instead, bring your attention to being more present and focus on the next step.

- Remember that, even if something doesn't work out, it's best to handle the problem when you have all the facts rather than pointlessly ruining right now (and making yourself suffer twice!).

- Remind yourself that you don't need to have all the answers and that you can handle whatever happens, even if it is unexpected.

Seek out discomfort

When you avoid discomfort, you're reinforcing the belief that you can't handle it, making yourself feel less capable and more scared. Spending your time trying to avoid discomfort stops you engaging fully with life. I want you to intentionally choose moments of discomfort, as a small amount of stress on your body lets you bring yourself in and out of the stress response in a controlled way and gradually gets your nervous system used to handling moderate levels of discomfort. This strengthens your resilience and your ability to cope, teaching you that you can safely manage and recover from discomfort.

Before you embark on Step Five (see page 241), make sure that you try some of the following:

- **Get out of breath:** Doing this mimics the stress response, increases your stress tolerance and helps you to get used to discomfort.
- **Persist in a struggle:** Sit with a difficult task rather than switching to something else.
- **Challenge your ideas:** Read a book that challenges your thinking and beliefs.
- **Try something new:** Taste a new food or learn to play a musical instrument.
- **Plunge in cold water:** Turn the shower temperature to cold for one minute.
- **Feel your emotions:** Accept sadness, guilt or stress rather than avoiding them.
- **Notice when you manage discomfort:** Notice when you experience and work through discomfort or manage a difficult situation.

Accept the waves

I love the TV show *Grand Designs,* which follows some of Britain's most ambitious house builds. When I first watched it, I used to think, 'How do they always manage to find these projects that go so wrong?' Then we did our own building project and I realized that this is just how projects go. This is a good metaphor for life: we can't eradicate struggle and difficulty. In fact, the idea that we can is bordering on delusional, and yet we all too often imagine we can do exactly that.

In many ways, the idea that we could have so much power over how the world works is another version of magical thinking. It lets us keep fear at bay and protects us from the reality of life, where we are vulnerable, death is inevitable and we do not have ultimate control. It's comforting to imagine that we can stop bad things happening, but when we overthink and try to be in control of our lives, we're trying to control the uncontrollable.

Trying to fight against the unpredictability and toughness of life is a bit like trying to stand up against fierce ocean waves as they break on the shore – they just knock you down. It's better to accept that the waves will always keep coming, and to launch yourself out to swim with the current.

When things are difficult, remember this is how life is: it is hard, it is stressful, but you're not unlucky or doing anything wrong. Suffering is part of life, a common experience, not something specific to you.

Try these techniques:

Not everything is down to you

It is not your responsibility to make life run smoothly. You are forgetting about all the other external factors, as well as the other people involved and their shared responsibility. What you did or didn't do was not the deciding factor in what happened. Try drawing a pie chart and adding sections for everyone and everything that had an impact. Weigh each factor in percentage terms.

Draw your circle of control

Take control of what you can and let go of the rest. You don't have to be in control of everything for life to happen: you can let things happen of their own accord. Take a moment to think of all the amazing things that have worked out through chance or without a plan. I love the Serenity Prayer as a reminder of this idea: 'Grant me the serenity to accept the things I cannot change, the courage to change the things I can, and the wisdom to know the difference.'[79]

Using the diagram opposite as a guide, draw your circle of control. Inside the circle, place all the things you can control. Outside the circle, place all the things you want to let go of.

People-pleasers

Many overthinkers also struggle with people-pleasing. If you're someone who is highly attuned to other people and tends to put other people's needs before your own, there's more information to help you understand yourself better and strategies to tackle this problem on page 295.

The circle of control

I CANNOT CONTROL

The ups and downs of life   Natural disasters   Other people's moods

What others do, say, think or feel   What others think of me

Death and illness   External situations

The past   **I CAN CONTROL**   The future

How I view life   My boundaries

How I act in my relationships   Screen time

Whether I ask for help   How much I read the news

How I treat others   My mindset and expectations

How I move on from mistakes and failure   My attitude

Who I follow on social media   How I speak to myself

The amount of effort I give   How I spend my time

Self-care   Being present in this moment

My response   Inner peace

Global political issues   The economy

Other people's happiness   Strangers on social media

What happens around me   The outcome of my efforts

Other people's motives   The way other people treat me

Stop asking: 'Am I living my best life?'

Trying to live our best life and trying to be perfect are both connected to a desire to be in total control. Both promise to make us feel good about ourselves – that if we live our best life or if we're perfect, we can feel good all of the time. These desires often come wrapped up in subtle questions: 'Am I making the most of life? Am I enjoying things enough? Am I working hard enough? Am I reaching my potential?'

When we aspire to such high standards, it leaves us constantly falling short and feeling ashamed of ourselves. It is the exact concoction of corrosive and toxic that overthinking loves so much. It also feeds overthinking's favourite topics (self-esteem, self-worth and identity) and pulls us into comparing, which, as you've already seen, brings with it even more problems.

These standards don't just drive us, they drive how we treat ourselves. When we inevitably can't meet them, it kicks off a downward spiral of self-criticism, diminishes self-worth and makes us feel deficient. Some people even tell me that they deserve to feel bad if they don't do well. They then resolve to work harder or do better and become further entrenched in these views.

Try these techniques:

Live the life you have now

There is no perfect formula that can make life always fun and joyful. No one is living their best life at all times. I love the Buddhist saying that encapsulates this:

Before enlightenment,

chop wood carry water.

After enlightenment,

chop wood carry water.

———————————

It's not trying to be perfect or living your best life that matters, it's how you live day to day that's most important. When we focus on what's ahead, it can blind us to all that we already have. Try to remember that it's the process that matters, not the outcome. See life as an adventure packed full of experiences and lessons. Make the most of the good times and accept that the difficult bits are unavoidable.

Write a note to yourself that encapsulates this idea and updates your old belief. For example:

- No one is living their best life 24-7.
- Perfect does not exist, so aiming for it puts you under pressure and only brings unhappiness and disappointment.
- It's not reaching your goals that matters, but how you get there.

Embrace a give-it-a-go mindset

Done is better than perfect. I'm not suggesting you aim any less high, but wouldn't it be better to work towards your goals without the anxiety, insecurity and self-doubt that perfectionism brings? Switch perfect for a give-it-a-go mindset. Take the pressure off and do things just to see where they lead.

Think about this in terms of efficiency. Doing everything perfectly is not an effective use of your time. The extra time you spend stewing over tiny details is not worth it. You create an imaginary end point that tricks you into believing that, if you work on it more, it will finally be perfect, but in fact this leaves you stuck in a loop of overthinking and delaying. Instead of aiming for 100 per cent, aim for 80 per cent and stop agonizing over the last 20 per cent. Work doesn't need to be completely 'right' before you share it. To put this into practice, try these suggestions:

- Start handing in, posting, launching or sharing your work when you consider it 80 per cent done. When you're too close to a project, you don't have a clear view of it – let someone else have a look.
- Think of 'good enough' as the optimal point – you've done enough, and any extra effort beyond this point gives diminishing returns.
- Put in the time and effort that a project or task deserves based on its merit and difficulty level.
- Start with small goals, as getting something done is better than avoiding, procrastinating or abandoning your work.

You'll quickly see that cutting back on perfectionism makes little difference to anyone else. Yet the extra time you have for rest or pleasure will make your life more enjoyable and can even improve productivity and performance.

Remember that people aren't loved because they're perfect

You do not need to be perfect, special or the best. That is not what makes you loved or worthwhile – and it is another standard that doesn't match up to the reality of life. When you let go of this idea, it doesn't make you any less valuable, but it does take the pressure off and frees you to enjoy your life. You can be yourself, have fun, change your mind, make mistakes, try new things, or do something embarrassing without it feeling like the end of the world if it doesn't work out. It also allows you to open up and connect with others on a deeper level.

I don't know about you, but my favourite people are definitely not living their best life and they certainly aren't perfect. If I'm completely honest, I don't warm to people who give the impression of these things. I want to know all of someone, flaws included, otherwise it's difficult to relate, because my life is so far from perfect! Perfection keeps closeness and understanding at bay.

- Write a flashcard to remind yourself of this idea: 'Real is so much better than perfect.'

There's no perfect route through life

No matter what you choose in life, there will be some advantages and disadvantages. You never get a choice that's all advantages or all good, whether you're considering which university to go to, whether to take the job or not, moving abroad or having a baby. Don't waver or imagine there was a better alternative, as this is what leads to overthinking.

We make our decisions based on a prediction: we try to predict whether life will be better if we make a certain choice. When we regret decisions, we're presuming that the other choice would have been better, but you have no idea of what that life might have been. It could have been better, worse or the same.

I find this process really helpful to take the pressure off when I'm making a life decision:

- Make the choice.
- Focus on making the choice work and seeing the good in the decision.
- Know that there will be hard times, but that you can persist and build resilience and knowledge.

Break free from the fear of failing

When we try to be perfect or live our best life, it means failure is not an option. Even the idea of failure feels too humiliating. We'll do anything to avoid the disappointment and shame, which can push us into overdrive and overwork, or the other way into avoidance and procrastination.

Avoidance is understandable: it's a sign that something feels emotionally risky. Our minds are trying to be helpful by keeping us safe from discomfort and vulnerability. We avoid something because it matters, because the prospect of failure or rejection feels too awful. We might also avoid something we need to do because it's difficult or boring, or because it brings up discomfort. When we can't bear discomfort, we try to escape.

The brain does a cost–benefit analysis and, if it estimates the task is 'high effort, low reward', you're more likely to avoid it or procrastinate. However, the brain misses from the calculation how much better you'll feel once you begin the task, and how bad overthinking makes you feel. Avoidance brings temporary relief, which can make us believe we've done the right thing, but it's a short-term gain for long-term pain – and it feeds overthinking and shame. You might let opportunities pass you by, or pretend you don't care, rather than work hard and risk things not working out as you want. In a warped way, this can maintain the belief that you could have been brilliant if you'd tried: 'I did badly because I didn't study,' 'I could have done better, but I didn't train,' or 'I had a brilliant idea, but I never got round to doing anything about it.' It can also be a way of avoiding potential criticism or negative feedback, but staying 'safe' shrinks our world. Growth is doing these things in spite of feeling scared. It's trying that matters, not succeeding. You'll see more on this in the next step, as it's key to curing overthinking.

Avoidance can come in many different forms:

- Avoiding difficult situations, never taking risks and staying under the radar.
- Cancelling plans.
- Not investing in your relationships.
- Not putting yourself forward and not trying new things.
- Not caring, because if you don't care it doesn't matter what happens.
- Failing to ask for help.
- Procrastination, under-preparing, turning up late or not completing work.
- People-pleasing and struggling to be assertive.
- Undermining your success.
- Self-destructive behaviours, such as substance misuse, skin-picking and binge-eating.
- Starting over and never staying in one place for long, by swapping jobs, moving cities or changing friends.

When we overestimate the risks and underestimate our ability to cope, it's as if our insurance premiums are too high.

Try these techniques for overcoming a fear of failure:

Seek out failure

When I researched fear of failure, I couldn't find a single biography where failure or difficulty wasn't part of the story. Our successes are achieved through trying, yet trying often ends in mistakes and failure. As much as it might not always look like it, failure is part of the story of success, not separate from it.

Our efforts won't always work out, we may not reach our goals first time, but when we push ourselves, we have a chance to see what we are capable of. It's scary to take the next step, but much scarier to be standing in exactly the same place a year later. It's only really a failure if you never try.

Seek out stories of failure. It's easy to imagine how good people's lives are when you see only the finished product:

- Ask friends to tell you about their failures and what they learned from them, so you see you are not alone.
- Listen to podcasts that share people's stories, such as: *How to Fail, Desert Island Discs, Young Again, Oprah's Super Soul* or *We Can Do Hard Things*.
- Research famous people's lives. I loved the TV show *Succession*, starring the Scottish actor Brian Cox. His is a good example of life not being straightforward. His father died of pancreatic cancer when Brian was eight, leaving only £10 in the bank and pushing the family into poverty. His mother had a nervous breakdown, so Brian's three sisters helped bring him up. They shared one toilet between five families. Brian left school when he was 15. His first job was washing the stage at the local theatre, but he gradually moved up the ranks. His first big break was when he was nearly 40, and he became an international name for his role

in *Succession* when he was 72. Success certainly didn't come easily to him: it came after years of hard work.

Give yourself permission to fail and then learn from it

Just because you've failed at something, it doesn't make you a failure. When you think about it, most things we learn in life come from making mistakes. Many of the things we're now good at, we were once bad at. Expect failure and see it as an important part of life – it builds resilience and helps us get to know ourselves better. Failure provides us with an opportunity to learn how to cope with tough situations, which builds self-confidence. It lets us see that mistakes, failure and rejection are never as scary as we think, so we are no longer so afraid of things going wrong. It can even lead to something better, as many of the world's most impressive inventions were created by people who were trying to make something totally different!

I can see the truth of this in my own life. After writing the *This Book Will . . .* series with a co-author, I tried writing several book proposals without a co-author, but none were accepted. These failures encouraged me to develop my writing skills and gain the experience I needed. When the opportunity to write *The Imposter Cure* came along, the time I'd spent working on the previous ideas and developing as a psychologist and writer meant that, this time, I was offered a book deal.

Going forward, I would like you to keep a mistakes, failures and disappointments diary so that you can see clearly the gains that come from these things. Each time something difficult happens that feels like a failure (or that you might overthink), write it down. Leave space below for writing what you learned from it later on. You could try this format for your diary:

- Write down the failure, how you felt because of it and your
  fears about its impact.
- After one month, look back at what you wrote, then add
  whether your fears came true and what you learned from
  the experience.
- After three months, come back to the diary again – and
  write down something good that happened because of
  that failure.

Slowly, you'll begin to see the benefit of mistakes and failures, from increased knowledge to growth. This provides further evidence to stop overthinking. You may even discover that you begin to feel less fearful of failure.

Don't hold yourself to a different standard

It shouldn't be one rule for you and one rule for everyone else. If you wouldn't see it as a failure for someone else, it doesn't count as a failure for you either. Ask yourself:

- Am I blaming myself for something that isn't my fault?
- Is how I'm seeing this fair?
- Would I think about this the same way if it was a friend?

Check what's behind the fear

David Conroy studied college athletes who had a fear of failure.[80] But he discovered they weren't actually afraid of *failing at the sport*. Underneath the feeling were five specific fears.

Try to identify which one of these fears is affecting you, so you can target it appropriately to overcome it.

FEAR OF	ANSWER IT BACK
Shame – if I fail, it will be really embarrassing.	It's not great to be embarrassed, but I've felt that way before and got through it, and I could get through it again if I needed to. It's worth the risk for the potential reward.
Devaluing the way I see myself – if I fail, it means I'm not the person I thought I was.	I must not define myself by my successes or failures, but by the fact that I keep trying.
An uncertain future – if I fail, it will derail my future hopes.	Avoiding this is giving me a false sense of control over the future, but in fact this is getting in the way of the future I want.
Changing the way that other people see me – if I fail, my friends won't want to hang out with me anymore.	I deserve to have people in my life who love me for me, not for my performance.
Upsetting other people – if I fail, my parents will be disappointed.	Other people will always have opinions and feelings about who I am and what I do, but it's my opinions and feelings that matter the most, as I'm the one who lives with them.

Don't avoid your feelings

It might seem counterintuitive, but I've noticed that people who overthink tend not to express their emotions. Emotions can feel overwhelming, and overthinking acts as a form of avoidance, keeping us in our heads and away from truly feeling the discomfort, pain or vulnerability underneath. Our minds race with endless thoughts and analysis, replaying the past or imagining future scenarios, or we might jump to being rational, leaving no space for our emotions – all to avoid sitting with what's really going on inside. Yet the feelings will pop up in our reactions to day-to-day issues, and can become disproportionate.

We might get stuck on minor daily problems as these provide a 'hook' to hang the emotion on (I'll be asking you to think about what your hooks might be in the strategy on page 239).

When you're stuck overthinking, it's hard to see it for what it is – avoidance. Although you don't feel good at the time, in some ways it is a convenient distraction from your real concerns, which are more uncertain and harder to resolve. You're trying to change how you feel internally with an external change (I'll do it when I . . . get a new job/promotion/partner/feel fitter/get through this busy period/get the house sorted/have more money/ sort out my life), and this gets in the way of looking at how you're actually feeling and doing something about it. Focus on what you can do today.

I worked with a wonderful woman called Melissa, whose life had been marked by difficult events over the past four years. Melissa's father, who she admired and to whom she was incredibly close, had to have open-heart surgery. Thankfully, he recovered, but three years later he was diagnosed with stage-four lung cancer and, despite rigorous treatment, he very sadly died later that year. During this period, Melissa was working in a challenging job, then was reassigned to a new job and had a baby. This is how she felt:

> *I've always been the person who supports everyone else, but therapy helped me see that I had ignored my own feelings. It had reached the point where I no longer felt interested in anything or even knew what I liked doing. I was physically exhausted and mentally drained, and I felt profoundly sad about everything that had happened. I just wanted to withdraw from life. I'd stopped doing anything for myself. I just wanted to eat junk food and be on my own. It was like I was punishing myself.*
>
> *I became really controlling, but the tighter control I took, the more out of control everything felt in my life. I felt so responsible; it was like a heavy weight. It left me feeling helpless. I was fixated on my work and my day-to-day concern was about how I was doing in my job, but as I*

started to talk about everything, it became clear that there was much more going on. My brain had fixed on work as it felt like something I could solve and improve, while many of the changes I'd experienced over the past four years were out of my control.

Melissa had coped amazingly well with everything that had happened, but it had reached a point where she was understandably overwhelmed. She began to see that overthinking had been a way to avoid dealing with the loss and grief she'd experienced. After her father died, she had become extremely anxious and felt guilty: 'What if there was more I could have done to save him?' Melissa could also see that she had compassion for everyone except herself. When she noticed the thoughts, she chose to move away from overthinking and find self-compassion. This allowed her to make space for her feelings and for looking after herself.

Melissa gave herself permission to do the things she loved again. She wrote letters to her father to express her grief and say the things she would if he were still here. She challenged the thoughts that said she could have done more to save him. Melissa was able to see that what happened was not under her control, but she had faced it to the best of her ability. Therapy allowed Melissa to review her life, re-evaluate and remember her strengths. I felt honoured to work with her and see the changes she was able to make to her life.

Try these techniques to help you express your feelings:

Allow yourself to feel

Your feelings are a bit like clouds: they're around for a while before moving on. Although you might prefer what we term 'good' feelings, all feelings are valid, and experiencing the full range of emotions is what makes us human. When you have darker feelings, remember that how you feel does not necessarily reflect how things are. Instead of identifying with or fighting with these emotions, remind yourself that your feelings are not permanent and they do not define you.

Ultimately, we need to allow ourselves to feel – this is key to all the ideas in this chapter. When we observe and acknowledge our feelings without judgement, we stop the overthinking cycle, giving ourselves a chance to experience the emotion and work through it without getting stuck.

When you have a 'difficult' feeling, try these steps:

- Pause and notice the feeling instead of becoming entangled.
- Be curious: enquire and feel what is there.
- Name the feeling and say it out loud: 'I'm feeling anxious right now.' Naming it takes away its power.

The aim is to allow feelings and create a space between the feeling and your reaction. It is this that leads to recovery and growth, allowing the sun to break through.

Write down how you're feeling

Reflection helps you to unpack what you're feeling, express your emotional experiences and learn from what you have done. It might seem counterintuitive, but looking at difficult feelings is the best way to allow them to pass. It will also help you to get to know yourself better.

- Set aside time in your day to write down your thoughts and feelings.
- Reflect on what's going on in your life. Take time to think about the good stuff, as well as the parts of life that are more difficult.
- Note down any avoidance patterns and become aware of how you react when you face difficult emotions, such as comfort-eating, skin-picking or shutting down.

Notice your hooks

Take a moment to think about what your 'hooks' might be. Melissa's hook was her work. Perhaps your hook is finding mess harder to put up with, or getting more irritable with your partner or kids when you've had a stressful day. Alternatively, you might become defensive when you feel vulnerable, or get annoyed by something minor when, underneath, you're really feeling sad. Watch out for strong emotional responses that don't quite add up. Feel where they sit and release them from your body. Is there anything beneath the upset – fear, shame, loss, anger, guilt, insecurity, loneliness, vulnerability? Deal with this feeling.

Are there any situations that trigger a disproportionate response in you? What is your feeling in these situations? Is there anything else going on: do you feel ignored, not cared for, worthless, not good enough, unappreciated or something different?

When you become more aware of your reactions and learn what your hooks are, you can use this to your advantage to gain greater awareness of how you're feeling and what's actually going on inside you. It's another way to broaden your spotlight of attention. It allows you to make a conscious choice, rather than just reacting, and to do something to look after yourself and the issues that are really troubling you.

Moving forward

Before you move on to the next step, I want you to set your expectations more fairly and remain flexible in your approach to life. Use the ideas, arguments and strategies in this chapter to do this. Ultimately, as an overthinker, you need to take the pressure off yourself and care less. You don't need to pay attention to *everything*, know the outcome or put 100 per cent into all you do. It just doesn't matter as much as you're imagining! Life will move along far more smoothly when you don't force it, and will be far more enjoyable without constant intervention or planning. When you give up the wish for things to be different and accept life as it is, it frees you. This will put you in the best position for the next step.

Step Four: Checklist

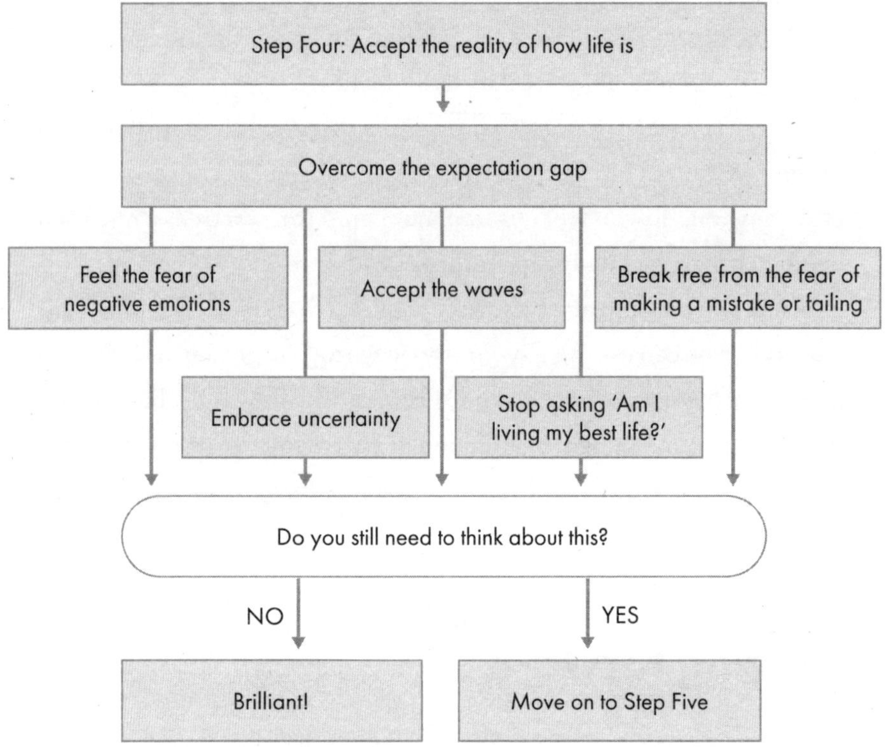

Chapter 14
Step five – face your fears

By the end of this chapter, you will:
- Take action and get back to doing the things that matter to you.
- See that your thoughts and feelings are not facts and gain evidence to help you talk back to your limiting beliefs.
- Cement your new ways of thinking.
- Keep your world bigger and make the day-to-day issues (that overthinking loves to get into) seem small.
- Seek out reality and experience life.

There's a reason why there are so many well-known quotes about the importance of facing your fears. If you avoid the things you fear, you will always be anxious about them. It's only when you face your fears that you can overcome them.

Step Five is crucial for curing overthinking. Knowing the theory isn't enough: it's only when you start facing the things that have been difficult that you can believe beyond any doubt that you can do it. It really is the only way to silence overthinking for good – and the rewards are seismic.

In this final step, it's time to open your life back up and make your words and actions congruent, so you are no longer the person who says one thing but does another. It's time to get back into the practice of doing what you say you're going to do and, more importantly, doing the things that matter to you.

When your thoughts say you can't do something, or tell you that you will be judged or you'll embarrass yourself, avoidance means you never have a chance to find out. Doing these things is the only way you will know for sure. The work you did in Step Four puts you in the best position to do this.

Face this step with compassion and back yourself. I know that you can do this – and that when you do, your life is going to be *so* much better and so much more satisfying.

Daring to change

Growth happens when we learn to embrace the risk. I find it helpful to remember that distress and growth can co-exist and are part of the same process. They are not in opposition, but are two dimensions of experience. Growth can feel uncomfortable, as it pushes you into places you haven't been, but it's here that you learn the most about yourself and build resilience. When we look at and feel our distress, we also create space for growth.

Humans are amazingly adaptable. Trust in yourself and your ability to work things out. When we move with change, stop fearing discomfort and stay curious about life, things flow more easily. These things may cause discomfort, but confronting it is the only way through. Otherwise, discomfort lingers over you like a cartoon raincloud. At least when you make a change, you can put an end to the overthinking and self-criticism. It's also helpful to remember that there's a lot of good stuff on the other side of discomfort – knowing yourself better, seeing your capability, proving you can cope with setbacks and knowing it's not as bad as you expected.

Amélie had been in a relationship for a long time and knew that it wasn't working anymore. Her partner had become gradually more critical and dismissive over the years, and often made Amélie the outlet for her upsets. Amélie had lost her confidence and, although she knew that she was unhappy, she felt scared to leave. She also felt guilt and worry about the impact her leaving would have on her partner.

She doesn't ask me about things and I no longer want to tell her. For so long I've tried to make her happy and to appease her, but she doesn't appreciate me. I've been in the relationship so long, it feels hard to imagine life differently. I feel intense anxiety and guilt that I want something different. I also feel a loss: 'Why didn't I do this earlier?' I've felt trapped for so long and starved of time and attention. It feels so hard leaving, and I feel so sad that it hasn't worked, but I'm starting to think about what I want, and I don't want to be treated like this anymore.

I've found a new place to live. I feel terrified, and the fear and uncertainty feel overwhelming at times. I hear the critical voice creeping in, but I think about all the things I've managed to do since starting therapy and the positive impact they've had. Joining a basketball club, seeing friends again, the upholstery course. If you'd said to me I could do those things, I wouldn't have believed it, yet I did and I felt terrified before each one. Especially the upholstery course; I've never done anything creative and I was daunted by who else would be there. I imagined they'd all be really experienced and far better than me, but they were so lovely and it's been amazing to try something new. It's helped me remember the different parts of myself.

Sometimes I wish I could go back to avoiding. It's hard at times, pushing yourself into all these new things. But then I remember how much better life is now, that I wasn't really living before and my world had become so small. Each time I've taken the next step and faced the things that I've been avoiding, it's made me feel more alive and it's given me the confidence to keep going. All my friends have noticed, too; they say I'm back to my old self. It gives me the confidence to take this next step, and there's this new part of me that feels excited about things again.

It was only when Amélie thought about what she wanted and faced her fears that she could change her situation. Remember, it's *doing* the thing that you gain from, not thinking about it. In fact, if you think about it too much, you'll only talk yourself out of it.

Relationships

If your overthinking is linked to your relationships and your communication, there is more specific information on this, as well as advice and strategies, on page 291.

Build new habits

The more practised you become at doing what you say and want – whether it's something big, like it was for Amélie, or something smaller – the easier it will become, because you will build new habits and new neural pathways in your brain. If you do a new thing enough times, you may not feel anxious about it anymore. There are also so many benefits, including greater life satisfaction, increased confidence, improved mood, less anxiety and less time to overthink, to name just a few.

Building a new habit typically takes anywhere from 18 to 254 days, with an average of about 66 days.[81,82] When I first started road cycling, I felt nervous every time I rode. It wasn't a case of doing it once and then the fear went away; it took somewhere over fifty times before I felt more at ease. When you do things that feel good or stimulating, it can give you a boost, so you do it again. I think about it as a net positive: there might be some difficult parts to what you're trying to do, but if overall the gains are greater, it's worth it!

As you work through this chapter, you need to plan for your 'worst self'. For example, consider the best way to approach facing your fears if you've had a really difficult or very busy day, or when you've slept badly or had an argument with a good friend, or when your child has had a meltdown. When we make plans, we normally plan for our 'best self', but we need to plan for the person we are, rather than the person we hope to be. This allows us to be prepared, and to put resources in place, for how we *actually* feel when we come to put our plans into action. For example, you could arrange support from friends and family, or plan to implement your new habit at the beginning of the day rather than at the end of the day, to ensure things go as well as possible. Keep the following ideas in mind to successfully build these new habits:

- **Write down your motivation**: Be clear on why you want to do this and the difference it will make to your life.
- **Start small**: Willpower is like a muscle; it gets fatigued, and motivation then drops. Start small with something you can easily do, then build up.
- **Aim to gradually improve**: Don't aim for amazing straight away. The pleasure of meeting your expectations will push you to keep going.
- **Break it down**: Break bigger goals into smaller steps. The key is to get started, because once you've started it's much easier to keep going.
- **Slip-ups are normal**: Bring self-compassion. Think in advance about what might go wrong or get in the way, and how you can bounce back quickly if you do go off track. Don't have an all-or-nothing attitude towards your plans: for example, just aim to never miss a class twice in a row.
- **Be patient**: Consistency and repetition are key. You'll need to do these things again and again, but each time you do them, you're making progress.

It's never as bad as you think

Reassure yourself that nothing is ever as terrifying as you think. As difficult as something might feel, in my experience – both professionally and personally – thinking about it is *always* worse than the reality. The period right before a change or new activity is always the worst bit, as it's filled with uncertainty. Expect the thoughts to come, and accept they will probably not be on your side. You're in limbo, and it's here the anticipatory anxiety grows. When we worry, we tend to miscalculate fear. Try to externalize the thoughts and step back from them. You could say, 'Here come my thoughts that I don't want to do this, but I know anxious predictions do not tell the truth.'

I also find it helpful to know that humans are terrible at making predictions! Social psychologist Professor Dan Gilbert looks at the pursuit of happiness and whether people can accurately predict which events will make them happy, by how much and for how long.[83] Will we enjoy the pizza or pasta more? Will it be more enjoyable to watch a play at the theatre or to watch a reality show on TV? Will going to university or doing an apprenticeship bring more happiness? Will getting married bring more or less happiness in the long run than living life as a single parent?

Gilbert became interested in this area after going through an incredibly difficult period: a divorce, a falling-out with his best friend, the unexpected death of his mentor and trouble with his teenage son. He was surprised that, although life was tough, he wasn't nearly as distraught as he would have imagined. It made him wonder whether he was alone. He joined up with psychologist Tim Wilson to research the topic. Their research challenges the idea that we will be miserable if we don't get what we want. It shows conclusively that we tend to overestimate how good we'll feel when things go right, and how bad we'll feel when things go wrong, as well as how long we'll feel awful for (it's never as long as you think).

In a similar study, psychologists at City University, London, spoke to people before taking their driving tests and asked how they might feel if they failed.[84] Those who failed their driving tests overestimated the duration of their disappointment – and this even included test-takers who had previously failed! In another study, college sports fans were asked to estimate how happy they'd be after their favourite team won the game, and how long the feelings of happiness would last.[85] Again they were shown to overestimate not only how happy they'd be but also how long it would last.

Our psychological immune system lets us feel truly happy even when things *don't* go as planned.[86]

Dan Gilbert's research also confirms that it's not making the perfect choice that makes you happier, it's just making a choice![87] Gilbert and Wilson got students to complete a photography course. At the end of the course, the students were given two photographs they had taken and were told that they could keep one and the course would keep one. It was a hard choice: they wanted to keep both. In the first group, they were told that, if they ever changed their mind, they could swap the photo. The second group were told their decision was final. They found that those who made an irrevocable decision were much happier with the choice they made.

In a follow-up study, the psychologists let people decide which group they wanted to be in. The majority chose the first group – they thought they would be happier if they could change their minds – but it was still those who made a final choice who were happier. When a decision isn't irrevocable, it means you can revisit it and change your mind, which leaves a huge amount of scope to overthink it. More choice made people less happy.

Once we've made a decision and taken action, the brain works to protect us from feeling bad. Our minds find a way to rationalize what's happened and reframe it to see why the decision we've made is better than the option we have dismissed. This means we feel better about ourselves and about the world in general. Remember this as you work through this chapter. Even if something doesn't work out, you'll be able to handle it better than you expect – and it may teach you something worth learning about yourself.

Don't decide what to do based on your feelings alone

How you're feeling right now is not an indication of how you will feel when you are doing something else at a different point in time. The two do not correlate.

I can think of a situation in my own life when this was proved very true. For the past year, I'd been looking forward to going to the Burning of the Clocks – an event held in the city where I live on 21 December, to mark the shortest day of the year. People make their own lanterns and, after parading through the city, they pass them into a blazing bonfire on the beach as a token of the year's end. Since moving to the city, we hadn't been able to attend, for various reasons, so I was really keen to see what it was like as I'd heard so many good things about it. Yet when it came to the day, the prospect of working out where to park, finding somewhere to stand and deciding who to meet, on top of an already busy holiday, felt overwhelming. I almost talked myself out of going. I was so focused on potential problems that I'd forgotten the excitement of the event itself! It was such a wonderful evening, but if I'd listened to how I felt before I went, I might not have gone.

We are not very good at predicting how we will feel about future events or experiences. Dan Gilbert suggests that this is due to a number of reasons:

- Our minds tend to subconciously add or remove details from imagined future scenarios, leading to inaccurate predictions. Often our spotlight focuses on just one small part of what we're going to be doing – and the potential problems that might come with it – and we forget about all the likely gains.

- How we feel now affects our prediction. When we imagine the things we want to do, our thoughts are often coloured by our present mood. We forget about the boost to our mood we may experience from doing these things.

- We underestimate how quicky our feelings can change and our ability to change them. Our lack of faith in our own resilience can lead us to incorrectly expect that negative emotions will always last longer than other feelings. This can lead us to take decisions that don't maximize our potential for satisfaction and enjoyment.

- The psychological immune system means that the brain is an expert at construing what happens to us in a positive light. It helps us cope with negative events, making them seem less painful than we initially anticipate.

Imagine you're sitting at home, feeling anxious about meeting a group of friends. The anxiety overrides what it will be like when you're there. You're on the wrong brain track, so it's difficult to remember all the times you haven't felt like going but were pleased when you did. How you feel now is not a reflection of how you will feel once you're there, when you'll be with your friends doing something enjoyable. Going and doing something is also an opportunity to boost your mood and it stops you having time to overthink. Keep in mind opposite action (see page 162) – if your mind says 'No', it's probably exactly what you need to do.

In addition, anticipatory anxiety is nearly always wrong because we tend to overestimate the risk of situations we fear and underestimate our ability to cope. In one study, participants were asked to write down their worries.[88] They were later asked to identify which of their anxious predictions came true. Eighty-five per cent of what people worried about never happened. Of the 15 per cent that did happen, 79 per cent of participants discovered that either they could handle the difficulty better than expected, or the difficulty taught them a lesson worth learning. Next time you're over-planning, remember that 97 per cent of what you worry about is your mind tricking you and scaring you with things that are highly unlikely to ever happen.

Try to separate your actions from your mood. Often, we link a bad mood to a bad day, feeling tired to not wanting to do much, and feeling nervous to thinking we should avoid something, but it's important to break these links. Feeling nervous doesn't mean you're unprepared or that an event is going to go badly. It just means you care about something beyond your control or are unsure about how it's going to go. Remind yourself it's OK to do it while you're nervous.

Rather than trying to eliminate discomfort, risk or uncertainty and control the outcomes, ask yourself, 'Do I know what I need to do?' You can then identify the action you need to take. On the whole, we already know what to do – and we need to do it even if we don't know the outcome. If you think of my Burning the Clocks example, overthinking left me trapped in 'what ifs' and potential problems – what if we can't find a parking space, what if we can't find a good place to stand – instead of identifying what I needed to do, which was go into town, locate a parking space and then find the best place to stand once we were there. I didn't need to think through all the potential outcomes, I just needed to shut down the thinking and go.

Instead of predicting how you think you'll feel, think of the times when you've taken action despite not feeling like it. How did it go? Were you glad you did it? This is the best prediction of how this occasion will go. You can also think about how you want to feel in the long run. To do this, get in touch with your future self. Make sure you're really clear about why you want to do what you're doing. How will it make things better for you in the future? Why will you benefit? Make your goals concrete and think about what you'll gain if you reach them. We need to fit our feelings into a wider picture, which includes our goals, values, what's meaningful to us and our general needs. It's so much better to look back and know you tried than to wonder, 'What if?'

Avoidance tells you that you'll feel better if you hide, but the real question is, 'Would I rather do this and get it over with, or not do it and feel worse?' We regret inaction more than action – the goals you didn't chase, the things you didn't say, the risks you didn't take – especially in the longer term.

This is your life, so take charge of the choices that matter to you. As you work through the next section and face your fears, keep in mind the following pointers:

- Expect the avoidant thoughts. You could say to yourself, 'When it comes to doing this, I'm going to think of every reason not to, but I know it's what I need to do.'

- Accept your mood. Acknowledge that you're feeling bad, tired or nervous. Don't try to fight it or resist it.

- Do not end things here, as you won't get a chance to see that you can do it and that it's not as bad as you thought. You'll also miss out on experiencing the relief, enjoyment and pride that comes from doing it.

- Use the idea 'both and': you can *both* want to do it *and* feel terrified about it. It doesn't need to be just one thing. It can feel difficult even though this is what you wanted, but that doesn't mean you shouldn't do it.

- Ask yourself, 'If I was at the end of my life looking back, what would I want to see and what would my biggest regrets be?' This lets you see the bigger picture and gives you the opportunity to really think about what's important to you.

Experiment and face your fears

Now it's time for action. Brainstorm a list of all the things you've been finding difficult and everything you've been avoiding. These things might show up as procrastination, isolating, not sharing how you feel, talking yourself out of things, not trying a new business idea, avoiding sending an email or not making a call.

Next, I want you to set each one up as an experiment, using the table on the following page as a guide:

- Start small and build up: organize your list so the easiest thing to do is at the top and the hardest last. Write them down in the table under 'Things I want to do'.

- For each thing, write down what your feared outcome is and identify the underlying fear. Step Four should have given you a better understanding of this (see Chapter Thirteen). Ask yourself what you are really afraid of: rejection, judgement, failure, the unknown? Once you're more aware of what's going on, it lessens its grip on you.

- For the most challenging items (found at the bottom of the list), remember to break them into manageable chunks so they feel more doable.

- Finally, work out the best time to do these things. I know that if I do something first thing in the morning, I'm less likely to talk myself out of it. Alternatively, I might have more success if I tag it on to something else that I'm already doing, or find some external accountability via a friend!

Things I want to do (easiest first, hardest last)	What's the underlying fear?	Can I break this down into easier steps?	When is best to try this?
Speak to someone I don't know	Fear of humiliation	Start small by saying 'Good morning' to the guy in the local shop when I buy my milk	In the morning so I don't have time to talk myself out of it
Be more open with my friends	Fear of rejection	Try it out with my best friend first so it's less pressure	When I'm on my own with them
Try dating on the apps	Fear of rejection	Get my friends to help me set up a profile. Try messaging first and build up to meeting	Meet in the day for coffee so it's a short date
Join a running group	Fear that I won't be good enough	Find out about a local group so it's near home. Remind myself that I can try it a few times and can always change my mind if I don't like it	Immediately – I just need to go for it and silence the 'will I, won't I' voice

Include your relationships

While you are thinking about facing your fears, make sure you focus on your relationships. Dare to bring your whole self to your relationships – be willing to be genuine and vulnerable. Say what you're thinking without thinking it first. Show affection and talk in greater depth. I know this is all scary, but it's the only way to see that you will be accepted exactly as you are. As you gradually take greater risks with the people you feel close to, you will build confidence in facing your fear. Be aware of anxiety and fear of rejection trying to block your relationships, and do bring compassion to these feelings. If you have been struggling with relationships, this will be hard, but it's one of the most rewarding places to invest your time and energy.

If you are struggling with social anxiety, there's more information on this and how it feeds into overthinking, as well as specific strategies to help you overcome it, on page 288. It's also important to seek out therapy to support you if this anxiety is at a level that is interfering with your day-to-day life.

List as many positive outcomes as you can

When we get caught up in overthinking, we give a huge amount of time to worst-case scenarios, living through them as if they are happening. But what about thinking of the positive scenarios? I know I normally tell you not to over-prepare, but bear with me . . .

It might go wrong, but what if it goes right?

When we see facing things as a positive rather than something to fear, then we become excited to see what happens. This prevents your brain from overestimating a negative outcome, by reminding you of all the potential positive outcomes it hasn't considered, broadening your spotlight of attention. Part of the reason why you're afraid of the future is your brain doesn't appreciate all the positive scenarios that are likely to play out. Gaining confidence isn't about denying what could go wrong, it's about recognizing what might go right. The more you practise this way of thinking, the more you'll strengthen that new neural pathway. It then becomes easier to think in these ways.

You could change your internal narrative and picture what you *want* to happen with visualization. This form of mental rehearsal is the one type of planning I'll allow. Athletes visualize their goals before a competition. They see themselves winning the game or running the fastest race. This increases the likelihood that it will go well (while imagining the worst can increase the likelihood that things will go wrong).

What you focus on and take deliberate steps towards is most likely to become a reality. Maybe you're giving a talk or you have an important meeting. Visualize it in advance: see yourself confidently walking into the room and clearly articulating what you want to say.

- Try spending a few minutes really thinking through what you want to happen.
- Write it down, engaging all five senses.
- Now see it as a film clip playing out just as you wish.
- As you visualize this, take deep breaths so you feel calm.
- Tell yourself you can do it.

Silence the 'will I, won't I' voice

As you work up to a new challenge or facing a fear, beware of 'will I, won't I' thoughts. Do not allow your brain to open up the idea of not doing this. Commit, and make each challenge non-negotiable so you close down any questioning thoughts. These thoughts can become all-consuming and use up the energy you need for actually doing these things.

Remind yourself that you've tried avoiding and it doesn't work. Think of your questioning thoughts as different radio stations, so you can tune out the station that says, 'I don't want to do this.' If you notice yourself debating, close it down and recommit to what you're doing: 'I'm not thinking about this, I'm doing it.' Or simply say 'Stop' or 'No' to the thoughts (using the strategy from Step Two; see page 171). You might even say to yourself, 'I *get* to do this' – as a way to reframe it as an opportunity rather than an obligation.

If it's helpful, think of other things you do without question. Can you bring the same approach to this? I never question going to work or taking the kids to school, yet I can talk myself out of doing things in the evening with surprising ease!

My kids do track racing (racing on bikes with no gears and no brakes) and so I decided to give it a go. Every week before racing, I'd get really nervous, and I'd make the mistake of starting to think about whether or not I was going to do it (the 'will I, won't I' voice). I'd check the weather and hope for rain so it would be cancelled. I must have been the only person hoping for rain in the summer! Or I'd think about how tired I was, and come up with different excuses for why I might not race.

To step out of this pattern, I made a commitment to myself to do the season, and I banned myself from checking the weather. This let me silence the 'will I, won't I' voice and left more room for me to enjoy the racing. If I was feeling unsure, I'd remind myself, 'If in doubt, just do it and remember that nobody but me cares how well I do.' I'd also remind myself how much I enjoyed seeing everyone, and how proud I felt of myself for trying something new.

Once I was cycling on the track for the warm-up, I knew I was happy to be there. I also wrote down how I felt after doing it so I could remind myself of how much I enjoyed it the next time I was nervous. There were some weeks when I still talked myself out of it, but rather than feel disappointed, I reminded myself I could try again the next week and that, if I decided at the end of the season I didn't want to do it, I could stop.

Taking action means we see the reality of our limitations. This is another part of acceptance. You might find that it's harder than you imagined; you might not win or do as well as you'd hoped. You might lose the fantasy that you once had, but this is the trade-off of living in the real world and engaging with life (rather than staying stuck in your head), and it's part of being human. It's doing things that we gain the most from, not thinking about things. Keep going and see where it leads.

Do it and take notes!

You could spend hours planning and preparing, but until you take that first step, it's all just theory and speculation. The fastest way to *know* if something will work for you is to try it. Clarity doesn't come before action; it comes from action. It's just about getting started and setting the wheels in motion.

There are no guarantees that the challenge will work out, but not trying will leave you feeling anxious, static and stuck – and will give you more time for overthinking. Trying means you at least have a chance of achieving what you're hoping for.

The best way to silence those thoughts is to just do it! As you do, track your outcomes and note down how you feel before and after. Use the table opposite as a model. Here are some tips for how to record your challenges:

- Challenge yourself to do one thing each day that pushes you out of your comfort zone. It doesn't matter how small.
- Write down what outcome you fear from the challenge, thinking deeply in the moment to decipher those fears.
- Before you do your challenge, make a note of how likely that outcome feels, and then how likely it logically is.
- Do it!
- Make a note of what the true outcome was, and how you feel you coped.

The last three columns in this table are the most revealing! We spend hours worrying in the lead-up to a challenge, living through it in our imaginations, overthinking what might go wrong, considering the worst outcomes, over-preparing or talking ourselves down, but we don't think enough about the reality of how it went, how we did and what it shows we're capable of. Fill in these columns straight away, as it's harder to

Things I want to do!	What is the feared outcome?	How likely does that outcome feel? (0–10)	How likely does that outcome logically seem? (0–10)	What was the actual outcome?	Was it better or worse than predicted?	How did you cope? 0 = terribly 5 = as well as I could hope
Make a phone call	What if I say the wrong thing? What if I don't know the answer? Fear of the unknown, fear of judgement	9	6	I really cringed, but it was OK	It was better than I expected, but I didn't like it	3
Give a talk	I'll do a bad job – fear of failure	9	5	It went really well	Much better. I was nervous before, but it was great	5
Share a feeling when I see friends	They'll think I'm pathetic – fear of judgement	8	7	I felt shy, but I managed to do it, and one of the others shared that she'd felt the same. I hadn't realized they felt like that too	I did find it hard, but I'm glad I did it, as I felt like I was being more real	4
Go out even if I don't feel like it	I'll be too tired and I'll be on bad form – fear of the unknown	7	5	I had a really good time and was so glad I went	Much better	5

accurately recall your mood and how it went when you're not in the feeling. This is a chance to update your fears. It's also good to talk to other people about it, so you really cement how you did in your brain. Just give your gut response and the best judgement of how you got on. When overthinking gets involved, it undoes how you did and you will over-analyse potential problems.

This is evidence you can use for future support when you do the next challenge, and the one after that. Often, we're so relieved that we've done a challenge that we switch off and move on to the next thing, which means we miss the opportunity to gather concrete evidence and update our anxious predictions. It's important to see in black and white that you did it and, although you thought it would go badly or you wouldn't cope, you were wrong.

Each time you fill in a row in the table, you are gathering more information: 'I felt like this last time, but I did it and I'm so glad I did.' It's also a chance to see that, the more you challenge yourself, the easier it gets.

Feeling stuck?

If you're feeling stuck, try asking yourself these three questions:

1. **What am I avoiding?** Apply opposite action (see page 162). You need to do it!
2. **Where do I start?** Break the challenge down, creating a step that you can take today. Just get started and see where you get.
3. **What obstacles are stopping me from getting to where I want to go?** Break them down, then move forward.

When I was asked to do TEDx, I couldn't believe people thought I'd be worth listening to. I felt incredibly flattered and excitedly said yes.

I looked forward to it as I prepared my talk, but as the date came closer, I started to dread it. I'd think to myself, 'Why have I said I'll do this? I'm not a public speaker, I'm a therapist. Why didn't I just stick to what I know and like? I don't even like public speaking; I'm so much better working with people one to one.'

In the days immediately before the talk, my anxiety increased and I slept badly. On the day itself, I felt so nervous, but I reminded myself that it's normal to be nervous and that, after this one time, I never had to do it again. After the first few minutes of giving the talk, I was able to settle into it and, although I still felt anxious, it was OK. Afterwards, I was so pleased I'd done it, as it had been a chance to try something new, challenge myself and share my experience and ideas. I loved listening to all the other talks, meeting people and hearing their experiences. I noted down how I felt and saved the feedback that people sent to me. This meant that I would remember the outcome if I was asked to give a talk again.

The next time I was asked to give a talk, I said yes, thinking that this time things would be different. But as the day approached, I felt almost exactly the same. The only difference was that, this time, I knew how glad I'd been and the sense of pride I'd felt on the first occasion. I remembered that I could both want to do it and feel nervous and question myself. It was really hard to link to this feeling in the midst of the anxiety, but I clung on to it. On the morning of the talk, I had the same thoughts about wishing I'd stuck to therapy, but I knew it had gone well the last time and that, deep down, I wanted to do it. I reminded myself that the hour before was the worst part, and silenced the 'will I, won't I' voice. I also took note of the change of heart: when I'd agreed I wanted to do it, this was my true feeling – the change of heart was just fear.

I've now done many talks, and it's something I really enjoy. I no longer have the dread beforehand, but it took a long time before I felt this way, and I do still feel nervous on the day. I know this is how I will always feel, but that it just means I'm getting prepared, that I care about what I'm doing and that I want to do a good job.

Don't let overthinking get in the way of you living your life. When your words and actions are congruent, it means you are participating in the world rather than watching it go by – and the most likely outcome is that you will make progress and feel good about yourself. The more you challenge yourself, the easier it will become, allowing you to shut down overthinking and open up to life.

Moving forward

Congratulations on completing the last step. You have done so well! Keep facing your fears – and push your boundaries if you dare. Do things that you know will be hard, seek out rejection, open up to others and dare to live life the way you want to. This is the ultimate way to stop overthinking and to enjoy life to the full.

Step Five: Checklist

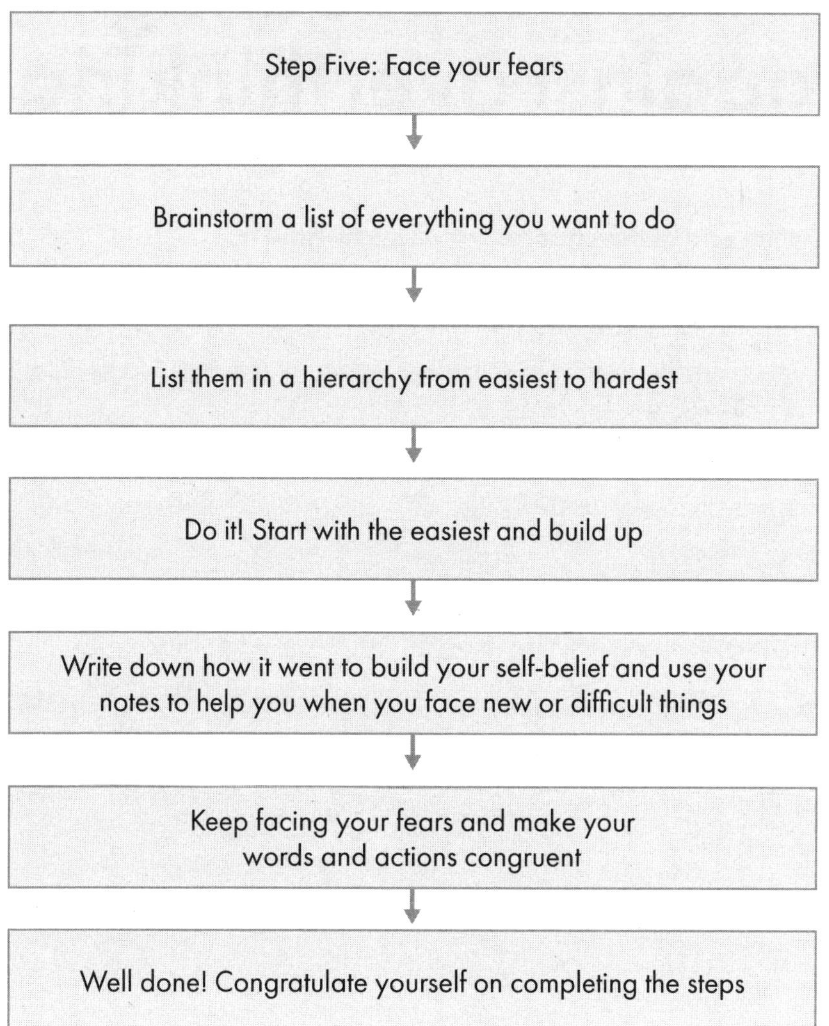

Chapter 15
Future-proofing against overthinking

By the end of this chapter, you'll know how to:
- Build your confidence.
- Find a place where this type of thinking can thrive.
- Make the most of being in life, instead of just thinking about it.

Build your confidence

One of the best ways to future-proof your life against overthinking is to build your self-confidence. Confidence is not something you're born with: it's best seen as a skill you can learn. Confidence helps you feel secure in your own thoughts and less concerned about what others think. It makes communication easier. You're also more likely to know what you want and make choices with your best interests in mind.

When your self-confidence is solid, it's like being in a sturdy boat. While you might prefer to sail in calm waters, if the sea does become rough, you can trust in yourself and your ability to cope. Even if you are thrown off-course, you know you can weather the storm; and a strong sense of your values can help steer you back on track.

It's important to tie how you feel to multiple areas, so you broaden your base of self-esteem. I like to think about these areas as floats for your boat, keeping you buoyant in difficult times. Even if something goes wrong, you are left less vulnerable as you have the other areas of your life to fall back on. If, however, you have only one thing that makes you feel good, when things are uncertain in that area it can cause you to capsize. This is why it's important to open up your world. The more buoyancy you have, the more secure your boat will be. Floats can be your relationships, work, activities, interests, hobbies or sources of support. The strategies you have learned also act as floats.

Shifting from external to internal validation

Most overthinkers rely on external validation to feel good enough or worthy. We all love positive feedback, but external validation on its own is precarious, as it's always reliant on someone or something else.

It might feel good in the moment, but before you know it, you're in need of more reassurance. When you think back to the sturdy boat, using external validation to feel more self-confident is like trying to row in a boat with holes – you'll soon be sunk. To future-proof yourself against overthinking, you need to shift to internal validation.

Internal validation comes from within. It takes in everything you are doing and allows you to see the full picture of who you are and what you're capable of (this is why it's so important to log what you've been doing, so you can add it to what you know about yourself). This helps you feel more secure within yourself, guides your choices, builds self-esteem, brings better mental health outcomes and makes life easier. You'll also be less affected by what others think. It's the perfect antidote to overthinking.

When you recognize your strengths and connect to them, you will no longer be reliant on external validation to feel good about yourself. It's your view that should inform your thoughts, actions and decisions. This information is also something you can draw on when you feel unsure of yourself: it provides useful information for your compassionate voice so you can encourage yourself and acknowledge your progress and effort.

Let's discuss what internal validation truly is. Internal validation:

- Incorporates your values, strengths and instincts, as well as the personal satisfaction that comes from knowing you've done well.
- Means being conscious of how you're doing, based on what *you* know about yourself.
- Means being in tune with what you want, like and need – and what you *don't* want.
- Allows you to internalize your achievements, strengths and successes, and to take on board positive feedback.

- Means noticing and accepting your feelings, as well as accepting your limitations, mistakes and failures with compassion.

To build internal validation, I want you to do the following:

Let your values guide your choices and behaviour

Your values form the foundations of what's important to you in life. Be clear about what really matters and let this inform your decisions. An easy way to identify your values is to ask yourself the following questions:

- What's important to me?
- What do I enjoy doing?
- What qualities do I admire in others?
- What sort of person do I want to be in my relationships, at work and in life generally?
- What do I want to be remembered for?

Use these questions to think about what success means to you and what you really want from your life. This is not what you think you *should* do, or what you imagine others expect, but what *you* want. Success is different for everyone, but in my mind it's not just about one thing. It's a layered experience that reflects how you integrate all the different elements of your life – your family, friends, work, interests, passions and downtime. Real success comes when you manage to include everything that is important to you.

When you act in line with your values and you know why you are doing things, it will matter less what others think and your life will be more meaningful. Meaning is the best buffer there is to stress, worry and low mood.

Maximize your strengths

Focusing on your strengths is the best investment of your time – and much more valuable than focusing on and trying to improve your perceived weaknesses. Don't just see yourself as an overthinker. Take a moment to think of all your positive character traits and skills:

- To start with, think about everything you've accomplished in the steps so far and what this shows about you.
- Think about the things you've done that you are proud of and the different things that make you who you are.
- Ask friends and family how they would describe you – you could ask them to write down their thoughts so you can keep them and look back at them.
- Look back at any positive feedback or accomplishments, no matter how big or small, and take these in so they become something you know about yourself.

Use this information to update your self-image. Really take on board this information so you can connect to it and it becomes something you know about yourself. This lets you look at the full picture of your life, rather than just the bits you are unhappy with. Praise and positive feedback are great in the moment, but you need to internalize them and build an inner measure of how you're doing. Otherwise, you'll only ever feel as good as whatever you're doing.

To keep going with this, write down the good things that happen, which will further widen your spotlight of attention. Each day, try to note down three things that went well. This is also useful information to bring to mind when you're in a doom spiral or when self-criticism is getting too loud.

It's also important to share your successes and the things that make you happy with the people you care about. Lots of people I see don't share the full story of what's going on for them – a holiday, a pregnancy, doing well on a project – as they are so concerned about making other people feel bad. This is misguided, as good friends can enjoy your success. It's important to share all your experiences, good and bad, to feel connected.

Think about yourself less

People who like themselves more think about themselves less, while those who dislike themselves are the opposite – they worry about how they'll be perceived by others. They focus on (what they see as) their flaws and can become fixated on how others view them. The thing is, confident people still have these thoughts – they might worry what others think about them, they'll cringe at a mistake, or think 'I wish I hadn't said that' – but they respond to those thoughts in a different way. Instead of dwelling on them, they accept them for what they are, find self-compassion and let the thoughts go.

Trust in yourself

Now that you have stopped overthinking, it leaves space for you to tune back in to your instincts and close the gap between what you show on the outside and how you feel inside. What you present to others should be closely aligned with how you feel inside. This lets you see you are accepted exactly as you are.

I want you to start to listen to your gut reactions. Go with your first thought or feeling (do *not* overthink it). This works for any decision you're taking, from small to big. Start with something easy and build up: you could put on the first outfit you choose; if you're ordering food, go with your first thought; when someone asks what you think, give your immediate response; or when you're gauging how something went, go with your first feeling. Here are some tips:

- Listen to your first thought.
- Don't take long to decide (less than a minute).
- Don't prepare.
- Trust in what you like and go with what you think is best.
- Don't try to second-guess what others think: do what you want, not what other people think you should do. Ask yourself, 'If I didn't care what anyone else said, what would I do?'
- Don't worry about trying to look good or getting it 'right' (there is no right or wrong!).

Remember: no matter what you choose, there will be some advantages and some disadvantages. Even if it's not what you wanted or doesn't work out as you expect, you've learned something about yourself.

Going with your first feeling doesn't always mean making the most rational choice. For example, when I decided to pursue psychology as a career, it meant giving up my job and moving out of the flat I was renting so I could go back to university. Most people around me didn't think it was a good move, and when I looked at the pros and cons of the change, there were definitely more cons. Yet instead of focusing on the negatives and paying attention to the opinions of others, I looked at the weight of each pro and con and how each made me feel. It was the same for having a third child. Rationally, it didn't make any sense, but it felt right.

Channel this skill somewhere it can thrive!

The flip side of overthinking is that it means you are someone who is analytical, has a questioning brain, loves thinking about and putting ideas together, can persevere with problems and can channel your attention into challenges. To future-proof yourself against overthinking, I want you to redirect this skill and put it to good use. Find a project or something positive to think about so you create a good space for your mind to go to.

At the moment, I'm working with an incredibly special lady who has a chronic and very serious health condition. She recently signed up for a university course and has found that studying has opened up her world and put her brains skills to excellent use. The course itself has bought structure and stability. It's been amazing to see her love of the subject blossom. Here's how she feels about it:

I'm so happy I signed up to the course. Since it began, my brain has been caught up in reading and studying, and it's reignited my passion for creative writing and poetry. I think about the subject all the time, read books and listen to podcasts on the topics. It's also linked me up with like-minded people and challenged my thinking. Even when I'm not doing the course or studying, it gives my brain a great place to wander to. The discussions dance in my mind as I contemplate new ideas and bring different concepts together to make sense of them. I look forward to the sessions and I feel so much happier.

Where could you channel your amazing brain? Find the perfect place for this type of thinking. Pick your thing, surround yourself with people who can support you – and keep doing it!

Keep your world bigger

Finding meaning and purpose in life is one of the most consistent and strong predictors of psychological wellbeing and happiness. When you know why you're doing things and have a clear picture of what makes your life meaningful, it's a guiding light. It helps you define your life, cope with adversity, find inner strength and form a clear picture of the future you wish to strive toward. Bad days won't disappear, but meaning is brilliantly buoyant, giving you an underlying sense of purpose and belonging. When life threatens to throw you off-course, there is something stronger to keep you steady, enabling you to weather the storms.

I want you to think about how to move forward with meaning, so you are *living* life, rather than constantly taking lessons. How we spend our time is one of the most important decisions any of us makes. In terms of happiness, meaning and fulfilment, it's what we do every day that makes the biggest difference.

Sonja Lyubomirsky, a professor of psychology at the University of California, Riverside, has devoted her career to studying happiness. She finds that 40 per cent of our happiness is determined by our behaviour.[89] I love this research, as it really backs up the idea that it is not what happens to us that determines how we feel (this accounts for only 10 per cent of our happiness, while the other 50 per cent is down to genetics). It is proof that not overthinking about things is key, and that you can make happiness happen. It's a really hopeful message that shows we can increase or sustain our happiness through our intentional daily activities and the choices we make.

Sonja found that the happiest people devote a great amount of time to their family and friends, are comfortable expressing gratitude, help others, practise optimism, forgive, savour life's pleasures, try to live in the present moment, exercise regularly, and are committed to lifelong goals and ambitions. Guess what they didn't do? Overthink!

Try these techniques to live a happier life:

Take each day a little slower

When you're dragged along by life and feel like you can barely breathe, it's hard to keep objectivity and perspective. It's only when you slow down physically and mentally that you can make conscious choices, pay attention to the people and things that matter to you, and enjoy and feel grateful for your life.

Keep some empty time

Don't keep your time so filled that you don't have a second to sit back and take it all in. It's important to prioritize some quiet and alone time. All your time does not need to be productive, as we're not machines – we don't need to be constantly doing or thinking. Rest and recovery are essential parts of a healthy and happy life.

Find natural highs

These are the things that make you feel alive. It's not the big things that matter; it's the day-to-day stuff that really counts. Pay attention to what makes you feel good, finding positive sources of dopamine, oxytocin and serotonin to incorporate every day. Here are a few of my positive sources to give you some ideas: walking to school through the park with my girls, the outdoors, hearing birds singing, chats in the car with my son, doing well at work, a bright sunny day, time with my husband, cycling with friends, getting the giggles, jokes with my kids, enjoying a cup of coffee, running, seeing the sea, finding a parking space easily, volunteering, my favourite music turned up loud, catching up with friends, eating good food, a hug, appreciating beauty, holding hands.

Look outside yourself and give back

Giving back is one of the best sources of natural highs and is essential to future-proof against overthinking. Acts of kindness are proven to reduce distress, improve feelings of social connection, improve life satisfaction and increase meaning in life.[90,91] We need to get out of our heads and think about others more. This can includes our personal relationships as well as being part of something bigger than us. It's important to connect to the things that matter to you, whether that means charity, community or a cause closer to home. Connection is key to wellbeing, as it stimulates the release of endorphins. There's a strong relationship between community activity and increased self-esteem and self-worth. Giving back can also give you a more realistic outlook on life, helping you remember that life is bigger than you. Try to do something kind every day.

Begin living life now

Rather than putting life off, make the most of the opportunities that matter. You only get one chance at life. Death is something we are often discouraged from thinking about, but doing so can be empowering. It can clarify focus and act as a reminder that it is not materialism or external success that is most important. When we become obsessed by a particular external goal – thinking, hoping and scheming about what's ahead – it can blind us to all that we already have and the importance of having a daily life that fulfils us. We should not wait for a time that never comes. Now you've come up with some ideas of what you'd like to do, you need to put them into practice. Don't research them or plan the perfect way to do it, just start and try it out.

This will give you the best information about whether it's the right thing for you.

Build a routine that includes activities that will open up your world and bring you meaning. Close the gap between what you show on the outside and how you feel on the inside: try to live your life with your inner and outer lives in sync. Structure and routine are important for overthinkers, as they help to cut down on decision-making. Even if it's just a few minutes each day, these activities need to be part of your week so you can decompress, boost your mood and gain perspective.

When you do these activities, it's important to keep Step Four in mind – acceptance. It doesn't matter how much you think it through or how hard you try, you won't always say the right thing at the right time, or get the promotion, or choose the best place to stay. That's OK.

Long-term satisfaction includes short-term challenges and struggle. If you're doing a training programme or working on a project, you won't feel like doing it every time, but you'll be happy when you complete the goal. When I'm working on a book and trying to pull all the different parts together, I'm not happy. Even when I'm absorbed in what I'm doing and working hard, it's not always happiness – that's why aiming for meaning (not happiness) is so important. What makes it worthwhile is the process of doing it, the sense of purpose and the satisfaction when it does come together.

Being human means getting things wrong, putting your foot in it and finding things hard. But the joy that can come from trying these things, from our experiences and from building close friendships, is far more than you'll ever get from deliberating. Even when things don't work out, there can be a gain. Life is hard; that's why we have to enjoy the good bits and embrace all of it. That's what makes everything worth it.

Accept life as it is and yourself as you are

You don't need to focus on being the best or being exceptional. Just focus on doing the things that matter to you and bringing all of yourself to what you do. If you are struggling, come back to this book and remind yourself of what was helpful. You will have negative thoughts, emotions, memories and worries. This is normal: it's how you respond to them that's important, not whether you have them or not. Even when you are doing everything right, some days will be difficult. You're not getting it wrong; this is just how life works.

Live life as an adventure

Life isn't something we should try to control; instead, it's an adventure packed full of experiences and lessons. I love the poem 'Ithaka' by C P Cavafy,[92] which really sums this up. When I'm caught up by life, I read it (and I really recommend that you read it, too) as a reminder that life is best lived as an adventure. An adventure should be meaningful and enriching, but accomplishments or ticking off a checklist are not what makes it worthwhile. It's *how* you travel through your life that's most important.

Living life as an adventure means being in it and experiencing what it has to offer. Everyone's adventure will be different, but no matter which direction you take, you'll experience good days and bad. Remember, this is not you getting it wrong, it's just how adventures go – and like any great adventure, it's a process that never ends. Cherish the good times, take chances, make time for the things and people that matter to you, find joy in the small things and embrace the everyday.

Review

Now you have reached the end of the book, but before closing these pages, I want you to take some time to review everything you have done. At the end of therapy, I do this with the people I see, to help consolidate all the new ideas and insights while they are fresh in the mind. If you write down a review of what you have learned and achieved, it will give you something to look at when you need it, so you have an easy reminder without having to flick back through everything in this book.

You have created a new framework for how you want to live your life and to ensure that you give up overthinking for good. This framework is a more compassionate, realistic and fair understanding of what you should expect for yourself and from your life in general. This framework is accepting of how difficult life can be and of our limitations. It is a framework that won't lead to living your best life every day, but will lead to a more sure-footed understanding of yourself and a happier and more contented approach to life.

There will be times in the future when you're not feeling so good, and it might be tempting to return to overthinking. This is when you will need this review the most – when you feel bad, it's much harder to believe in your new framework. You could even write that down: 'You probably won't believe this when you read it, but you have to do it to break the habit.'

Take your time writing your review. Make use of the notes pages at the back of this book so you can easily refer to it. Use these pointers as you write:

- When you read the book, which ideas resonated most with you?
- Which chapters really struck a chord?

- Which skills and strategies did you find particularly helpful? Write down each one that worked well for you, as well as the type of thinking they work best on.

- If you had to choose a top five, which strategies would they be? Think of these as your fail-safes.

- Write down your motivation and reasons for keeping going with this work. Include why you want to give up overthinking, the mental and physical health benefits of not overthinking, and the difference it's made when you've used these strategies.

- What compassionate phrases can you use to support yourself and to keep this new thinking in mind? What can you remind yourself of if you're feeling bad?

- How can you take care of yourself and ensure you keep your capacity in good shape? This will give you space to face the daily struggles that inevitably come up in life.

- How will you future-proof your life against overthinking?

- Who can support you?

- What are your hopes?

Now write down an action plan for what to do to break the habit if you get stuck overthinking. Make a commitment to yourself that you will put this into practice next time you notice a mood change or realize that you're overthinking. Think of the five steps as you write your plan:

1. **Notice:** What are the best ways for you to increase your awareness? What triggers do you need to be aware of?

2. **Choose:** Which strategies worked best to reduce your focus on overthinking, broaden your spotlight of attention and boost your mood?

3. **Challenge:** What's the best way to continue to track and challenge your thoughts?

4. **Accept:** What are your new life mottos, and how can you ensure you remember these when things get difficult?

5. **Face your fears:** Is there something you're avoiding or worrying about that you can do?

Remember these key ideas

To end with, I have listed below some of my favourite lessons, tips and strategies from the book. Use this as a quick summary to remind you of the gains you have made if you feel overthinking coming back into your life.

Overthinking is the problem, not the solution. You can't think your way out of a negative feeling. Overthinking is the second arrow and causes huge amounts of pain and distress. You can't change what happens to you, but you can change your response. Those who don't overthink are happier. Make yourself one of them.

Keep compassion with you at all times. Be kind to yourself and others. Give yourself the space and room to learn, evolve and grow. Move with change, rather than against it. Remember that you're good enough exactly as you are.

Choose your reality. What do you want to let into your awareness? Choose where you focus your time and attention. Remember thoughts and feelings aren't facts; they're just your interpretation of what's going on. When you're not feeling good, your mind will work against you.

Never think about things when you feel bad. It's much harder to think differently when you're on a negative network. Boost your mood and broaden your spotlight of attention first. When your mood is higher, it makes everything better, and it's so much easier to see more than just one perspective.

Get out of your head and into the world. Use mindfulness to really engage in your life and with the people around you. And get off your phone!

There's no right decision. Make conscious choices that are aligned with what's important to you and the person you want to become. Then make the best of whatever decision you take.

Zoom out to find perspective and think about yourself less. Zoom out from your feelings, zoom out from the scrutiny you put yourself under, zoom out from thinking about yourself, zoom out from bad days. Keep everything in context and remember the bigger picture. Life is bigger than you.

Is it worth it? Is this issue worth your time and energy? If not, let it go.

Live your life. Don't get sucked into other people's lives, and do not compare. No one, and I mean absolutely no one, is living their 'best life' at all times. Remember that no one feels great every day and it's normal to feel the full range of emotions. Some days it will seem easy, and other days it will feel hard. The difficult days are when you will need to remember these new ideas most.

Reset your expectations. Once you release your expectations, you're free to enjoy things as they are rather than as you think they should be.

Life isn't under your control, and we can never be 100 per cent certain. Let life come to you. You don't have to have it all worked out to enjoy it. Think of all the amazing things that happen without any intervention. Trust that you will work it out.

Face your fears and update your anxious predictions. Action is the antidote to overthinking – it's never as bad as you fear, and it's the only way to gain the most from life. If in doubt, just do it.

What you do every day makes the biggest difference. It's the small steps that lead to the greatest changes. Forty per cent of how you feel is down to what you do. Use this to your advantage! Look outside of yourself, give back and remember life is bigger than you.

Appendix

In this next section, I'm going to give you a whistle-stop tour of some of the common overthinking problems I see. Overthinking often shows up as health anxiety, social anxiety, issues with relationships and communication, people-pleasing and intrusive thoughts.

The ideas I offer for each issue are intended as a starting point to manage these thoughts, with specific ideas and strategies. However, if these problems are at a level that is causing you significant distress, it's important to see your doctor or to find a therapist.

For each area of difficulty, it's important to first review and then follow Step One:

- Notice what is in your spotlight (see page 155).
- Carry out a thought audit (see page 156).
- Externalize the thoughts (see page 158).
- Recognize and manage your triggers and cues (see page 162).
- Differentiate between productive and unproductive thinking (see page 164).

Health anxiety

At times, we all worry about our health, ageing and even death. The most common fears related to this are serious health problems or mental illness. Some people have a feeling that something's not quite right. When you feel really anxious about these things, you may have panic attacks, which can also become something to fear.

The problems start when you become overly focused on your body and tuned in to any sensations or changes. If you pay close attention to your body or look out for signs of ill health, you begin to notice things that other people wouldn't pay attention to. This can amplify the intensity of the signs.

Please note that the advice that is given in these pages is for those suffering from health anxiety. It is not a substitute for professional medical advice and regular check-ups. You should always follow the national health guidelines.[93]

Health anxiety makes you misinterpret what the symptoms mean and overestimate the likelihood that something is seriously wrong, because it feels too terrifying to ignore. For example, you may worry that, because your grandmother had cancer, you're going to get it too, or that a headache could be a brain tumour, or that forgetfulness could be early-onset dementia.

Health anxiety can also make you ignore or discount other, less-catastrophic explanations for your symptoms (your old friend confirmation bias). For example, you may be feeling tired and rundown and worrying that it's chronic fatigue syndrome, while ignoring the fact that you haven't slept well and work has been stressful. Health anxiety makes it very difficult to consider a less worrying reason for how you're feeling!

To understand this, take a moment to tune in to and really focus on your feet. Close your eyes and just focus on how your feet feel. What do you notice? Did you notice it before? When I do this, I notice my toes start to tingle. It's not something I normally notice, but when you focus on a particular body part, you bring it into your field of attention.

The way you respond to your health anxiety can make it worse:

- Checking or seeking reassurance to reduce your worry can bring temporary relief, but it keeps you submerged in the problem.
- Avoiding your normal routines (for example, staying off work, stopping exercise, not seeing friends) for fear that you're not well enough gives you more time to overthink and excessively worry.
- Worrying increases anxiety symptoms and keeps the vicious cycle going.

It's the conclusion you jump to that's the problem

If you diagnose yourself with something terrible, it sets off a negative chain reaction – and then these physical symptoms are not all in your head. Now you are feeling them (as the foot experiment shows), but as you focus on the feeling, you amplify it. This makes you worry, which triggers your fight-or-flight response. So you will experience physical symptoms, and these physical symptoms can feel terrifying because they mimic many serious health conditions. As with panic, this can be incredibly debilitating and, over a period of time, can lead to a number of avoidance behaviours.

What to do

The following suggestions will help with addressing your health anxiety, but if you are struggling to shake your fears, make sure you see a therapist. These types of thoughts can be difficult to tackle on your own.

The health-anxiety panic cycle

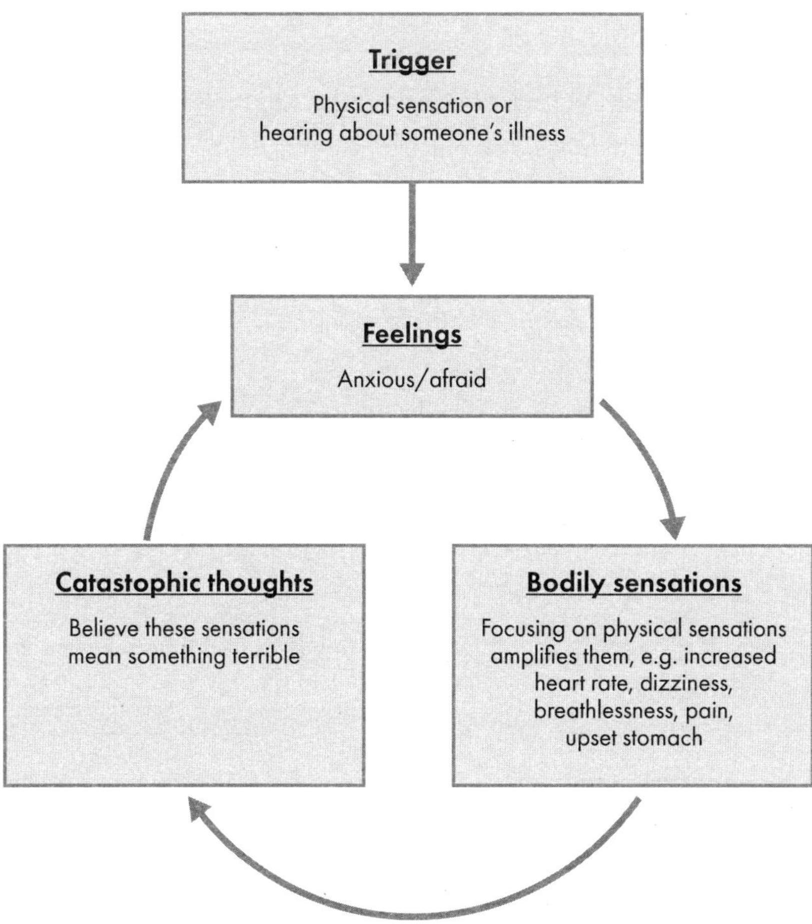

Step Two: choose

Zoom out and retrain your attention: Our bodies are amazing: they are always working and there is always something going on inside. When you're over-vigilant, you'll set off the fight-or-flight response or tune in to things that are perfectly normal. Try to reduce the amount of time you spend focusing on your worries. Use the attention training from Step Two to switch off from overly focusing on your body.

Stop daily checking, reassurance-seeking and body-scanning: The relief this behaviour brings is only temporary, and it keeps your mind focused on frightening diseases and illness. The more you check or seek reassurance, the less practice you have at tolerating discomfort and accepting that our health can never have a 100 per cent guarantee. Say no to checks such as asking friends about your symptoms, either in person or online, and frequently asking for medical tests. Follow the national guidelines, unless your doctor advises otherwise.

Ditch Dr Google: You will not find any useful answers there. Thanks to confirmation bias, we are drawn to the worst prognosis, and no one on the forums ever bothers to come back and update with good news. The amount of time you're spending researching your health could be put to much better use.

Set a worry time to delay thoughts: Set yourself a fixed time each day to worry. I recommend no more than 20 minutes – and don't do it before bed. If worries come up at other times, tell yourself you'll think about it during your worry time. If you run out of time, remind yourself you can come back to it the next day. Often people notice that the topics always tend to be the same and, by thinking about them less, they cause fewer problems.

Step Three: challenge

Write down all the most likely reasons for how you're feeling: If you've got a headache, put down: dehydration, lack of sleep, tension, stress, hangover, hormones, hunger, cold, virus, etc. Then rank them in order of likelihood and give a percentage for how likely each is. Put them all on a pie chart and see what's left over for your fears.

See this as a worry problem: Rather than thinking you have a serious problem, tell yourself you are worried you have a serious illness, but you don't.

Ask yourself if the symptoms go away when you're busy doing other things: Do you forget about the symptoms when you're distracted? This is good evidence that this is a worry problem.

Step Four: accept

Update your ideas about health:

- It's normal to feel sensations in your body.
- Anxiety symptoms can be felt strongly, but they can't hurt or harm you.
- Even healthy people experience aches, pains and changes in their bodies.
- Thinking about illness or being alert to it at all times is unhelpful and makes you feel bad.
- It's better to focus on a healthy lifestyle than to focus on your body.

Step Five: face your fears

Anxiety can't harm you: Think about when someone gives you a shock, or if you've ever had a near miss with a car. Anxiety is extremely physical, so you will feel strong symptoms in your body. Reassure yourself that it's nothing to worry about. Keep your life going and keep up with your normal routines.

Wait a day: If you'd normally book a doctor's appointment straight away, give it a day or two. If you'd usually seek immediate reassurance, disengage from this. Often, after a day or two, the symptom is no longer an issue. The only research you should do during these days is to read the national guidelines online, as this is the best advice based on research.

Social anxiety

Social situations can be really challenging for overthinkers. The fear of acting in a way that is boring or embarrassing, combined with the fear of being scrutinized and judged by others, can make social situations feel like something to avoid at all costs. This can be especially hard if you're particularly sensitive to other people or very empathic.

It's another chicken-and-egg situation: good relationships are the best cure for social anxiety, but social anxiety can prevent you from developing close connections. The actions you take to try to make social situations go well – preparing what to say, thinking through how it will go, thinking about what to say to the next person when you're talking to someone else, or avoiding it altogether – generally have the opposite effect and keep the problem going. Social anxiety makes it much harder to relate to others or feel connected, and prevents you from seeing that others won't judge you as you fear.

Preparing for social situations will make you more wooden and you'll find yourself trying to shoehorn pre-prepared topics into a conversation, which can mean it doesn't flow. If you're thinking so much about what to say, it can mean that you can't respond to questions or speak up. You might then end up seeming standoffish, shy or even bored, which is exactly what you're trying to avoid.

What to do

The following ideas will help you face social situations, but if you are struggling with social anxiety over a long period, make sure you see a therapist. It can be difficult to tackle on your own.

Step Two: choose

Get out of your head: Shift your focus and attention away from yourself by really listening to what's being said. It gets you out of your head and away from your thoughts, but it also means you can respond genuinely to what's being said. It's impossible to have a conversation if you have a commentary going on in your head. Imagine if I stood next to you and talked to you while you were trying to chat with someone – it wouldn't be easy to respond to the other person or really take in what they were saying.

Step Three: challenge

Think about what makes an enjoyable time with someone else: For me, it's how I'm left feeling afterward, finding out more about the other person and feeling they are engaged in the conversation. They don't even need to have the same opinion as me! If someone just talks at me it's far less enjoyable, even if their anecdotes are funny, as having to listen and laugh along all evening is draining.

Eavesdrop on other people's conversations: Next time you're waiting for a bus or sitting on a train, listen in to other people (without looking too strange!). No one is talking about anything that exciting: it's usually just catching up and hearing how things have been.

Step Four: accept

You are paying far more attention to yourself than other people are: Most people are more focused on themselves than on what you're doing.

How you feel is not what other people see: Even when we're nervous, it's not obvious to other people. It's also helpful to remember that we're all similar under the surface, and there is so much overlap in people's insecurities and fears. No one is on top of everything.

One awkward moment doesn't define you: I can still vividly remember cringe moments from my past, but rather than dwelling on them, I bring self-compassion. We all do embarrassing things occasionally. Everyone has awkward moments.

Step Five: face your fears

If you're unsure of what to say, ask the other person questions: Most people love talking about themselves.

Do not engage in a post-mortem: Replaying a social event after it's over is a waste of time. Remember how you felt straight afterward, before overthinking had a chance to undo things.

Feel better knowing the research: Studies have shown that, the more two people see each other, the more they'll like one another. It's called the exposure effect. So just seeing someone regularly, even if you don't speak, makes a difference.[94]

Relationships and communication

How can it be possible to love someone so much, but also find them the most annoying person in the world? The reality is that true love will only get you so far.

I always say that the top three requirements for any relationship to function well are communication, communication and communication. It's the foundation of any good relationship, and one of the best ways to strengthen connection, build trust, foster understanding and empathy, and resolve conflicts. Communication is also a great way to stop the passive aggression, resentment and internal arguments that can plague overthinkers. If you are feeling angry with someone – communicate with them!

It sounds simple, but most people find it incredibly difficult to communicate well as it requires being vulnerable. It will also be harder if your family weren't great at communicating because it's not something you've had a chance to learn. The good news is it's never too late to start communicating, and it will make a *huge* difference to your life.

A common theme that comes up in relationships is when one partner believes the other doesn't understand all they do and doesn't feel appreciated. For example, women often describe to me the weight of carrying the mental and emotional load, and they feel this invisible labour goes unnoticed. Men can also feel their work goes unseen. I worked with a fantastic guy called Dylan. He was outwardly laid back, but internally he felt very differently. He felt responsible for his family and carried the emotional burden of supporting everyone else. This meant that he frequently took on too much and ended up being overloaded. This is how he felt:

I've noticed that when there's an upset at home or I feel fed up or unappreciated, I can become passive aggressive. I spend the day rehearsing mental arguments, resenting how much I have to do for my family and the fact that I've had to move my entire life around to fit in with what everyone else needs. The anger gives me tunnel vision; I find myself thinking of all the things they've done wrong or they said they'd do, but didn't. When I'm stuck overthinking, I feel like I do much more than everyone else and I get annoyed with my family and see them as ungrateful and spoilt.

When we slowed things down in the session, it gave Dylan a chance to calm his body and think about things again. He could see that, although he believed this to be the truth in his angry moments, it wasn't a fair picture. Talking about how he was feeling also gave him space to think about the other side of things – what other people did for him, how loved he was by his family, and the different ways everyone in the family contributed. It also let him see that, at times, life was hard and he and his partner could both struggle. Now, instead of focusing on who was having a harder time, he could think about how they could support each other.

Dylan managed to open up to his partner and realized she'd had no idea he was feeling that way. Once she was more aware of what was going on for him, she was able to have greater empathy and they both felt more connected to each other. In time, he began to see that, even though wanting to do everything came from a good place, it left him feeling resentful. He began to speak up sooner, stopping things spiralling out of control. Of course, this reset didn't avoid upsets completely, but it did reduce their intensity. It also let him see that, when he was stuck in anger, it hurt him the most.

Good communication short-circuits overthinking and helps your reactions stay proportionate. It does this in three ways:

1. When you speak up, you stop mentally rehearsing arguments, which prevents the feeling getting bigger.
2. When you say it out loud, you have a chance to process it and gain perspective.
3. Discussing it when you feel calmer gives the other person an opportunity to respond and to change their behaviour.

What to do

The following ideas will help you address your overthinking around relationships. If you need more support, do seek the help of a therapist.

Step Two: choose

Love is a doing word: Keep doing loving things and saying kind and complimentary things about each other. Keep a broader spotlight of attention: don't narrow in on what hasn't been done or what you're unhappy with, but pull the beam wider and keep an awareness of all the good things in your relationship. Recognize what your partner is doing instead of trying to point out that you are doing more. Boost the good feelings and notice when your partner is being kind, appreciative, helpful or funny. To express your gratitude, name specific things your partner does for you. Notice and respond to bids for attention and move towards your partner when they're trying to connect with you.

The magic ratio is five to one: The Gottman Institute's advice[95] for couples to maintain healthy relationships is that, for every one negative feeling or interaction between partners, there must be five positive feelings or interactions. Be mindful of your behaviours and attitude towards your partner. Be compassionate and accepting of their strengths and weaknesses. Only give advice if it's asked for.

If the load is uneven: Write down everything that you are both doing and discuss a better way to manage or divide up the list.

Step Three: challenge

If in doubt, ask! Worried what someone is thinking? Ask them. Worried that someone is going to give up on you? Try talking to them. Speaking to people works best.

Hear what the other person is saying: Don't just focus on getting your point across. Communication needs to be two ways. Try to give them the benefit of the doubt; so think to yourself, 'What's the most generous interpretation?', and put yourself in their shoes.

Keep your anger specific to what has just happened: Don't let it spread like wildfire and light up any previous memory of wrongdoing. When you keep it concrete, you have a chance to step out of the feeling more quickly and make changes. If there are repeating topics that come up, try talking about it when you're both feeling calm. Try to keep away from blame, and do be clear, concise and specific. And remember that there are always two sides to the story.

Step Four: accept

Whose rule is it anyway? Be careful of the expectations you place on others. Unsolicited advice is never a good idea. Just because you like to do things a certain way, it doesn't mean they will too. It is their right to act however they wish, and your choice to be their partner (or friend). Remember that they're your rules and the other person hasn't signed up to them. In all likelihood, their behaviour is not a personal slight or meant to annoy you; they're just different from you and probably think differently too. If it's a problem that you keep coming up against, then discuss it and see if you can work out a compromise.

Step Five: face your fears

Say it when you feel it: Don't wait too long to share an upset. Try to speak up long before it gets to the point of rupture. This lets out some of the feeling, so you don't suddenly erupt, and gives overthinking an outlet. For example, if your partner upsets you, rather than thinking about it and rehearsing arguments in your head, I want you to try telling your partner that they have upset you.

Put it into words: Don't imagine someone knows what you're thinking – you need to tell the other person and remember that no one can read minds. Think about *how* you say things and keep in mind that you're speaking to someone you love. I often think how kindly people will talk to someone on the phone that they've never met (if, for example, they're making an enquiry) and how horribly words can come out with those you care about. The people who matter most to you deserve your best.

People-pleasing

People-pleasers are particularly prone to overthinking. They are highly attuned to other people and, as a result, can neglect their own emotional needs. They find it hard to show their true feelings and struggle saying no.

You might have picked up on some of these themes in Dylan's thoughts (see page 291). People-pleasing can stem from insecurity and pinning your self-esteem on what others think of you. External validation is a way to feel good, but it's precarious to base your self-worth on approval from others.

Doing whatever it takes to make others happy can leave you not feeling so good about yourself and, if you're doing things reluctantly or out of obligation, it can lead to anger and resentment. This behaviour means you don't get a chance to see that you would be accepted by the people who matter without always going the extra mile. It can also leave you anxious or stressed – and it's the perfect breeding ground for overthinking.

What to do

Try the following ideas, which will help you to stop overthinking other people's happiness – and to learn that sometimes you can say no.

Step Two: choose

Go with your first feeling: Choose not to overthink what you should do. Get used to choosing the things you want without over-analysing – deciding which film to see, agreeing where you want to meet. Reconnect with your instincts so you can get to know yourself again. It's OK to be assertive: you're not inconveniencing the other person or bothering them. It's good to say what you want and need.

Step Three: challenge

You are not responsible for other people's happiness: That is their responsibility. Be careful of holding on to other people's feelings. Only they can change how they feel.

Other people's moods are not always about you: Remember that things don't start and end with you. Someone else's mood is not directly linked to what you have done. They can be in a bad mood because they're having a bad day. Say to yourself, 'It's OK for them to feel like this, it's not because of me.' Consciously step away from feeling like you need to fix it.

Step Four: accept

Not everyone thinks the same way as you: People-pleasers are so good at thinking about what other people need that they can feel let down if they don't get the same in return. It's not that the other person didn't want to do what you needed, it's just that it didn't even cross their mind.

Relationships should work both ways: The best relationships are mutually beneficial, with give and take. Allowing people to do things for you is an important part of feeling accepted and connected, and leads to deeper, more authentic and satisfying relationships. If the relationship doesn't last when you start expecting more, it's a sign that it wasn't good in the first place, not a reflection on you.

You can't be everyone's cup of tea, or you'd be a mug: If you're liked by everyone, the chances are you don't like yourself very much. Accept that not everyone will like you and that's OK; you probably don't like everyone you meet either.

Step Five: face your fears

Learn to say no: You don't have to do everything everyone asks. Get the no in early, as it can be tempting to say yes to avoid making the other person unhappy, but late cancellations risk upsetting people more. If you need to buy some time, say you'll check, so you have time to work out if you want to do it.

Put boundaries in place: It's good to prioritise your needs. Decide what is enough in your relationships and try to stick to it. If you're always the first or last at work, or you're always the one to pick up the slack, it's time to change this. When you know your worth, people will respect and appreciate you more.

Don't suppress your feelings: You don't have to be OK with everything. Stop associating being a good person with how much you're willing to self-sacrifice. You can be a kind person or a good friend without being a doormat.

Dare to be yourself and let others in: Don't try so hard to be liked by everyone that you no longer like yourself. When you act like a social chameleon and try to adapt yourself to what you think others need, it leaves you feeling accepted on fake terms. Dare to be you. The difference this will make to the quality of your friendships is immeasurable.

Stop apologizing: Don't prefix everything with 'sorry', as it weakens your confidence in what you're saying, and most people actually find it really annoying!

Only do it if it brings you pleasure: Don't do something for approval, to get something back or to be liked. It will only fuel resentment. Make a habit of thinking about what you want and need first, before thinking about others. Don't think about what you think you *should* do or be swayed by FOMO (fear of missing out). Listen to your gut reaction and learn to tune in to your instincts.

Intrusive thoughts, urges and impulses

We all have intrusive thoughts, urges and impulses from time to time. Common themes include checking and rechecking the door is locked, worrying about germs or having an urge to crash into the central reservation or jump in front of a train. You might have an impulse to say something rude or embarrassing. Sometimes, a saying or song will keep coming back to you over and over again. It can even be overthinking itself – an intrusive thought or urge can trigger obsessive thinking as a form of mental checking to relieve the anxiety from these intrusive thoughts.

Everyone experiences these thoughts. Negative thoughts and feelings are completely normal. We have around 4,000 thoughts a day, so it makes sense that some of them may be negative or random – particularly considering the brain's role as a threat detector. These thoughts only become a problem when you believe the thought has importance or means something about you. As you'll see, this is simply not the case.

Back in 1992, Purdon and Clark surveyed 293 students (none of whom had a diagnosed mental health problem) and asked them to report their most upsetting intrusive thought from the past three months.[96] The most common intrusive thoughts include:

- Ideas about harming yourself or someone you care about, or other acts of violence, such as running your car off the road, hitting animals or people, or killing someone.
- Thoughts about contamination from germs, disease, dirt or radiation.
- Thoughts of causing danger or harm by leaving something crucial undone, such as leaving the stove on, forgetting to lock the door, or forgetting to turn off an electrical appliance.

- Sexual thoughts that are contrary to your desires, such as disturbing sexual images, sexual thoughts about a family member or child, or acts against your sexual preference.

The only issue with intrusive thoughts is how much significance you give the thought and what it means to you. If you're unbothered by these thoughts, you might just think, 'Urgh, that's a weird thought.' You're then much more likely to not get stuck thinking about it.

It's your reaction to intrusive thoughts that's the problem:

Intrusive thoughts

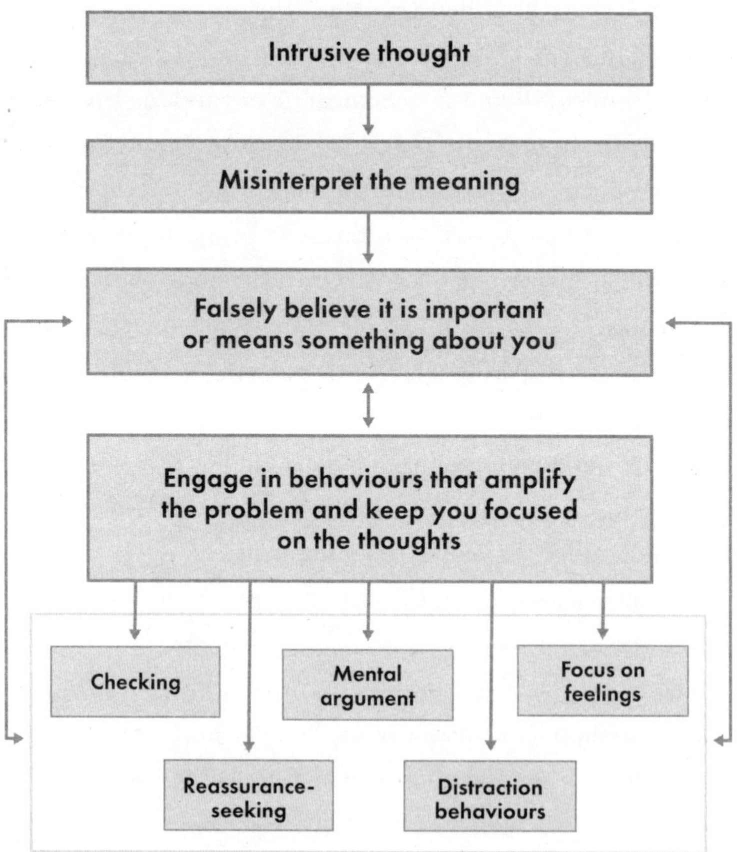

What to do

Intrusive thoughts are common, but it's important to see your doctor or a therapist if you are struggling with them.

Step Two: choose

Don't overthink it: Just dwelling on these thoughts and giving them consideration puts them in your spotlight of attention and makes them seem more important than they really are. Remember, it's only you that is making them important. Ask yourself, 'Am I paying too much attention to this thought?'

See your thoughts as just thoughts: Let your thoughts come. It doesn't mean anything about you and it's not important. Think of all the random thoughts that pop into your head in a day. Don't treat these troubling thoughts any differently!

Step Three: challenge

Change your interpretation of these thoughts: You know these thoughts are normal, so you don't need to worry about them, check, seek reassurance or feel ashamed. This takes the power out of the thoughts and takes the focus off them. You can't control or stop intrusive thoughts, but it doesn't mean you agree with them or that they are true. The thoughts are meaningless.

Intrusive thoughts prey on the things that matter to you: The reason you respond so strongly to these thoughts is because they go *against* what you value and want.

Thoughts and actions are not inextricably linked: It's important to remember that having the thought is not equivalent to carrying out the thought, and that having a thought does not increase the likelihood of it happening. Thoughts cannot have a direct influence on events in the real world.

It's OK to have negative thoughts about other people: Having the thought is not what makes you a good or bad person. I might feel like shouting and screaming at someone, but it's what I ultimately do that counts. Having these thoughts is not the same as acting on them.

Step Four: accept

Intrusive thoughts do not discriminate: Research in 2014 assessed 777 university students at 15 sites in 13 countries across 6 continents.[97] Results showed that nearly all participants (93.6 per cent) reported experiencing at least one intrusive thought during the previous three months. Doubting intrusive thoughts (e.g. worry that you didn't lock the front door or left on the gas or your hair straighteners) were the most commonly reported category.

The findings show how common intrusive thoughts are in the general population, and that the thoughts are similar in content to those seen in OCD. This emphasizes that it is not the intrusive thought that is the problem, but how you interpret it and your reaction to it. Knowing how normal these thoughts are and that, in fact, they are no different from any other thoughts we have can take away their power and importance.

Don't strive for certainty about these thoughts: Sometimes it feels like we need absolute certainty about a thought to reduce doubt or the fear of negative outcomes, but it's striving for certainty that causes anxiety, not the uncertainty itself. I also think that if we *did* know every outcome in advance, life would be pretty boring!

Step Five: face your fears

Allow the thoughts: Don't suppress them, as they will just come back stronger. Attempting to consciously avoid or stop unwanted thoughts has a paradoxical effect: it actually makes them increase. If you try *not* thinking of a pink elephant, you'll see what I mean.

Just because you have a thought, doesn't mean you have to act on it: When you don't do what the thought says, you break the anxious cycle and get to see that things are still OK. Tell yourself, 'I don't need to do one more check. One more check is not going to prevent something bad from happening, and it will only make me feel worse.'

Acknowledgements

A huge thank you to my brilliant editor, Jessica. This book would never have happened without you. I've loved working with you! Thank you for persuading me to write this book and coming up with such an important topic. Your thoughtful ideas and insights, coupled with your encouragement and enthusiasm, have made such a difference to me and this book. Thanks also to Leanne for seamlessly preparing the book for print and to everyone involved at Octopus. I feel incredibly fortunate to be part of such an excellent team.

Thank you to my fantastic agent, Jane, for your continued support. Your experience and knowledge are invaluable. To the psychologists who have inspired me and to the amazing people I work with in my clinic, thank you for letting me into your lives and teaching me so much about life. Many people imagine that being a psychologist is depressing, but it's the opposite; it fills you with hope and shows you how remarkable people are.

Most importantly, thank you to my wonderful family. First, a thank you to my incredible parents, John and Deborah, who have done so much for me. I'm so grateful to have your unwavering support – I love you and appreciate you both very much! To Heather and John, my fantastic in-laws, thank you for all you do.

Saving the best until last, Jack, Max, Edie and Bibi – the loves of my life – you fill my days with so much joy, and I'm so lucky to have you. Thank you, Max, Edie and Bibi for being the three greatest kids I could ever have dreamed of. You are smart, funny and the best company, always teaching me something new and keeping me on my toes. I couldn't be prouder of you. I love *you* more (if it's in print, surely it's final?!).

Jack, my number-one cheerleader, thanks for always supporting me in whatever I do and never questioning it (or my sanity). Despite saying I'd *never* do another book, here we are again (even sooner than expected!). When we met, 19 years ago, I could never have imagined all that lay ahead of us, but meeting you is the best thing that ever happened to me.

Endnotes

The overthinking cure

1   Dr Susan Nolen-Hoeksema, *Women Who Think Too Much: How to Break Free of Overthinking and Reclaim Your Life*, Piatkus Books, London, 2004.

2   Felicia K Zerwas, Brett Q Ford, Oliver P John and Iris B Mauss, 'Unpacking the Pursuit of Happiness: Being Concerned About Happiness but Not Aspiring to Happiness is Linked with Negative Meta-Emotions and Worse Well-Being', *Emotion* 24(8), 2024, https://www.apa.org/pubs/journals/releases/emo-emo0001381.pdf

3   Edward R Watkins and Henrietta Roberts, 'Reflecting on Rumination: Consequences, Causes, Mechanisms and Treatment of Rumination', *Behaviour Research and Therapy Journal* 127(7), 2020, 10.1016/j.brat.2020.103573, https://pubmed.ncbi.nlm.nih.gov/32087393.

4   Thomas Curran and Andrew P Hill, 'Perfectionism is Increasing Over Time: A Meta-Analysis of Birth Cohort Differences from 1989 to 2016', *Psychological Bulletin* 145(4), 2017, www.apa.org/pubs/journals/releases/bul-bul0000138.pdf.

5   Thich Nhat Hanh, *No Mud, No Lotus: The Art of Transforming Suffering*, Parallax Press, Berkeley, 2015.

How to use this book

6   Pedro Mateos-Aparicio and Antonio Rodriguez-Moreno, 'The Impact of Studying Brain Plasticity', *Frontiers in Cellular Neuroscience*, February 2019, www.frontiersin.org/journals/cellular-neuroscience/articles/10.3389/fncel.2019.00066/full.

Chapter 1: Overthinking is the problem, not the solution!

7   Susan Nolen-Hoeksema and Jannay Morrow, 'Effects of Rumination and Distraction on Naturally Occurring Depressed Mood', *Cognition and Emotion* 7(6), 1992: 561–570, www.tandfonline.com/doi/abs/10.1080/02699939308409206.

Chapter 2: The root of overthinking

8   Edward R Watkins and Henrietta Roberts, 'Reflecting on
      Rumination: Consequences, Causes, Mechanisms and Treatment
      of Rumination', *Behaviour Research and Therapy Journal* 127(7),
      2020, 10.1016/j.brat.2020.103573, https://pubmed.ncbi.nlm.nih.
      gov/32087393.

9   Dr Jessamy Hibberd, *How to Overcome Trauma and Find Yourself
      Again: Seven Steps to Grow from Pain*, Aster, London, 2023.

10   Peter Kinderman *et al*, 'Causal and Mediating Factors for Anxiety,
      Depression and Well-Being', *The British Journal of Psychiatry* 206(6),
      2015: 456–460, doi: 10.1192/bjp.bp.114.147553.

11   Ed Watkins *et al*, 'Processing Mode Causally Influences Emotional
      Reactivity: Distinct Effects of Abstract Versus Concrete Construal
      on Emotional Response', *Emotion* 8(3), 2008: 364–78, doi: 10.1037/
      1528-3542.8.3.364.

12   Gordon L Flett *et al*, 'Perfectionism Cognitions, Rumination,
      and Psychological Distress', *Journal of Rational-Emotive and
      Cognitive-Behavior Therapy* 20(1), March 2002: 33–47, https://
      psycnet.apa.org/record/2002-15040-003.

13   Erin E McKenney *et al*, 'Repetitive Negative Thinking as a
      Transdiagnostic Prospective Predictor of Depression and Anxiety
      Symptoms in Neurodiverse First-Semester College Students',
      Autism in Adulthood 5(4), 2023: 374–388, https://doi.org/10.1089/
      aut.2022.0078.

14   Ahmet Koyuncu, Tuğba Ayan, Ezgi Ince Guliyev, Seda Erbilgin
      and Erdem Deveci, 'ADHD and Anxiety Disorder Comorbidity
      in Children and Adults: Diagnostic and Therapeutic Challenges',
      Anxiety Disorders 24(2), 2022: 129–140, https://pubmed.ncbi.nlm.nih.
      gov/35076887/.

15   Katherine A Pearson *et al*, 'Rejection Sensitivity Prospectively
      Predicts Increased Rumination', *Behaviour Research and Therapy*
      49(10), 2011: 597–605, https://pubmed.ncbi.nlm.nih.gov/21764037/

16   Daniel J Siegel, *Mind: A Journey to the Heart of Being Human*, W W Norton and Company, New York, 2016.

17   Lee A Kirkpatrick and Bruce J Ellis, 'An Evolutionary-Psychological Approach to Self-Esteem: Multiple Domains and Multiple Functions', *Blackwell Handbook of Social Psychology: Interpersonal Processes,* Wiley Blackwell, 2003: 409–436.

18   Mark Williams, John Teasdale, Zindel Segal and Jon Kabat-Zinn, *The Mindful Way through Depression: Freeing Yourself from Chronic Unhappiness,* Guilford Press, New York, 2007.

19   Ivanka Savic, 'Structural Changes of the Brain in Relation to Occupational Stress', *Cerebral Cortex* 25(6), 2015, 10.1093/cercor/bht348, https://pubmed.ncbi.nlm.nih.gov/24352030.

20   S Lyubomirsky and S Nolen-Hoeksema, 'Self-Perpetuating Properties of Dysphoric Rumination', *Journal of Personality and Social Psychology* 65(2), 1993: 339–49, https://pubmed.ncbi.nlm.nih.gov/8366423.

21   S Lyubomirsky and S Nolen-Hoeksema, 'Effects of Self-Focused Rumination on Negative Thinking and Interpersonal Problem Solving', *Journal of Personality and Social Psychology* 69(1), 1995: 176–90. https://pubmed.ncbi.nlm.nih.gov/7643299.

Chapter 3: The spotlight of attention

22   Haemin Sunim, *The Things You Can See Only When You Slow Down,* Penguin Life, London, 2017.

23   Peter Kinderman *et al,* 'Causal and Mediating Factors for Anxiety, Depression and Well-Being', *The British Journal of Psychiatry* 206(6), 2015: 456–460. doi: 10.1192/bjp.bp.114.147553.

24   Leon Festinger, *A Theory of Cognitive Dissonance*, Stanford University Press, Stanford, 1957.

Chapter 4: Classic overthinking traps

25   Barry Schwartz, 'The Paradox of Choice', 2005, www.ted.com/talks/barry_schwartz_the_paradox_of_choice?language=en.

Chapter 5: Why is overthinking so prevalent?

26   'Mental Health Facts and Statistics', *Mind*, www.mind.org.uk/
      information-support/types-of-mental-health-problems/
      mental-health-facts-and-statistics.

27   'Quick Facts and Statistics about Mental Health', *Mental
      Health America*, https://mhanational.org/resources/
      quick-facts-and-statistics-about-mental-health.

28   James Davies *et al*, 'Reversing the Rate of Antidepressant
      Prescribing', *British Medical Journal* 383, 2023, https://collegeofme
      dicine.org.uk/wp-content/uploads/2023/12/BMJ-FINAL.pdf.

29   David G Blanchflower, Alex Bryson and Xiaowei Xu,
      'The Declining Mental Health of the Young and the Global
      Disappearance of the Hump Shape in Age Unhappiness', *National
      Bureau of Economic Research Working Paper* No. w32337, 16 April 2024,
      https://papers.ssrn.com/sol3/papers.cfm?abstract_id=4794387.

30   Graph reproduced with thanks to David G Blanchflower,
      Alex Bryson and Xiaowei Xu.

31   'Mental Health of Children and Young People in
      England, 2023', Mental Health of Children and Young
      People Surveys, *NHS Digital*, https://digital.nhs.
      uk/data-and-information/publications/statistical/
      mental-health-of-children-and-young-people-in-
      england/2023-wave-4-follow-up.

32   Joseph L Ward *et al*, 'Admission to Acute Medical Wards for Mental
      Health Concerns Among Children and Young People
      in England from 2012 to 2022: A Cohort Study', *The Lancet Child and
      Adolescent Health* 9(2), 2025: 112–120. www.thelancet.com/journals/
      lanchi/article/PIIS2352-4642(24)00333-X/fulltext.

33   Eduin Latimer, Freddie Pflanz and Tom Waters, 'Health-Related
      Benefit Claims Post-Pandemic: UK Trends and Global Context',
      Institute for Fiscal Studies, https://ifs.org.uk/sites/default/files/
      2024-09/Health-related-benefit-claims-post-pandemic_2.pdf.

34 The *PLoS* Medicine Editors, 'The Paradox of Mental Health: Over-Treatment and Under-Recognition', *PLoS Med* 10(5), 2013: e1001456, https://pmc.ncbi.nlm.nih.gov/articles/PMC3665855.

Chapter 6: Blame your brain!

35 'Hebb's Law', *ScienceDirect*, www.sciencedirect.com/topics/neuroscience/hebbian-theory.

36 Eun Joo Kim, Blake Pellman and Jeansok J Kim, 'Stress Effects on the Hippocampus: A Critical Review', *Learning and Memory*, 22(9), 2015: 411–416, doi: 10.1101/lm.037291.114, https://pmc.ncbi.nlm.nih.gov/articles/PMC4561403/.

37 Norman Doidge, *The Brain That Changes Itself: Stories of Personal Triumph from the Frontiers of Brain Science*, Penguin, New York, 2008.

38 Barbara L Fredrickson *et al*, 'The Undoing Effect of Positive Emotions', *Motivation and Emotion* 24(4), 2000: 237–258, doi: 10.1023/a:1010796329158, https://pmc.ncbi.nlm.nih.gov/articles/PMC3128334.

Chapter 7: Self-criticism

39 Theodore A Powers, Richard Koestner and David C Suroff, 'Self-Criticism, Goal Motivation, and Goal Progress', *Journal of Social and Clinical Psychology* 26(7), 2007: 826–840, https://selfdeterminationtheory.org/SDT/documents/2007_PowersKoestnerZuroff_JSCP.pdf.

40 Kelly McGonigal, K. *The Willpower Instinct: How Self-Control Works, Why It Matters, and What You Can Do to Get More of It*, Avery, New York, 2011.

41 Mark R Leary *et al*, 'Self-Compassion and Reactions to Unpleasant Self-Relevant Events: The Implications of Treating Oneself Kindly', *Journal of Personal and Social Psychology* 92(5), 2007: 887–904, doi: 10.1037/0022-3514.92.5.887, https://pubmed.ncbi.nlm.nih.gov/17484611.

42 Paul Gilbert, *The Compassionate Mind*, Constable, London, 2010; 'Compassion: From its Evolution to a Psychotherapy', *Frontiers in*

Psychology 11, 2020, https://doi.org/10.3389/fpsyg.2020.586161; 'Creating a Compassionate World', *Frontiers in Psychology* 11, 2021, https://doi.org/10.3389/fpsyg.2020.582090; Compassionate Mind Foundation, 'Overview of Compassionate World Interview Series by Prof Paul Gilbert OBE', www.youtube.com/playlist?list=PL15t-W6V_jQjYZa9j7sRywtbxNb7TMpqD.

43   The Compassionate Mind Foundation, www.compassionatemind.co.uk.

Chapter 8: Unfairly comparing

44   M R Leary, 'Commentary on Self-Esteem as an Interpersonal Monitor: The Sociometer Hypothesis', *Psychological Inquiry* 14 (3–4), 2003: 270–274.

45   Leon Festinger, 'A Theory of Social Comparison', *Sage Journals* 7(2), 1954, https://journals.sagepub.com/doi/10.1177/001872675400700202.

46   Richard Joiner *et al*, 'The Effect of Different Types of TikTok Dance Challenge Videos on Young Women's Body Satisfaction', *Computers in Human Behaviour* 147, 2023, https://researchportal.bath.ac.uk/en/publications/the-effect-of-different-types-of-tiktok-dance-challenge-videos-on.

47   R Rodgers and H Chabrol, 'The Impact of Exposure to Images of Ideally Thin Models on Body Dissatisfaction in Young French and Italian Women', *L'Encéphale* 35(3), 2009: 262–8, doi: 10.1016/j.encep.2008.05.003, https://pubmed.ncbi.nlm.nih.gov/19540413/.

48   Armand Chatard *et al*, 'The Woman Who Wasn't There: Converging Evidence That Subliminal Social Comparison Affects Self-Evaluation', *Journal of Experimental Social Psychology* 73, November 2017: 1–13, https://www.sciencedirect.com/science/article/pii/S0022103116308447.

49   T Kasser and A Ahuvia, 'Materialistic Values and Well-Being in Business Students', *European Journal of Social Psychology* 32(1),

2002: 137–146, https://selfdeterminationtheory.org/SDT/
documents/2002_KasserAhuvia_EJSP.pdf.

50   Tim Kasser, *The High Price of Materialism*, MIT Press, Cambridge,
2003.

51   Adam Alter, *Irresistible: Why You Are Addicted to Technology and
How to Set Yourself Free*, Vintage, London, 2017.

52   Jonathan Haidt, *The Anxious Generation: How the Great Rewiring
of Childhood Is Causing an Epidemic of Mental Illness*, Allen Lane,
London, 2024.

53   Adam Alter, 'Why Our Screens Make Us Less Happy', 2017,
www.ted.com/talks/adam_alter_why_our_screens_make_
us_less_happy?subtitle=en.

Chapter 9: Take a capacity check

54   C J Price and C Hooven, 'Interoceptive Awareness Skills for Emotion
Regulation: Theory and Approach of Mindful Awareness in Body-
Oriented Therapy (MABT)', *Frontiers in Psychology* 9, 2018: 798,
https://pubmed.ncbi.nlm.nih.gov/29892247.

Chapter 11: Step two – choose your response

55   J Mark G Williams, 'Mindfulness, Depression and Modes of Mind',
Cognitive Therapy and Research 32(6), August 2008: 721–733, https://
link.springer.com/article/10.1007/s10608-008-9204-z.

56   Istvan Schreiner and James P Malcolm, 'The Benefits of
Mindfulness Meditation: Changes in Emotional States of
Depression, Anxiety and Stress', *Behaviour Change* 25(3), February
2012, www.cambridge.org/core/journals/behaviour-change/
article/abs/benefits-of-mindfulness-meditation-changes-
in-emotional-states-of-depression-anxiety-and-
stress/16CEFE3661C9173067A32827CE8F6010.

57   James Carmody and Ruth A Baer, 'Relationships Between
Mindfulness Practice and Levels of Mindfulness, Medical and
Psychological Symptoms and Well-Being in a Mindfulness-Based

Stress Reduction Program', *Journal of Behavioural Medicine* 31, September 2007: 22–33, https://link.springer.com/article/10.1007/s10865-007-9130-7.

58   'Nature: How Connecting with Nature Benefits Our Mental Health', *Mental Health Foundation*, www.mentalhealth.org.uk.

59   Lucy Jones, *Losing Eden: Why Our Minds Need the Wild*, Penguin Books, London, 2021.

60   Tanya G K Bentley *et al*, 'Breathing Practices for Stress and Anxiety Reduction: Conceptual Framework of Implementation Guidelines Based on a Systematic Review of the Published Literature', *Brain Sciences* 13(12), November 2023: 1612, https://pmc.ncbi.nlm.nih.gov/articles/PMC10741869.

61   I M Engelhard and M A van den Hout, 'How does EMDR work?', *Journal of Experimental Psychopathology* 3(5), 2012: 724–738, doi: 10.5127/jep.028212, https://journals.sagepub.com/doi/10.5127/jep.028212.

62   J Firth *et al*, 'A Meta-Review of "Lifestyle Psychiatry": The Role of Exercise, Smoking, Diet and Sleep in the Prevention and Treatment of Mental Disorders', *World Psychiatry* 19(3), 2020: 360–380, https://onlinelibrary.wiley.com/doi/pdf/10.1002/wps.20773.

63   B Stubbs *et al*, 'EPA Guidance on Physical Activity as a Treatment for Severe Mental Illness: A Meta-Review of the Evidence and Position Statement from the European Psychiatric Association (EPA), Supported by the International Organization of Physical Therapists in Mental Health (IOPTMH)', *European Psychiatry* 54, 2018: 124–144, https://www.europsy.net/ app/uploads/2018/12/2018-EPA-Guidance-Paper-on-Physical-Activity.pdf.

64   L Mandolesi *et al*, 'Effects of Physical Exercise on Cognitive Functioning and Wellbeing: Biological and Psychological Benefits', *Frontiers in Psychology* ('Movement Science and Sport Psychology' section) 19, 2018, https://www.frontiersin.org/articles/10.3389/fpsyg.2018.00509/full.

65   A A Kandola and D P J Osborn *et al*, 'Individual and Combined
      Associations Between Cardiorespiratory Fitness and Grip Strength
      With Common Mental Disorders: A Prospective Cohort Study in the
      UK Biobank', *BMC Medicine* 18, 2020: 303, https://doi.org/10.1186/
      s12916-020-01782-9.

66   Matthew P Herring and Jacob D Meyer, 'Resistance Exercise for
      Anxiety and Depression: Efficacy and Plausible Mechanisms',
      Trends in Molecular Medicine 30(2), 2024: 204–206.

67   Leandro Z Agudelo *et al*, 'Skeletal Muscle PGC-1 α1 Modulates
      Kynurenine Metabolism and Mediates Resilience to Stress-Induced
      Depression', *Cell* 159(1), 2014: 33–45. doi: 10.1016/j.cell.2014.07.051.

Chapter 12: Step three – challenge your thinking

68   D P McAdams, 'Narrative Identity: What Is It? What Does It Do?
      How Do You Measure It?', *Imagination, Cognition and Personality:
      Consciousness in Theory, Research and Clinical Practice* 37(3), 2018:
      359–372, www.self-definingmemories.com/Narrative_Identity_
      shaped_by_SDM.pdf.

69   Adapted from Melisa Robichaud *et al*, *Cognitive-Behavioral Treatment
      for Generalized Anxiety Disorder*, Routledge, New York, 2019.

70   C Witvliet *et al*, 'Granting Forgiveness or Harboring Grudges:
      Implications for Emotion, Physiology, and Health', *Psychological
      Science* 12(2), 2001: 117–123, https:// pubmed.ncbi.nlm.nih.
      gov/11340919.

71   E Messias *et al*, 'Bearing Grudges and Physical Health: Relationship
      to Smoking, Cardiovascular Health and Ulcers', *Social Psychiatry and
      Psychiatric Epidemiology* 45(2), 2010: 183–187, https://psycnet. apa.org/
      record/2010-02913-005.

72   Desmond Tutu, *No Future Without Forgiveness*, Rider, London,
      2000.

73   Robert A Emmons, *Thanks! How the New Science of Gratitude Can
      Make You Happier*, Houghton Mifflin Harcourt, Boston, 2007.

74   R A Emmons and M E McCullough, 'Counting Blessings
      Versus Burdens: An Experimental Investigation of Gratitude
      and Subjective Well-Being in Daily Life', *Journal of Personality
      and Social Psychology* 84(2), 2003: 377–89.

75   Adam Grant and Jane Dutton, 'Beneficiary or Benefactor:
      Are People More Prosocial When They Reflect on Receiving or
      Giving?', *Psychological Science* 23(9), 2012: 1033–1039, https://faculty.
      wharton.upenn.edu/wp-content/uploads/2013/04/GrantDutton_
      PsychScience2012.pdf.

Chapter 13: Step four – accept the reality of how life is

76   Archie O de Berker *et al*, 'Computations of Uncertainty Mediate
      Acute Stress Responses in Humans', *Nature Communications*,
      7 (10996), 2016, www.nature.com/articles/ncomms10996.

77   Heather Lanier, '"Good" and "Bad" Are Incomplete
      Stories We Tell Ourselves', www.ted.com/talks/heather_
      lanier_good_and_bad_are_incomplete_stories_we_
      tell_ourselves.

78   Sandra J Llera and Michelle G Newman, 'Worry Impairs the
      Problem-Solving Process: Results from an Experimental Study'.
      Behaviour Research and Therapy 135 (103759), 2020, https://pmc.
      ncbi.nlm.nih.gov/articles/PMC7703801/.

79   'The Serenity Prayer', www.lords-prayer-words.com/famous_
      prayers/god_grant_me_the_serenity.html.

80   David E Conroy *et al*, 'Measurement: The Performance Failure
      Appraisal Inventory', *Applied Sport Psychology* 14(2), 2002, www.
      tandfonline.com/doi/abs/10.1080/10413200252907752.

Chapter 14: Step five – face your fears

81   Jocelyn Solis-Moreira, 'How Long Does It Really Take
      to Form a Habit?', *Scientific American*, 24 January 2024,
      www.scientificamerican.com.

82   P Lally, C van Jaarsveld, H Potts and J Wardle, 'How Are Habits
      Formed: Modelling Habit Formation in the Real World', *European*

Journal of Social Psychology 40(6), 2009, doi: 10.1002/ejsp.674, https://onlinelibrary.wiley.com/doi/abs/10.1002/ejsp.674.

83   Timothy D Wilson and Daniel T Gilbert, 'Affective Forecasting', *Advances in Experimental Social Psychology* 5, 2003: 345–411 https://dtg.sites.fas.harvard.edu/Wilson%20&%20Gilbert%20 %28Advances%29.pdf.

84   Peter Ayton, Alice Pott and Najat Elwakili, 'Affective Forecasting: Why Can't People Predict their Emotions?' *Thinking and Reasoning* 13, 2007: 62–80, https://doi.org/10.1080/13546780600872726.

85   T D Wilson, T Wheatley, J M Meyers, D T Gilbert and D Axsom, 'Focalism: A Source of Durability Bias in Affective Forecasting', *Journal of Personality and Social Psychology* 78(5), 2000: 821–836, https://doi.org/10.1037/0022-3514.78.5.821.

86   Daniel Gilbert, 'The Surprising Science of Happiness', https://www.ted.com/talks/dan_gilbert_the_surprising_ science_of_happiness.

87   Daniel Gilbert, *Stumbling on Happiness*, Harper Perennial, New York, 2007.

88   Robert L Leahy, *The Worry Cure: Stop Worrying and Start Living*, Piatkus Books, London, 2006.

Chapter 15: Future-proofing against overthinking

89   Sonja Lyubomirsky, *The How of Happiness: A New Approach to Getting the Life You Want*, Penguin, New York, 2008.

90   David R Cregg and Jennifer S Cheavens, 'Healing Through Helping: An Experimental Investigation of Kindness, Social Activities, and Reappraisal as Well-Being Interventions', *The Journal of Positive Psychology* 18(6), 2022, www.tandfonline.com/doi/full/10.1080/ 17439760.2022.2154695.

91   W T Harbaugh, U Myer and D R Burghart, 'Neural Responses to Taxation and Voluntary Giving Reveal Motives for Charitable Donations', *Science*, 2007: 316, 1622–1625, https://pubmed.ncbi. nlm.nih.gov/17569866/.

92 C P Cavafy, 'Ithaka', *Collected Poems*, Princeton University Press, Princeton, 1975, www.poetryfoundation.org/poems/51296/ithaka-56d22eef917ec.

Appendix

93 'Conditions A to Z', *NHS*, www.nhs.uk/conditions.

94 Harry T Reis and Susan Sprecher (Eds), 'Proximity and attraction', *Encyclopedia of Human Relationships*, 2009, 1298–1299, https://doi.org/10.4135/9781412958479.n420

95 The Gottman Institute, www.gottman.com/blog/the-magic-relationship-ratio-according-science.

96 C Purdon and D A Clark, 'Obsessive Intrusive Thoughts in Nonclinical Subjects. Part 1 Content and Relation with Depressive, Anxious and Obsessional Symptoms', *Behaviour Research and Therapy* 31(8), 1992: 713–720, https://pubmed.ncbi.nlm.nih.gov/8257402/.

97 Adam S Radomsky *et al*, 'You Can Run But You Can't Hide: Intrusive Thoughts on Six Continents', *Journal of Obsessive-Compulsive and Related Disorders* 3(3), 2014: 269–279, https://jonabram.web.unc.edu/wp-content/uploads/sites/2968/2015/01/IITIS-Part-1-2014.pdf.

Index

Page numbers in **bold** refer to illustrations

About the author

Dr Jessamy Hibberd (BSc, MSc, DClinPsy, PgDip, PgCert) is a highly respected chartered clinical psychologist, author and commentator. She gained her Doctorate in Clinical Psychology at Royal Holloway, University of London, and completed her accreditation in CBT at the world-renowned Institute of Psychiatry, Psychology and Neuroscience, Kings College London. Jessamy also completed her training in schema therapy, and most recently completed a post-graduate certificate at The Tavistock and Portman in child, adolescent and family mental wellbeing. She is registered with the Health Professions Council and is a member of the British Psychological Society (BPS) and the British Association for Behavioural and Cognitive Psychotherapies (BABCP). Dr Jessamy has over 15 years' experience working in mental health (within the NHS and in her own practice), and is passionate about psychology and the benefits it can bring. Her TEDx talk 'Adventure of a Lifetime', where Dr Jessamy highlights three simple changes anyone can make to feel happier and live a more fulfilling daily life, has been watched by thousands.

www.drjessamy.com
drjessamy
@drjessamy
@drjessamy

'The definitive guide to understanding and beating imposter syndrome'
The Sunday Times

Beat insecurites and gain self-belief

The Imposter Cure

You are not a fraud

You deserve success

You can believe in yourself

DR JESSAMY HIBBERD

Also by this author

ISBN: 978-1-78325-627-3

RAISING READERS
Books Build Bright Futures

Dear Reader,

We'd love your attention for one more page to tell you about the crisis in children's reading, and what we can all do.

Studies have shown that reading for fun is the **single biggest predictor of a child's future life chances** – more than family circumstance, parents' educational background or income. It improves academic results, mental health, wealth, communication skills, ambition and happiness.[1]

The number of children reading for fun is in rapid decline. Young people have a lot of competition for their time. In 2024, 1 in 10 children and young people in the UK aged 5 to 18 did not own a single book at home.[2]

Hachette works extensively with schools, libraries and literacy charities, but here are some ways we can all raise more readers:

- Reading to children for just 10 minutes a day makes a difference
- Don't give up if children aren't regular readers – there will be books for them!
- Visit bookshops and libraries to get recommendations
- Encourage them to listen to audiobooks
- Support school libraries
- Give books as gifts

There's a lot more information about how to encourage children to read on our website: **www.RaisingReaders.co.uk**

Thank you for reading.

---

[1] OECD, '21st-Century Readers: Developing Literacy Skills in a Digital World', 2021, https://www.oecd.org/en/publications/21st-century-readers_a83d84cb-en.html

[2] National Literacy Trust, 'Book Ownership in 2024', November 2024, https://literacytrust.org.uk/research-services/research-reports/book-ownership-in-2024

Notes